THE
SUICIDAL
PATIENT

W9-BZT-791

Recognition,
Intervention,
Management

VICTOR
VICTOROFF

JASON ARONSON INC.
Northvale, New Jersey
London

THE MASTER WORK SERIES

First softcover edition 1996

Copyright © 1996 by Victor M. Victoroff

Library of Congress Cataloging-in-Publication Data

Victoroff, Victor M., 1918–
    The suicidal patient : recognition, intervention, management /
Victor M. Victoroff.
        p.   cm. (The Master work series)
    Originally published : Oradell, NJ : Medical Economics Books,
c1983.
    Includes bibliographical references and index.
    ISBN: 1-56821-810-9 (s/c : alk. paper)
    1. Suicidal behavior.   I. Title.   II. Series.
    [DNLM: 1. Suicide.   2. Crisis Intervention.   Not Acquired]
    RC569.V53   1996
    616.85'8445—dc20
    DNLM/DLC
    for Library of Congress   96-
7477

Manufactured in the United States of America. Jason Aronson Inc. offers books and cassettes. For information and catalog write to Jason Aronson Inc., 230 Livingston Street, Northvale, New Jersey 07647.

THE
SUICIDAL
PATIENT

To Elaine

About the Author

Victor M. Victoroff, M.D., graduated from New York University's College of Medicine in 1944, and served his internship at Bellevue Psychiatric Hospital. In 1988 Dr. Victoroff became medical director of the Geropsychiatric Unit of Meridia Huron Hospital in East Cleveland, Ohio, and was made chairman of the Department of Psychiatry in 1992. In late 1994 he was appointed emeritus chairman of the department and continues to see a wide range of patients at various hospitals and in his private practice.

Contents

Contents

Foreword

The subject of suicide is old yet ever new. The distant past provides us with such vivid and contrasting examples as the four acts of self-annihilation described in the Bible—Samson, Saul, Abimelech, and Achitophel—and Socrates's death, the latter furnishing a striking instance of execution by suicide. We hear or read in our own time of unusual forms of suicide, such as of the IRA prisoners in Northern Ireland. Their statements to the press are public suicide notes spread by modern media to all parts of the world. These IRA prisoners presented us with a deadly drama of mass suicide by self-imposed starvation. Thus, with suicides occurring from biblical times to our very own, it's apparent that this matter is truly timeless, and the appearance of this book is, therefore, quite timely.

The settings and circumstances of suicidal acts are extremely varied, as is illustrated by the following examples:

- the apparently normal college student who is found dead with a gunshot wound in his mouth and the fatal firearm clutched firmly in his right hand as a consequence of cadaveric spasm;
- the megamass-suicidal disaster in Jonestown by cyanide ingestion;
- the previously diagnosed, deeply depressed, withdrawn patient—a loner—who has repeatedly voiced such ominous thoughts as "the world will be better off without me" or "I can't face life anymore" found hanging from a rafter in his attic; and
- the mother who destroys her three small children with a shotgun and then places the lethal instrument to her chest and pulls the trigger.

The many types of persons who are inclined to commit suicide share one critically common predisposing factor—the twofold belief that death is preferable to life and that the struggle for existence is not worth the pain and effort it invariably demands from all of us. Apart from this factor, the underlying causes of attempted and successful suicides are extremely complex. Nothing so momentous as the act to destroy one's self can have a simple etiology. Accordingly, we can conclude that recognition—with appropriate intervention—and prevention of suicide are not easy. But they are possible.

This volume is based on the thesis that suicide can be combatted by searching out its causes and by instituting therapeutic measures before the illness reaches such overwhelming dimensions that it is at the point of lethality. As physicians and others intimately involved in providing health care, we know full well that prophylaxis is superior and thus preferable to therapy. In the matter of suicide, we are dealing with a life-and-death matter in which various modalities of therapy—psychiatric, occupational, pharmacologic, and the like—can avert the final fatal act.

The practicing physician is the first line of defense against suicide. On him falls the burden of dealing with it as it presents itself in clear and subtle manifestations. Few specialities in clinical medicine confer on their practitioners immunity from involvement with violent, self-initiated termination of life. Certainly, the family physician and the psychiatrist are the most frequently and most intimately concerned. But the patient of the orthopedic surgeon, the neurologist, the neurosurgeon, or the oncologist may have fleeting or persistent suicidal thoughts as a consequence of his or her organic injury or disease. And the organic lesion need not be excruciatingly painful, prolonged, or refractory to therapy for the seeds of the notion of doing away with one's self to be implanted and flourish in the mind of the vulnerable subject. The dynamics of suicide can be truly enigmatic and subtle, even when extensive background information is available to help alert the staff of a general hospital to the presence of a patient who is at serious risk of suicide as the "solution" to his seemingly insoluble problems.

If I were to sum up the message of this book for its readers, it would be this: Suicide has always been and always will be with us. Be aware, be alert, be responsive, be responsible. The sanctity of all human life and the reverence with which we regard it are—or should be—powerful motivating factors in eliciting our best unceasing efforts to minimize the number of these deeply disturbing irreversible tragedies.

Unfortunately but realistically, we must concede that the most energetic efforts of physicians, other members of the health team, families, friends, clergy, and others will never eliminate suicide. However, let's at least try to decrease its toll. Our motivation can be such as is expressed in the Talmudic admonition "He who saves one life, it is as though he has saved the world."

Lester Adelson, M.D.

Preface
to the 1996 printing

No serious book on the subject of human self-destruction can ignore the awful shadow of racial suicide that hangs over us as a real possibility in this nuclear age. The recent political changes in Russia, with the fading away of militant communism, have pushed the hands of the catastrophe clock back a few minutes, but the threat remains.

This new reprint is a welcome opportunity to again set before the public my description of the phenomenon of self-murder, and a careful review of why it may occur and what can be done to identify persons at risk; to provide some attempt to prevent the event; to deal with it expeditiously when it has occurred; and to care for the patient, the family, and the community when postvention time has come. Again, the message is not only for professionals involved with the occurrence of suicide but for anyone who may be even remotely associated with the phenomenon. It bears emphasis that most suicides are preventable and are prevented . . . because of reconsideration by the would-be suicidal person, self-rescue, and timely and appropriate intervention by family, friends, neighbors, authorities, employers, co-workers— indeed, anyone with a sense of belief in his or her own competence to be a "suicide-rescuer."

However, there are several issues, barely touched on in the original, out-of-print text, that now require recognition and mention.

The first is the mass media attention to popularizing the act of suicide as if it were a cult.

In the spring of 1991 Derek Humphrey published an evil little book, *Final Exit*, that purported to help people who wanted to die but didn't quite get the hang of it. Without a thought to assisting those who are distraught to find help, he encouraged the decision of the intended suicide to trust his or her own impulsive or torturously considered decision as final. A small but statistically valid increase in suicides in the State of New York in the year after the book was published is attributed to Mr. Humphrey's contribution. His premise and the context of his book have been spiritedly contradicted in the professional but not so much in the popular press.

Next is the burgeoning assumption of a messianic duty on the part of a small segment of the medical profession to help desperately ill persons, demanding immediate surcease of pain, by conspiring to help them die by suicide. This process is called *physician-assisted suicide.*

Dr. Jack Kevorkian, a retired pathologist, invented a suicide machine that he has used to assist (at this writing) at least twenty-seven patients to die. He is sole, formal chief of a new division of medical specialization called "obitiary," the ministration of death. For reasons of his own, Dr. Kevorkian has paraded as an angel of self-deliverance, but his agenda is that of a serial killer whose name is on the same list as Bundy, Manson, and Gacey. As an example of his "merciful logic," he promised to help kill a woman suffering from treatable migraine.

He has been on trial for murder, but his legal fate is still uncertain because Michigan, until recently, had no specific law against suicide. Despite specific orders of the court to stop, he has continued to make himself available to new victims of his private enthusiasm.

Dr. Kevorkian has established himself as judge of the suitability of candidates for suicide, and indirectly if not directly has been their executioner.

With the inspiration supplied by Humphrey and Kevorkian there has been intensification of the presence of the right-to-die movement. The Hemlock Society, Exit in Scotland, the Voluntary Euthanasia Society in England, and other groups in France and Germany are examples.

In Holland a serious experiment with euthanasia has been in progress in which physician-assisted suicide is a core factor. On examination, the malignant consequences are hardly acceptable. Guidelines imposed by the Netherlands Medical Society have been ignored. Physicians have not sought a required second opinion. There is no investigation. Patients are killed who have not agreed to euthanasia. In 61 percent of cases examined death was imposed without the patient's knowledge or consent. In 45 percent of cases the death was perpetrated without the consent or foreknowledge of the next of kin.

Addressing the issue of physician-assisted suicide professionally and ethically, the American Medical Association has established a task force to study "futile and inappropriate care." Virtually every hospital has an established Committee on Ethics that can assemble quickly on demand to discuss a specific case where the issue of pulling the plug—stopping life support—has come into question. I have served on this committee in the hospital where I devote most of my professional time, Meridia Huron Hospital in East Cleveland, Ohio. I have been impressed with the seriousness and sincerity of the members who have sat about the table and truly debated and reviewed all aspects of the case before agreeing not to terminate life, but, if appropriate, not to continue futile support.

Lastly, the high-tech search for biological markers for suicide has progressed. Serotonin level as a possible predictor of suicide has been studied intensively. Various tests identify chemical abnormalities in the brains of persons who have killed themselves or have made a serious, near-lethal attempt. Serotonin deficiency has been found in the brains of 95 percent of this population. Low serotonin levels have also been determined three times more frequently in those who carefully planned, in contrast to the impulsive suicides.

Low serotonin content of brain tissue is determined by both genetic and environmental factors. It will be a while before routine serotonin tests will be available outside the research laboratory, but when they are, the serotonin level as a marker, and others yet to be defined, will profitably be made available to define a population at risk which can then be vigorously approached by premonitory treatment.

The statistics in the original text of this book have held up fairly well. Adolescent suicide continues to increase in rate, but more slowly than ten years ago. The observation that older people are at highest risk for suicide of nonpsychotic populations has earned the attention of a large cohort of concerned professionals. The peaking of the incidence of suicidal behaviors in drug- and alcohol-habituated persons and those with severe personality disorders has led to a serious dilemma in this age of managed care.

The first victims of medical cost-containment have been this large group of vulnerable persons who live in the psychological limbo of "not-sane, not-insane" diagnostic categories. Reviewers for insurance companies, asked to precertify inpatient care, on hearing the patient was intoxicated or had a history of drug or alcoholism, allow minimal time in the hospital . . . or none. The needed therapeutic endeavor to protect these actively self-destructive patients is put beyond reach, with consequent morose prognoses.

We have a text—*Final Exit*—that is advertised as a do-it-yourself manual for the aspiring suicide. We do not have a specific instruction to the undecided—contemplating Hamlet's dilemma, "To be, or not to be . . .—how, and why, to stay alive. This is a lack that I shall endeavor to correct in the near future.

My thanks to my wonderful family, particularly my wife, Elaine, who is always patient and cogent in her critique of my work. Through the years my children, each uniquely gifted, have added their inspiration, helped assemble data, shared opinions, and pointed the way. These include Dr. Mark Alan Vlosky, psychologist; Dr. Michael Victoroff, family practitioner; Dr. Jeffrey Victoroff, neurologist; Gregory Victoroff, Esq., attorney; Debra Victoroff, author and film editor; Dr. Brian Victoroff, orthopedic surgeon; and Joshua Victoroff, high school student and superb athlete.

Finally, I must thank my patients, who really have been my best teachers.

Acknowledgments

As must any writer or researcher on the subject of suicide, I give first credit for source material and original thinking to Edwin S. Shneidman, Ph.D., who is professor of thanatology and director of the prestigious Laboratory for the Study of Life-Threatening Behavior, in the Department of Psychiatry, University of California at Los Angeles. On a par with him is his colleague Robert E. Litman, M.D., chief psychiatrist of the Los Angeles Suicide Prevention Center and professor of psychiatry, University of California at Los Angeles.

Although the bibliography lists their works, I want to note here certain authors whose exceptionally fine work has unquestionably influenced my own orientation. Herbert Hendin, M.D., for one, comes closer to Émile Durkheim than anyone in this generation with his contributions to the understanding of the correlation of sociologic factors and suicide.

Jerome A. Motto, M.D., and William K. Zung, M.D., have provided good foundations for constructing and validating scales and tests by which suicidal potential may be predicted. George E. Murphy, M.D., has done helpful studies on the identification of suicide risk and especially on the amplifying effect that alcohol and substance abuse have on vulnerability.

Richard H. Seiden, Ph.D., Norman Farberow, Ph.D., and Michael Peck, Ph.D., have been occupied with youth suicide on and off the campus. In revealing studies, Cynthia R. Pfeffer, M.D., forces us to accept the fact that very young children kill themselves. Nancy C. A. Roeske, M.D., director and undergraduate curriculum coordinator of medical education, Department of Psychiatry at Indiana University, was most kind to correspond with me concerning her keen interest in the stress of a medical career, particularly as it affects women.

A special note of appreciation is due Aaron R. Beck, M.D., not just from me, but from all physicians for his creative understanding of depression and his invention of cognitive therapy.

Closer to home, my appreciation is extended to Lester Adelson, M.D., chief deputy coroner, Cuyahoga County, Ohio, my ally and friend in the struggle for knowledge. With sapience and wit he has asked Socratic questions to which his passion as teacher has fired me to find the answers.

Fauntleroy Ayers, Ph.D., was among those who prompted me to begin this book. He and his associates, Mr. Robert Jenks and Miss Florinda Unique, have taught me how determination and fantasy are necessary for creative work of any kind.

Mr. Konrad Meyer, volunteer in the Psychiatric Division of Huron Road Hospital, provided basic research material. He and the hospital librarian, Ms. Mary Krichbaum, supplied me with all the raw data I needed to review the topic.

Mrs. Lucille Nolan, head of the Department of Volunteers at the hospital, organized a program of lectures to high school students, called "Medical Insights," which began my teaching adolescents why they should not kill themselves. She has been the initiator of much of the successful community interaction that Huron Road Hospital has enjoyed, as well as an amazingly successful recruitment officer for the hundreds of volunteers who are indispensable aides in the hospital.

Encomiums have not been invented which will do adequate service to the devotion, enthusiasm, and time that Elaine J. Victoroff, my wife, has donated to the conception, development, and maturation of this project. Every phase of this book has been touched by her affectionate insistence on self-discipline. If the quality of writing is acceptable and not overly prolix, she must accept the credit.

Mrs. Margaret Jump, expert philologist, grammarian, and stylist, helped read proof and is most gratefully thanked. Special appreciation is deservedly extended to Mrs. Tilda Paltza, who typed faultless pages under considerable pressure of time and did so with amiable good nature.

This book has been a family project. My love and thanks to all begin with my sons Mark Alan Vlosky, Ph.D., Michael Victoroff, M.D., and Jeffrey Victoroff, M.D. Mark Alan, a clinical psychologist, Michael, and Jeffrey have discussed and corresponded with me about many aspects of the text and have given frank observations I could not have obtained from anyone else. Jeff helped with research. Indeed, he spent an entire summer analyzing data abstracted from thousands of admissions at Huron Road Hospital.

Attorney Gregory T. Victoroff, another son, helped enormously in the gathering of information and collaborated on Chapter 15, Suicide and the law, and Appendix B. Debra C. Victoroff, daughter, artist and designer, offered helpful comment and criticism from her knowledge of disability and mental retardation. Brian N. Victoroff, the son now in medical school, helped correct copy and made appropriate criticism regarding the use of language in the text. Brian collected data from questionnaires submitted to school officials regarding their experience with suicide in adolescence.

Joshua Drew Victoroff, my youngest son, has been an inspiration to this work just by being who he is.

Introduction

The evidence is unmistakable. Injury and death due to self-inflicted trauma and illness are increasing. The rate of acceleration of suicidal acts for certain vulnerable populations is on a runaway course. In the United States from 1960 to 1979, suicide rates for men almost tripled among the 20- to 24-year-old population and about doubled for young women. Rates in other parts of the world are reported as having tripled or even quadrupled. Adolescent girls attempt suicide more frequently than boys, but are less efficient in the lethality of their attempts. However, for a variety of reasons, the rate of death for attempted suicide in women is increasing. In the early 1960s, each age group jumped upward in the statistical incidence of self-destruction and continued to carry each year they aged this same increased propensity to suicide. There is another factor that adds to the urgency of our concern: Suicide is a greatly underreported event. Thus, the already recognized surge of self-destructive morbidity and death is in fact worse than officially projected. It may be a flood yet to crest.

Perhaps you've been shocked to receive the unexpected news that one of your patients had killed himself. If you experienced guilt and perplexity for having failed to recognize the risk, your feelings are not unique. Physicians, for the most part, are crisis-oriented. They focus on the potential for morbidity and death that suicide attempters bring into emergency rooms and the hospital wards. But they have only peripheral vision for the self-destructive patient before he is carried unconscious into the hospital. Yet fully one-third of patients who take their lives have seen a physician within three months of their suicide.

Rationalizations and self-consolation are predictable—and wrong: "The patient never told me he was so depressed." "How was I to know he had assumed his cancer was going to kill him?" "It really isn't any of my business that his marriage was breaking up and his wife took the children and didn't say where she was going." "Suicide is an esoteric, psychiatrist-type of business 'way out of my experience.'" "Even if I had suspected, there's really nothing I could have done. There's nothing anyone can do when someone wants to take his life."

Physicians in other matters do not blame others or offer lame excuses when found in error. The gynecologist who had reassured his patient that the shotty nodules in her breast were benign would be appalled if a malignancy were found. He'd look to himself to improve his diagnostic skills, not just shrug off the missed diagnosis. We physicians don't sufficiently acknowledge that suicide is a biological hazard to the patient for which we are responsible exactly as we are for sepsis, hemorrhage, fractured bones, and endocrine disorders.

In this text, I describe the suicidal patient and the phenomenon of suicide as the doctor encounters this event. Insofar as through this book I play the role of consulting psychiatrist for nonpsychiatrist physicians and health professionals, I offer suggestions regarding how persons and institutions might respond constructively to the tragedy of suicide in general and the youthful suicide in particular.

This text had its genesis in 1968 when, as chief of the Division of Psychiatry at Huron Road Hospital in Cleveland, Ohio, I began to follow the incidence of psychiatric patients in emergency care. Over the next four years, the statistics showed that the number of patients admitted for self-destructive cause jumped from 25 to 100, a 400 percent increase. The mean age fell from the low 30s to the high 20s, with a peak at approximately 16 years. The ratio of females to males increased to a peak of about 70 percent female.

The case load, while it has not continued to accelerate at quite the rate it did for the first four years, does continue to increase. Particularly affected are adolescents and young adults, and lately we are admitting young children who have made suicidal attempts. It's a wrenching experience for hospital personnel and for the attending physician to examine and care for a 12-year-old boy who has turned a pistol to his head and destroyed one eye. The shock reactions of the medical staff as well as of the family make it apparent that the psychiatrist called for consultation has the responsibility to help persons peripheral to the suicide as well as the patient.

I've lectured to many high school and college audiences on suicide. I offer the facts about epidemic suicide and then appeal to my audience to enter into partnership with their parents, teachers, and the health profession to help stop the rise in morbidity and mortality to which they are vulnerable. The lecture series has been expanded to involve school principals, psychologists, counselors, and teachers.

I have also developed a course for physicians in suicide recognition and prevention, with the hope that this program may help to reduce the malignant increase of suicide. In giving the course, it has become apparent that there is a significant lack of confidence in dealing with the self-destructive patient. This is not surprising. There is less-than-adequate preparation of the physician in detecting, understanding, and coping with suicide in patients—and in dealing with the dark face of suicide in his own mirror.

This book is an elaboration of these lectures, seminars, and courses. The inspiration that motivates the writing of it comes from a conviction that suicide may be the most readily preventable lethal disease in all of medicine—if only we learn how to recognize and treat its potential victims.

PART I

The phenomenon of suicide

CHAPTER 1

Kinds of suicide

Suicide is difficult to define. It's not a diagnosable disease, but, like skin rash, low homatocrit, and papilledema, a sign of many.

A middle-aged woman slashes her throat with a butcher knife. A teen-age boy points a gun into his mouth and pulls the trigger. An elderly man starts his car in a locked garage. These are examples of undeniable suicide.

Other cases are not so obvious. A recently jilted young man joins a sky-diving club. A middle-aged spinster whose mother has just died after a lingering illness begins to take long walks alone at night through high-crime areas. A teacher who has just lost his job because he exposed his genitals to one of his students drives his car at 90 mph on a limited access highway. If any of these should die, would it be suicide?

On another level, is the soldier committing suicide who throws himself on a grenade in an evident self-sacrificial attempt to save the lives of his comrades? How about the mother who can't swim and drowns attempting to save her child who has fallen into the water? Also, high school youth who take street drugs in any available quantity, or who climb water towers to paint their initials on them may be engaged in death-seeking behavior. If they die, is it by chance or by design?

An overweight patient who has just survived coronary bypass surgery, but ignores his diet and smokes two or more packs of cigarettes a day may claim he doesn't want to give up the good things in life. But if he dies, could his death be rightly attributed to suicide?

When a hysterical woman in confrontation with her husband impulsively swallows 30 five-grain aspirin tablets, she may not really expect to die but may be acting out the ritual of suicide. But if this woman should succumb to salicylate poisoning, she might be signed out by the coroner as a suicide even if her intentions were only to dramatize for her husband the depth of her mental anguish.

Socrates provoked the people of Athens, who then forced him to drink hemlock. A woman persuades her son to disconnect the life-support device while the nurse steps out of the room. Both manipulated others to cause them to die but they aren't classified as suicides.

Most of you can recall situations like this: You're attending a patient in acute illness, but not sick enough to warrant your anxiety about survival. But he announces to you with dire emphasis, "Doctor, I'm going to die tonight." Despite your reassurances and good care he does succumb. Similarly, old people, seemingly in good health, may predict their imminent death with quiet certitude. Then, as if keeping a promise, they die, confounding incredulous relatives and their physicians and raising a question if there's been a self-fulfilled prophecy. Such deaths aren't always explicable on the autopsy table. In attempting to account for these deaths, we're inclined to say, "The patient gave up his will to live," assuming a voluntary decision had been made to die. Abandoning the psychic state consistent with life and accepting a state of mind inclining to death is a form of suicide.

If we define suicide as a voluntary, deliberate act by an individual intended to cause his death, we won't include many self-inflicted illnesses and injuries that result in death. The simplistic definition fails to account for self-destructive acts not specifically intended by the victim to end with morbid result but nonetheless kill. It doesn't include the death of a person who had contrived with or persuaded another to kill him. It doesn't make provision for behavior that others judge to be self-destructive but is not intended by the victim to end in death.

For example, a rejected, despondent lover subjects himself to risky behavior. He doesn't intend to commit suicide simply, but

4

makes a contract with God or Fate: "I'll ride my motorcycle until I hit 100 miles per hour, then I'll slow down. If it's determined that I should die, then I'll die. But if I escape danger, then I'll understand that I'm expected to survive and I'll go on with my life." Such arrangements that result in death may be defined as conditional suicide.

A politician turned out of office by the fickleness of his constituency may suffer so much psychic pain because of the repudiation that he may surrender his ideals and his mature judgment. Where he was kind, he becomes rude; where honest, he is cynical; where trusting, suspicious. His selflessness degenerates to selfishness. His courage turns inside out to meanly retreat. Even his physical self-care deteriorates: He dresses slovenly, he overeats, quits exercise, and begins to drink excessively. This example of such a major decompensation of personality may be termed minisuicide, equivalent suicide, or partial suicide.

Before Mark David Chapman, a 25-year-old security guard, left Hawaii for New York, he signed himself out on his last day at work as "John Lennon." His shooting of the ex-Beatle superstar shocked the world. Lennon's death was totally unpredictable and unpreventable. It was, of course, a murder by a seemingly mentally deranged individual, but it may have been suicide by proxy. Mark Chapman may have been impelled to kill himself. Then, in a state of pathological identification, in the act of destroying John Lennon, Chapman may have symbolically committed suicide. Public figures are particularly vulnerable to this formula and may never have known the murderers who would use them as surrogates for their own malignant self-hatred.

Other substitutions for one's own self-destruction or mutilation may involve objects. Not only the cutting of one's wrists and autocastration, but also their substitutions—the smashing of prized belongings and the unexpected resignation from a long-held prestigious position—may signify a desperately dysphoric mood and might be examples of symbolic suicide.

If a couple of experienced, well-equipped scuba diving buddies go ice diving, lose their way trying to get back to the point of entry, run out of air and drown, in the absence of any clue to suicidal wish, their deaths may be described as unintentional suicide.

Intention and awareness

Sometimes the question is raised with regard to unsuccessful suicide attempts: "But was it a serious attempt? Did she really mean to die or was she just trying to scare everybody?" Implied in the question is another question: "If these wounds are really trivial, should the patient be considered as a true suicidal risk or as a manipulative blackmailer who presumably should be admonished for her infantile tactics?"

The intention to die may be presumed with acts of high lethality, but the seriousness of any act of suicide is correlated with the mental state of the patient and never can be summarily dismissed as trivial. A sensible definition of suicide must then include two variables: the degrees of *intention* and *awareness*. Knowing to what extent the person expects his act to result in death and how conscious he is of the consequences of his suicidal act has clinical relevance to prevention, identification of persons at risk, and treatment.

Assessment of intention is often related to the degree of lethality implicit in a suicidal act. If a man puts his head on a railroad track and is beheaded, we presume a high level of lethality for his act. A youngster who neglects his anticonvulsant medication, goes rock climbing, and falls to his death may have died by accident or by reason of indifference to whether he lives or dies. Such an act may exemplify equivocal lethality. A girl who impulsively empties bottles of her mother's medicine into her palm and swallows a mix of quinidine and methyldopa may not really expect to die; therefore, the intentional lethality of the act may be quite low.

The correlation between intention to die and lethality of a suicidal act is not always congruent. A bullet in the head, obviously expected to be highly lethal, may not result in death; swallowing ant poison might not have been intended by the victim to be more than a histrionic gesture of low lethality, yet could result in death.

Definitions

To understand suicide in general, it helps to know what the several kinds of suicide are. The following definitions should help.

6

Intentional suicide: An act or pattern of self-destructive behavior of high lethality, deliberately planned by the subject to result in his death.

Subintentional suicide: An act or pattern of self-destructive behavior of low or uncertain lethality, not clearly perceived by the subject as likely to result in his death.

Unintentional suicide: An act or pattern of self-destructive behavior of variable levels of lethality, not consciously expected by the subject to result in his death.

Parasuicide: An act designed by the subject to simulate suicide but characterized by low expectation of lethal outcome.

Euthanasia: An act that results in the death of a person by at least one other person; the motive is declared to be merciful and the means are as painless as possible. Euthanasia may be brought about by the direct request of the patient who consciously directs others to consummate his death. It may be called for by others who presume that the patient wishes to die. It may also be imposed upon a person who may not agree or might even object to termination of his life. Passive euthanasia occurs when interventions that could prolong life are suspended and the patient is allowed to die. Active euthanasia occurs when means are employed to end the life of a suffering person.

Chronic suicide: Instances of self-destructive behavior carried over an extended period, resulting in deterioration of health and/or decompensation of mental stability, and eventually ending in death.

Suicide attempters: Persons who at any time have made an intentional or subintentional suicide attempt.

Suicide contemplators: Those persons who manifest suicide ideation.

Suicide ideation: Thoughts, contemplations, reveries, fantasies, and obsessions in which a person invents themes and

7

stories with his suicidal death as an essential element. Vague premonitions of death or phobic apprehension of dying don't satisfy the definition. Examples are scenarios that include the subject's provoking an act of aggression or covertly managing a seeming accident that results in his being killed or that portray himself being stricken with a fatal disease.

Psychosomatic suicide: Severe ulcerative colitis, bronchial asthma, massive urticaria, hypertension, and anorexia nervosa are some of the diseases that under certain circumstances may be unconscious means of suicide.

Dyadic suicide: The event of murder followed by suicide is relatively rare, affecting fewer than 1,000 victims annually. It usually occurs in dyadic pathological relationships. Sometimes the mental disturbance contaminates an entire family, which is at risk for one of its members to institute a massacre. Physicians usually don't have the opportunity to pick up the vulnerable family as do school officials, local police, social agencies, employers, and friends. Some family members may be seen in psychiatric or psychological consultation, often referred by the courts for previous physical abuse against one or another.

Certain psychological patterns are suggestive of coming lethal violence. A psychotic with messianic delusions is a risk, such as a mother who believes she should die and take her children with her to rescue them from an ugly cruel world. Also dangerous is a severely dependent individual whose passivity hides fantasies of powerful, aggressive vengeance. An example would be a man who is extremely jealous of his wife, involved in an erotic, love-hate pattern of behavior with her. When he is rejected, he may kill her, the children, and everyone in sight.

The adolescent who sees himself as different from all other members of the family and rejected by the primary parent may experience a pattern of failure to win approval. Under sudden stress, such as an incident of ridicule in school, he may commit an ultimate act of murder and suicide.

Paradoxical suicidal behavior: Suicidal acts, frequently seen in children, manifest the continual and probably unconscious wish for maternal protection and help and may eventually become the cry for help of a suicidal act.

8

CHAPTER 2

Statistics and trends

It's helpful to be aware of certain statistical information in order to know what populations are at special risk for suicide. This information shows what factors may incline persons to consider self-destructive behavior. It can also disclose trends and patterns of suicide in our society and suggest how they probably will continue to change.

However, we have to be cautious about statistics of suicide. Many deaths that are unambiguously intentional are never discovered, recognized, or admitted as suicide. Others that are acknowledged never are officially reported as such. Suicides that are either not fully intended or are altogether unintended are not considered at all in vital statistics on self-destructive acts. Considering all this, tables that purport to display raw numbers of suicides are underreported. And it's tempting to say they are grossly underreported.

Many writers naively offer estimates of how inexact official tabulations really are. For example, after admitting we don't know and can never know how many vehicular fatal accidents are masked suicides, writers who claim that "up to 15 percent are suicides" are merely conjecturing and may be simply silly. Perhaps more vehicular deaths, except the most obvious accidents that the victims could not possibly have predicted, such as being hit by a truck careening downhill with failed brakes, are suicides; perhaps none are. By backtracking over the information available in case histories—doing a "suicide autopsy" of persons who have died of seeming driver error—some fatalities not counted in the suicide statistics may very well be found to have been intended. Many suicides are probably buried in sport, industrial, and household accidents. Some may skew statistics of suicide in young children out of refusal to believe youngsters would die by their own hands.

Because of the time involved in collecting raw data, culling out contradictory or irrelevant input, subjecting the refined material to mathematical analysis, then restating what has been learned, published statistics about suicide are out-of-date by at least two years. The *World Almanac* in 1982 gives vital statistics dated 1978. An article on the subject of suicide by psychiatrists appears in the *Journal of Clinical Psychiatry*, August 1980. The journal's findings are based on information on physician deaths that had been obtained from the American Medical Association in 1967–1972.

In the early 1970s, suicide rates from 1936 to 1968 were collated in the United States. Studies on the data determined that during this time suicide rates had decreased. This news was reassuring and could have supported a complacent attitude, delaying research and tending to minimize the need for aggressive public health attention to suicidal behavior. The medical community was reporting such encouraging news at a time precisely when suicide rates, especially for young people, were ascending rapidly.

It may be said in time that the alarm that in part has inspired the writing and publishing of this book was an overstatement—if statistics then show a reduction in suicide.

That prospect is unlikely, as a new research tool, called "cohort analysis," shows. This technique is used to study the manner in which an age-specific group, such as 20- to 25-year-olds, change the likelihood of suicidal behavior as the group itself ages. Recent studies tentatively indicate that younger groups are thinking about suicide, making nonlethal and lethal attempts, and succeeding in suicide at a higher rate which persists as the group or cohort ages. It's true that the rate of increase may slow or level off at older ages, but if the trends continue the higher incidence will eventually affect older persons as the young, more vulnerable cohorts age.

Because the data aren't well-documented, certain trends and tendencies demonstrated by suicidal persons cannot be accurately placed on numerical scales. What can be done is to offer you tentative inferences as markers for your own practice, which if you use with discretion and common sense can be helpful in considering a particular patient's vulnerability at a specific time in his life. As the factors that incline the patient to suicide add up, each raises the likelihood of suicide. The breaking point, the moment when defenses against self-murder crumble, depends on the strength of personality in managing stress and the power of the destructive influences, intrinsic and extrinsic, that are bearing down on the patient.

Populations at risk are described briefly in this chapter. In a later chapter, their characteristics will be more fully identified. In the brief descriptions, there is just the minimum of classifying suicidal behavior by specific numbers. You need a more pragmatic approach in order to estimate suicidal potential in your patients. For example, it's probably enough for you to know that the middle-aged, alcoholic man in respiratory arrest after self-induced carbon monoxide poisoning falls into one of the highest categories of suicide risk. With that information, you can devise a treatment plan that may include a request for psychiatric consultation, the use of restraints, and appropriate advice to the staff on protocol for dealing with relatives and visitors.

Marital status. Being married is a powerful protection against suicide. The ratio of suicide attempts and successes for the married is about half what it is for single persons. Losing a spouse through death more than doubles suicide potential. Ending a marriage by divorce almost triples the risk, and the susceptibility to suicide is much greater for men who are divorced as compared to women. The suicide rate increases only slightly for ex-wives, but it's almost sixfold for ex-husbands. Although suicide is less frequent among married persons, there is an exception. The rate of suicide in married persons under age 20, both men and women, is higher than for single individuals.

Mental illness. The risk for suicide attempts and success is at least 30 times greater for depressed patients with a history of

11

psychiatric hospitalization than for persons in the general population. This includes patients suffering neurotic as well as psychotic depression. The risk for schizophrenics is about nine times that of nonschizophrenics.

Depressed patients, particularly those who are psychotic and diagnosed as having bipolar and unipolar affect disorders, together with chronic alcoholics who communicate suicidal ideas, constitute approximately half of all suicides.

Violence. The sum of deaths for suicide, homicide, and accident exceeds all other causes of death in persons aged one to 39. Many deaths attributable to homicide are actually the result of victim-precipitated homicides. Many injuries and deaths recorded as accidental are actually masked suicide.

Children. Death by suicide is unusual among children up to 15 years of age. However, the relatively low fatality totals are attributable more to ignorance about how to commit a lethal act efficiently than to low intensity of intent.

The wish to die is expressed by many depressed youth. Children—even younger than 10—who are mentally retarded, those with antisocial tendencies or who suffer thought disorders or psychotic symptoms, and youngsters who are drug or alcohol users constitute a readily identifiable cadre of susceptibles. Not so obvious in this category, however, are the children of professional families, particularly physicians' children.

Self-destructive behavior in children five to 10 years of age does occur. Physicians should be especially wary when examining youngsters who have suffered seemingly accidental injuries due to self-poisoning, gun-related incidents, burns, and falls. More than half the number of six- to 12-year-olds admitted to a psychiatric hospital acknowledged preoccupation with suicide or threatened or attempted to kill themselves.

Adolescents and early adults. The increase in the rate of suicides and unsuccessful attempts among 15- to 24-year-olds has been epidemic. The incidence for boys has tripled since 1960 and has about doubled for girls. Although fatalities among boys are greater than for girls, the gap may be narrowing.

The study of cohorts seems to indicate that as the age groups mature, they carry with them their higher propensity to suicide, which leads to the conclusion that, unless a reversal occurs, the incidence of suicide will continue to increase in years to come. But the outlook may not be so pessimistic. Cohort studies done before publication of this book are based on demographic data up to 1977. A comparison of the vital statistics from 1978 with those from 1977 shows a slight but distinctly lower incidence of actual suicide in all age groups up to those 75–79 years old. Whether the trend toward increased suicide has peaked, whether the present statistical analyses are in error, or whether small differences are irrelevant, is unclear.

Apart from the cold data, insofar as physicians and those in other health-care professions are concerned, the number of young people who are attempting and succeeding in killing themselves is a tragic problem for the community, particularly for the emotionally ravaged immediate families.

Women. The peak incidence for suicide attempts and deaths occurs for women between the ages of 50–54. Women make suicide attempts three times more often than men, but attempts by men are more lethal and end in death more often.

There is an increased incidence of suicide attempts and successes during the week before menstruation. These events may have little or no demonstrable connection with psychological stress or trauma.

Depression, social isolation, and verbalizations about suicide in adult women are correlated with more frequent attempts and more serious lethality.

The suicide rate in pregnancy is minuscule compared with nonpregnant women of comparable age. There has been a sevenfold decrease in suicide during pregnancy in the last 30 years, and an additional twofold decrease in suicide during pregnancy since the availability of abortion on demand.

When it does occur during pregnancy, suicide is more common in young women, particularly teenagers. Suicides are more likely to occur in the first trimester and in the final month of pregnancy, particularly in unmarried women. Although postpartum suicides do occur, they are more likely several months after the delivery than immediately after birth.

Men. Suicidal acts increase for each male cohort. There is a slight decline in suicidal frequency from ages 30–45, but the rates rise again, peaking at 75–79 years. Generally, males are three times more successful than women in suicide attempts. At every age, males commit suicide with higher incidence than women.

Prior attempters. The number of living Americans with suicidal histories may be as great as 10 million. Conservatively speaking, there are probably 500,000 to one million suicide attempts annually.

As many as 90 percent of patients who have made an unsuccessful suicide attempt experience recurring urges to self-destruction in the convalescent period after returning home from the hospital and before getting back to work and assuming the life pattern natural to themselves and before once again regaining emotional balance.

At least 10 percent of persons who have survived an attempted suicide will die of suicide. Multiple attempters may increase the lethal quality of their successive attempts. Therefore, the more unsuccessful attempts, the more likely the following one will be fatal.

Religion. In the United States, Protestants are represented highest in the groups of suicide. Catholics and Jews are next. Last are Americans practicing religions of the Orient, such as Buddhism, Islam, and Hinduism.

Relatively few suicidal persons are encouraged or inhibited strongly by religious affiliation. More relevant is the personal philosophy the individual has about the value of life, the meaning of his existence, the possibility of reward or punishment in an afterlife, and the possibility of reincarnation. A Zen Buddhist who may believe his life is disagreeable and can be logically surrendered for a chance at another is at greater risk for suicide than the Baptist who grew up with a vivid picture of hell or the Catholic who was taught that suicide is a mortal sin.

Physicians and their families. Male physicians generally, up to the age of retirement, kill themselves at a somewhat higher rate than the national norms. Women physicians, however, have a much higher rate of suicide, perhaps double the rate for males. The suicide rate for women doctors may be about three times that for American women of the same age. Most doctor suicides occur before the age of 45. The single woman physician under age 35 and the woman in training are at special risk.

Physicians at retirement age are considerably more likely to kill themselves than nonphysicians of the same age. Psychiatrists are especially vulnerable to suicide, more so than other physicians. Doctors who have suffered disciplinary action and have been placed on probation by examining boards are at high risk for suicide.

High intelligence and familiarity with lethal means are no doubt associated with increased mortality in physician populations, including members of their families.

American Indians and Alaskans. American Indian and Alaskan youths have higher rates of death-intended behavior than the general population. As the cohorts age to about 45, the incidence is higher, then levels off. Deaths related to alcoholism, which may well be included in both overt and subintentional suicide, are many times greater than in the general population.

Blacks. Although suicide rates for whites exceed those for blacks, the difference between the races has been closing. Suicide rates among young blacks has increased slightly faster than for whites, particularly among 15- to 19-year-old males. The homicide rate, which may reflect suicide intention in part, is far greater in blacks than in whites.

Young black females are actually at greater risk than black males up to age 17, although in adult years, black females are distinctly lower in attempts and successes than black males.

Epileptics. The rate for initial and repeated suicidal attempts for epileptics is considerably greater than general population prevalence rates for nonepileptics at all ages. Men epileptics are much more likely to commit suicide than women epileptics. As might be expected, epileptics often use their anticonvulsant drugs, especially barbiturates, for self-destructive acts, frequently using alcohol in addition to the medications. Many epileptics are depressed because of the economic penalties their illness imposes. They are affected by prejudice and an inability to achieve in education, marriage, or employment. Some have a severely negative self-image.

The patient suffering from temporal-lobe epilepsy frequently manifests personality disturbances. About 10 percent of patients suffering from temporal-lobe epilepsy with psychomotor seizures attempt suicide. Males are slightly more likely to try than females, and are more likely to make multiple attempts.

Substance abusers. There is a tremendously higher incidence of suicidal behavior among drug and alcohol users and abusers than in the general population. This is particularly true for unsuccessful and multiple attempters. The proportion of suicidal attempts that end fatally is higher than for nonusers of alcohol and drugs. Blacks, whites, and other ethnic groups tend to be less differentiated among suicide attempters if they are drug and alcohol users. However, the study findings may be skewed by the fact that a substantial number of substance abusers are veterans of the Vietnam War.

The risk of death by suicide is formidable among those who drink to excess, increasing generally with the severity of the alcoholism and its duration. Alcoholic intoxication is involved in approximately one-third of successful suicides. At least one in every 10 chronic alcoholics dies of intentional suicide. Many more die of subintentional or unintended suicide.

Prisoners. Most suicides in jails and prisons occur within 48 hours of incarceration. The population of greatest risk are first-term male offenders. The severity of charges for which the prisoner is held varies widely and does not seem to correlate with the likelihood of suicide. Most attempts at death occur by hanging, for the obvious reason that asphyxia by an article of clothing is the means most available to the prisoner.

After examination by physicians. Almost three-fourths of all suicides have been examined by a physician within a year of death. About a third have been seen by a doctor within three weeks of self-destruction. Almost half the number of psychiatric patients who commit suicide have been seen in psychiatric out-patient departments within 30 days of death, and of these, the percentage of men and women is about equal.

Relation to murder. Sixteen percent of suicides have previously committed murder.

Relation to inner aggression. It's probable that the suicide rate in some degree is tied to guilt and aggression. Cultures in which childrearing practices emphasize guilt and suppress normal aggression are likely to have high rates of suicide. The highest susceptibility to suicide occurs in upper, middle, professional, and managerial classes, particularly among artists, intellectuals, and scientists, all of whom are less likely to express aggression. The lowest suicide rates are generally among those least professionally skilled, least organizationally involved, and least constrained in expressions of aggression.

Methods. Use of guns for suicide carries with it the greatest likelihood of death. Poisons, including drugs, are the next most lethal device. Deaths by self-inflicted cuts and stabs, jumping from high places, carbon monoxide, methane, propane, and other toxic gases that may be inhaled, hanging, and drowning follow in order of frequency. A variety of bizarre techniques include self-electrocution, injection with paraffin, cooking oil, peanut butter, mercury, deodorant, or mayonnaise, walking into the propeller of an airplane, hammering a nail or barbecue spit into the skull, boring a hole in the head, sawing off a limb, and intentional rock climbing falls.

Persons younger than 30 years of age seem more inclined to slit their wrists than those in older age groups. Adults are more likely to use poisons or exhaust or illuminating gas. Persons who are younger than 50 years are more likely to use drugs in overdose.

The most frequently used instruments of death among males who successfully suicide are firearms. Asphyxia by strangulation is the next most frequent technique, closely followed by poisoning. Among females, poisoning is the most common means of suicide. Cervical compression and firearms follow. Drowning and jumping from high places occur relatively infrequently in both sexes, but are significantly higher in females than males. Jumping is fantasized by young children.

Overdose by prescribed drugs is by far the most frequent means of suicidal attempt. The drugs used most frequently are the benzodiazepines, with diazepam (Valium) heading the list. In following order of frequency are analgesics, tricyclic antidepressants, phenothiazines, hypnotics, anticonvulsants, and barbiturates.

17

From the mid 1960s through the early 1970s, there was more than 100 percent increase in the number of drug-overdose suicide attempts. Most of these occurred among young adults. The trend since has included even younger persons in the adolescent and preadolescent years. The number of attempts and successful drug-overdose suicides since the mid 1970s seems to be slightly decreasing in most age levels but continues to rise among adolescents and in children.

Antipsychotic drug overdose has increased with the greater availability and variety of these drugs and with the greater recourse general practitioners and psychiatrists have to them as therapeutic agents. The lethal potential of psychotrophic drugs is considerably increased when these agents are used in mixed injections or combined with alcohol.

Mellaril, Thorazine, and Prolixin are major phenothiazine-derivative tranquilizers. Other neuroleptic drugs or tricyclic antidepressants combined with them are frequently employed in suicide attempts. Triavil, a combination antipsychotic and tricyclic antidepressant, is frequently mixed with central system depressants, such as phenobarbital, diazepam, and glutethimide in suicide attempts.

Although women tend to avoid mutilating methods for suicide, they are slightly more likely than men to jump from high places and cause severe body disfigurement. It may merely be that they give no thought to the consequence of jumping from a high place.

Geosuicide. One thousand suicides per day are reported to the World Health Organization. The city with the highest suicide rate in the world is West Berlin. Austria and Hungary, by a substantial margin, have the highest incidence of suicide, followed by Switzerland, Denmark, West Germany, and Sweden. Japan, France, Belgium, and the United States occupy the middle level of incidence. At the lowest level stand Norway, the Netherlands, Portugal, the United Kingdom, and, at the lowest, Ireland.

In every country, suicide trends described for the United States generally seem to be duplicated for men but are different for women. Suicide rates go up generally with age and are lower for women. The peak age for suicide among men is 65 or older, except for Denmark, where the peak is at 45 to 64, and Ireland where it is at 25 to 44. Rates for women 15 to 19 are much higher in Japan than in the United States, nearly equal to men.

Among women, the suicide rates peak at 45 to 64 in the United States, Denmark, Ireland, Norway, Sweden, and Switzerland. Women 65 and older have the highest rate for suicide in Austria, Belgium, France, Japan, the Netherlands, and Portugal. In the United Kingdom, the death rates for female suicides are identical in the 45-to-64 and 65-and-older groups.

There has been an international rise in suicide rates. From the 1940s to the 1970s, the British reported a 3,000-percent increase in the rate of suicide attempts. Comparing the change in rates in 1964 with 1953, of 13 selected countries only Austria, Japan, and Italy showed a slight decline in the rate. France showed no change. At that time, there was an eight percent increase in the United States. In the worldwide upsurge in suicide seen at the time, the largest increase was registered among young persons. In most English-speaking countries, the largest increase in male suicide was at the ages of 15 to 24. Among nonwhite males in the United States, the rate rose by more than 80 percent. In Austria, Poland, Hungary, and Australia, the largest increases among males was reported at ages 25 to 44.

In every country where the overall suicide rates for females increased, the most substantial rate was for ages under 45. The rate doubled in England at ages 15 to 24 and increased almost as much at these ages and at 25 to 44 in Australia and among nonwhite females in the United States.

When these statistics are compared with the international statistics for 1977, the latest available, it is obvious that the escalation of suicide has continued. In Austria, the German Federal Republic, Sweden, Japan, France, Belgium, and the United States, there has been substantial increase. In no country has there been a regression.

Manifestly, whatever forces are at work increasing the propensity to suicide, it affects almost all nations of the world equally.

Economic factors. The suicide rate decreases in wartime and during times of prosperity. It rises in peacetime, particularly during economic depressions, and it affects higher income groups to a greater degree than those of moderate and low income.

Seasonal factors. The fewest suicides in America and Northern Europe seem to occur in December. Most attempts occur in April and May. These inferences are not valuable, since suicide seems also to be influenced by geography, mobility of population, and climatic changes. For example, suicides at Niagara Falls are more likely to occur in August and September, concurrent with the heaviest tourist traffic.

Suicide in children and adolescents occurs twice as often during the fall months of September through December than during the other eight months combined.

Relation to child abuse. There is no straightforward correlation between child abuse and attempted suicide; however, parents who attempt suicide are somewhat more likely than others to abuse their children.

Intimates. There is a striking increase in the likelihood of suicidal attempts and successes by persons who have been exposed to the suicide of some person close to them.

Sequential and simultaneous suicide attempts among family members, among groups, and in organizational settings are a formidable hazard. There is some suggestion of genetic predisposition to such suicidal behavior. Hemingway died of a self-inflicted shotgun blast. His father shot himself to death when the author was 29. Hemingway's sister died of a drug overdose, presumed a suicide.

When Freddie Prinze and Marilyn Monroe died, presumably of suicide, there were numerous suicide attempts among persons in populations identified with them. After public figures kill themselves there is a distinct probability that there will be an increase in overt suicides and in fatalities that may be disguised suicides, such as in automobile accidents.

Conspicuous persons. Literary, artistic, and theatrical people are at greater risk for suicide than persons who are engaged in more inconspicuous professions. Examples include Virginia Woolf, novelist; Hart Crane, poet; Ernest Hemingway, novelist; Marilyn Monroe, movie star; Freddie Prinze, TV comic; Sylvia Plath, poet; Ann Sexton, writer; Charles Boyer, movie star; Yukio Mishima, novelist; Dave Garroway, TV personality; Inger Stevens, movie star; and Phil Ochs, singer.

Threateners. Contrary to the often-repeated maxim "Those who say they will, never do it," a high proportion of persons who commit suicide have a history of prior suicidal threats.

Attempters. Suicide attempts are not tabulated. Estimates vary widely. There are anywhere from eight to 90 times as many attempts as there are completed suicides. Attempts are more frequent among young persons, and successful suicide is more likely in older persons, particularly males.

Suicide in nonpsychiatric hospitals. Suicide rates and trends in nonpsychiatric hospital facilities are noted here with the caution that, though they are from the best available data, the studies they come from are five to 30 years old. The rate of suicide seems to be as much as three and one-half times that of the general population and 10 times higher than in psychiatric hospitals. However, when patients diagnosed as mentally ill who are treated on the medical and surgical facilities and make suicide attempts are removed from the count, the rates for suicide within the hospital fall to a level closer to the rates that prevail outside the hospital for those same groups.

Patients suffering from severe chronic diseases affecting the respiratory, cardiac, and renal systems and those suffering intractable pain or with marked loss of functional efficiency and independence are at greatest risk. Many suffer organic brain disorders. Although this fact would seem to suggest that most suicides in hospitals occur to older persons, the age groups below 34 may have the highest suicide rates. Patients admitted as victims of assault, suicidal acts, or accidents and those suffering from circulatory disorders seem to be at highest risk, followed by patients with respiratory illness. At lower incidence are the patients suffering from endocrine, metabolic, nutritional, and neoplastic diseases.

About three-quarters of hospital suicides die in the hospital environment, and one-quarter while out on leave. Most patients die by jumping from a high place in the hospital: window, roof, ventilating shaft, or stairwell. Hanging from curtain rods, clothes hooks, shower rods, grilles, and pipes is the next-preferred suicidal method. Most of those patients who made suicide attempts while on pass or leave did so with guns. Jumping in front of a vehicle and drowning were the next two frequently used methods. These data have been derived from experiences in Veterans Administration hospitals. Other studies regarding patients in general hospitals do not indicate a high number of suicides on leave, probably because fewer patients are let out on leave from medical and surgical units of general hospitals than from government-managed hospitals.

Hospitalized patients most often kill themselves in their own rooms, next often in an unattended area and in washrooms. In a majority of attempted and completed suicides in hospitals, psychiatric consultation was neither requested nor obtained.

CHAPTER 3

Motives for suicide

The bartender recognized the depressed demeanor of the patron: a disconsolate young man who sat hunched over his drink. One hand held his shot glass, the other clutched his coat together under his chin. After a bit of friendly encouragement, the young man hoarsely told his sad situation. His mother had died and left her fortune to his younger brother; his wife, disgusted by that, took the children and left him; his company had just laid him off; at the last moment he had switched his bet at the race track from the horse that won to a loser.

With a commiserative shake of his head, the bartender volunteered, "I can see why you're so down. If that happened to me, I'd cut my throat."

With a raspy sigh, the customer opened his collar. "Me too," he agreed, exposing his slashed neck.

The familiar joke illustrates the common impression that suicidal behavior is the result of situational stress. Certainly, some acts of suicide are a reaction to imminent crisis; however, the usual reaction of surprise and bewilderment that follows the news of many suicide attempts is consistent with obscure and probably unknowable motivation. The less insight observers have why a victim attempted suicide, the greater the shock. "She had everything to live for" contrasts with "If I were in her position, I might have done the same."

Establishing why people kill themselves is not easy. The principal witness of successful suicide, of course, cannot give direct testimony, and suicide notes are suspect. Many attempters may embellish, distort, minimize, exaggerate, or conceal reasons for suicide. In a majority of cases, however, reasons for suicide are freely acknowledged or readily obtained by direct interview or in psychiatric consultation.

Aside from the patient, useful information can be obtained from intimates such as family, friends, employers, and co-workers. Casual acquaintances with no ax to grind may sometimes make observations that can be helpful. With the patient's consent, information may be solicited from physicians, psychiatrists, psychologists, and case workers who have treated him.

Karl Menninger has identified three elements that motivate suicidal acts in whole or in part. The first is the *wish to be dead*. This is an almost universal accompaniment to dysphoria and reveals a kind of melancholy, dispirited reaction to the burdensome quality of life and to the seductive tranquility death would bring. On being asked, "How many of you can recollect having, at any time in your lives, a wish you were dead?" most members of an audience would raise their hands.

The *wish to die* (be killed) is quite different from the wish to be dead. It includes a hostile element and strongly implies self-hatred. The wish is to be moved passively from a state of living to a state of death.

The *wish to kill* as the third factor that motivates suicide is derived from the psychodynamic insight that some suicidal acts are murders turned against the self.

We can begin the process of categorizing the reasons for suicide by dividing the triers into two broad groups: *psychotics*, those who have lost or have suffered severely compromised access to mental reality, and *nonpsychotics*, those who retain the ability to think and reason consistent with what is real.

There are many stages and kinds of mental illness that don't conform to this simple dichotomy. Patients who suffer chronic psychosis in remission may be quite logical and reality-oriented. Patients who are classified as psychoneurotic may, in periods of severe dissociation, be so confused that they cannot think logically. A phobic but nonpsychotic patient may in a state of panic attempt to jump from an airplane, terrified of being in flight and fearful that the plane may crash.

24

The psychotic patient's motives for suicide may emerge from his misconception of what's happening in real life. He may be suffering from persecutory delusions. For example, a man who tried to hang himself believed that he was the victim of a plot that would result in the death of all women in the world, leaving him the target of sexual demands of all the surviving men who would force him into unspeakable homosexual acts. Auditory hallucinations, "the voice of my dead father," ordered a 16-year-old high school senior girl to drink a can of lighter fluid. "Kill yourself," ordered the angry voice. These are false sensory cues that the psychotic person cannot, by reason of his illness, subject to reasonable examination and that may directly lead to suicide.

Patients suffering organic brain disorders may commit suicide. Everything from toxic reaction to alcohol and drugs, postsurgical anesthesia, cerebral depression, arteriosclerotic brain disease, metabolic disturbances such as diabetic ketosis or respiratory alkalosis, hypoxia due to blood loss, trauma to the brain, brain tumor, endocrine diseases such as hypothyroidism, or postconvulsive confusional states may result in sensory and cognitive misperception by the patient to the effect that he is in a threatened state, hopelessly ill, or that the hospital staff intends to kill him.

The motivation for suicide in the patient driven by internal stimuli may be to escape from or to give in to the perceived overwhelming command. It may be the inspired self-sacrifice of the victim told by "the voices" that on her death "the world will be cleansed of its filth" or, as a consequence of pouring gasoline on her body and igniting it, that her soul "will ascend to heaven." In bizarre self-mutilation, the psychotic patient may believe that at the instant he cuts off his arm or his penis or plucks out his eye, all his enemies will simultaneously die and he will receive complete exoneration for all the wrongs he has ever committed.

But there are nonpsychotics, too, who commit suicide, as these headlines attest:

- Father of five, unable to feed family, seeks death by fire
- Black businessman attacks police officer and is shot to death
- Television program canceled, youth leaps to death
- Just divorced physician found dead by suicide

- Murder suspect found hanged in basement after 18 days
- Teen computer whiz dies of suicide: gunshot wound to the head
- Woman drives car off pier, drowns self and two children

What are the motivations that overwhelm the powerful instinct of all living beings to survive?

Certain conditions are common to all suicides in varying degrees. A useful comparison may be made with infection. The degree of morbidity or the possibility of fatal effect is decided by the resistance of the host, the virulence of the agent, and the circumstances of the infection. Similarly, the likelihood that a suicide attempt will occur is determined by the nature of the causative agent or agents, the vulnerability of the victim, and the intensity of exposure.

Just before a person performs a suicidal act, he may perceive himself in grave and escalating danger—the causative agent. (*My boss examined the books. He knows I've been stealing.*) As a result, he becomes terribly distraught—vulnerability. (*I'll be caught. I never felt so terrified.*) His thought processes become obsessed with insufferable anguish so that he is unable to consider alternatives—intensity of exposure. (*I can't bear the shame. I must die.*) Impelled by desperate urgency to end this torment, he chooses death.

Causative agents

Social difficulties. Friction with spouse, friend, family, or fellow workers, job instability, financial dependency, legal problems.

Recent loss. Bereavement due to death of a loved person, separation from important figures, such as from one's children after divorce, the breakup of a love affair.

Guilt and shame. Engendered in betrayal of a trust, involvement in an extramarital affair, or public humiliation, such as arrest and conviction for crime.

Birthdays. Celebration of a birthday, particularly in America, constitutes a potentially stressful event. Children and adolescents who feel a deep need for recognition and yearn for loving expressions from their parents, siblings, and peers focus on the event of the birthday as a time when the usual business of the family and social life ceases and each intimate person concerned takes special notice of the birthday. The anticipation of gifts, cards, a party, a birthday cake with candles, special privileges, and congratulatory expressions of devotion and affection are sometimes built up to far beyond what might reasonably be expected, and it's all too often doomed to disappointment.

The frequency of suicidal acts at the time of birthdays for young people is not known, but clinical experience suggests that it may be more likely around that time.

For older persons, birthdays may have poignant meaning. They may reflect back on days when they were ignored or rejected, and a pattern of anniversary depression may occur. Narcissistic individuals see the accretion of birthdays as portentiously marking their decline to loss of functional efficiency, aging, and death. Along with anniversaries and holidays, birthdays impose a definite stress, increasing the likelihood of suicide in susceptibles.

Fear. Caused by real or imagined threats to body integrity or to life itself as might come with the belief that one is marked for assassination, suffering disease with fatal prognosis, or going insane.

Loss of control of the environment. As happens when a person enters military service or is relocated by his company, or as might be felt when an undesirable pregnancy occurs.

Pain. Unremitting anguish without the possibility of relief, or a threat of unendurable pain, such as the prospect of chronic, increasingly painful disease.

Altruism. The seeking of death to benefit another, as in the instances of chronic invalids who believe that when they die they will relieve their families of the emotional and financial burdens. Martyrs who sacrifice themselves for others.

Failure. As with the bankruptcy of a business, or in the belief that a cause will be lost because of one's error. Suspension from school because of poor grades or behavior may result in such loss of pride as to make death appealing.

Hereditary factors. A high family incidence of suicide may be more likely due to imitative behavior and psychological identification than to biological or genetic factors. However, studies of adoptive children whose natural parents manifested affective mental illness and schizophrenia tentatively suggest that, despite a comfortable and supportive environmental setting, they may be genetically disposed to be at high risk for suicide.

Biological markers for suicide. Preliminary but promising research suggests that monoamine oxidase levels in platelets may offer a biological marker suggestive of suicide proclivity. Those with low MAO levels in the platelets may be at considerably higher risk for suicide than those in mid-range.

In other studies, patients with low 5-hydroxyindoleacetic acid (5-HIAA) are shown to attempt suicide more often than those who have higher values and supposedly use more violent means. It's possible that the low 5-HIAA levels are linked to genetic determinants that cause increased vulnerability to many psychiatric illnesses as well as suicidal impulsive behavior.

Studies of this nature are highly tentative and have mainly been done in research on depressed patients.

Psychosocial factors. Psychosocial damage in some individuals leads to extremely poor social skills, inability to hold employment or to learn, mental retardation, and dyslexia. Extreme lack of trust in the environment may predispose to suicide as an escape.

The common psychological effector in nearly all suicides is depression, the despairing mood, the anomie that bleaches the color from life. Chronically depressed individuals who have "never known a day of happiness" live with an inconsolable disappointment and sadness that make existence meaningless.

Narcissistic persons who believe they come first and that society must obey their whims and fill their demands perseverate the psychological set called infantile omnipotence. They are incapable of dealing with frustration and may flee from a situation that refuses to respond to their cue.

Melancholic persons are convinced that they are at the mercy of forces inimical to their existence. On a more severe level, manic-depressive patients in the depressed phase—now categorized as bipolar or unipolar affect disorder—are a population highly vulnerable to self-destruction.

The flagrant misconstructions of the world perceived by the schizophrenic include paranoid suspicions. His dread of plots and evil mischief creates a universe of peril from which he may try to escape by suicide.

Vulnerability of the victim

It's unlikely that a person in good mental health will commit suicide. There may be exceptions whereby the person able to survey his situation carefully and contemplate his resources for coping may arrive at the conclusion that suicide is the only rational choice. But universal or even widespread agreement with such a judgment is unlikely.

Most suicidal persons undergo transient episodes in which their suicidal impulsions become especially dangerous. For example, persons who have suffered loss in childhood of a parent or other loved person are more likely to suicide in adult years if again they experience significant loss.

Persons obsessed with high perfectionistic standards and those who have been brought up to believe that failure is intolerable and will result in loss of love or overt rejection cannot cope with their discerned inadequacies.

Those alienated from others, unable to socialize, or who feel ostracized are walled-off by psychological barriers from access to support from others in the community. Schizoid individuals are frequently devoid of the capacity of forming or maintaining warm and affectionate ties. They may be deprived from childhood of good social nurturance.

Aside from the neurotic, psychotic, and characterologically defective idea processing, brain function is also vulnerable to disease, injury, metabolic maladjustment, congenital defects, aging, and toxic influences. Alcoholism—as often as all the other maladaptive instances put together—is the agent most likely to lead to suicide.

When all the circumstances predisposing to suicide come together, the potential victim needs all his mental skills to discern the threat and seek alternatives, to fight or to flee. All too often, the response is mental paralysis.

As loss of alveoli in chronic obstructive lung disease makes breathing more difficult, so when dendritic connections are clogged and clotted by neurotic fears, panic, delusions, or drug or alcohol intoxication, rational thought is not free to deal with the impulse to escape the anguish, sometimes by suicide.

The conditions that lead to suicide are like tumblers in a safe lock when the dial is spun at random. By chance they all fall into place and the lock disengages. Similarly, the elements in a suicide bounce about, with no one factor sufficient in itself to provoke suicide. Then, especially if alcohol is added to the combination, lubricating the elements so they tumble more freely, they may come together to undo the victim's defenses. The door to his mental integrity falls ajar, and life is lost.

Suicide-prone persons experience a raging interior debate between the pessimistic ideation that says, "No choice, no other choice. Do it. Stop thinking. Do it now!" versus the executive component of a healthy ego that argues, "This is absolutely crazy thinking, stop it!"

Vulnerable people may be easily persuaded to kill themselves, and suicidal behavior may be an imitative phenomenon. Goethe wrote the poignant novel, *Sorrows of Young Werther*, in 1774, the story of a young man who shot himself because of unrequited love. A wave of suicides that subsequently occurred all over Europe was attributed to the novel, causing some countries to ban the book.

Richard Bach wrote in *Illusions* that life is a school from which dropping out—suicide—is not a disgrace. Jason Perrine, 16, and Dawn Swisher, his 15-year-old sweetheart, read *Illusions* and appropriated the message. Then Jason, with Dawn at his side, raced his car at 110 miles per hour and crashed through a cinder block wall near their high school. Jason died and Dawn was critically injured.

In France, the use of illuminating gas for suicide was so prevalent in the 1830s, it inspired the artist Octave Tassaert to paint *The Suicide*. His depiction of a mother and daughter in a garret dying of gas poisoning is poignantly realistic and gives instant visualization of the temper of the times, consistent with an epidemic of suicide. Emphasizing this melodrama, Tassaert himself died of illuminating gas poisoning. The bizarre tragedy in Jonestown, Guyana, in which more than 900 members of the People's Temple Commune died in mass suicides, brings epidemic suicide right into our time.

Psychohistorical forces

The reasons for the worldwide increase in suicide since the early '60s can only be conjectured: We can note the influences on our civilization, then judge whether any of them may make people more vulnerable. World War II, the curse of the Holocaust, the Korean conflict, the cold war with the U.S.S.R., the Vietnam War, the unrelenting menace of nuclear havoc, the brinkmanship of the Middle East, the apprehension of Soviet and Chinese open warfare, and the growth of terrorism have established a climate of dread and uncertainty, a sense of foreboding and doom, with a fear that the destiny of mankind is out of control. It's feared the fate of mankind is at the disposal of either stupid authorities or of random forces of incalculable power, which at any moment could sweep our civilization into crumbled destruction.

In America, the put-down by Sputnik, the assassinations of Martin Luther King Jr. and the Kennedy brothers, the disgrace of Watergate, and the loss of primacy in world affairs that the United States has suffered have added their malignant effects on our society.

Disillusionment with religion, government, the work ethic, patriotism, parenting, and education were inevitable with the demystification brought into the household daily with the evening news, undermining reverence, piety, respect for authority, and belief in charisma. Skepticism, loss of faith, increase in cynicism, and the decline of idealism have followed. An "after me, you first" egocentrism came to flourish with the energy of weeds, leading to selfish concern on the part of each group and each individual who asks in every social interaction, "What's in it for me?"

There has been increasing demand for social, economic, and political equal rights and renunciation of powerlessness by women, blacks, homosexuals, and other groups who have suffered discrimination. However meritorious these themes may be and consistent with democratic principles, they add to the current disequilibrium in our society.

Finding the stormy climate too difficult, pervaded by a sense of powerlessness to do anything about it, there has been escape into easily available drugs, alcohol, esoteric self-negating religions, casual sexuality, and suicide.

The population explosion has led to overcrowding, an increase in competition for too-few opportunities and a breakdown of family ties. This has caused a sense of isolation and anonymity that may be implicated in the rise of suicide, particularly in young people.

The flight from commitment and the denial of feeling—"Keep it cool, man"—have led to detachment from affectionate relationships and revulsion from passionate enterprises. Egalitarianism and the cult of mediocrity devaluates excellence in performance and discourages making the most of human potential, condemning ambition as elitist, the present-day anti-intellectual obscenity.

The divorce rate, which has tripled in the last 20 years and has put an increasing number of children at risk, peaked in 1979 at well over a million. Half the marriages in America are in trouble, with the likelihood that more than a third may end in divorce. On any scale of evaluation of stress, divorce is nearly the most devastating to parents and children in its immediate and long-range destructive effects, even when it cancels a malignant marriage.

Adolescent girls are expected to live up to standards of competitiveness with boys on the boys' turf, while at the same time satisfy the imperative of biological conditioning that impells them to become homemakers and mothers. And young men on the other hand are under pressure to perform flawlessly in the classroom, on the basketball court, on the job, and in the bedroom.

Parents are caught in contrary winds of self versus another's best interest. They can't make lots of money and be good parents at the same time. Many, outraged at the invasion of privacy and the compromise of personal fulfillment their children's needs force on them, reject in whole or in part their roles as parents.

The result is bad parenting, manifested by refusal to take their children seriously, hypercritical attitudes, inconsistent discipline, refusal to listen, and patronizing behavior. It progresses to abandonment through separation, divorce, or overt rejection. Hundreds of letters I've received from adolescents carry the

32

theme "My parents are never there when I need them," or "I can't talk to them, they just don't accept me as I am."

The information overload of our times through television, film, computer software, radio, and the printed word creates an illusion of instant and comprehensive wisdom available at the flick of a switch. Children are promoted from one grade to another and seldom given fair or truthful feedback from their teachers and schools regarding their proficiency or lack of it. Only when first they fail a challenge do they discover their lack of preparation and lack of talent. On radio and TV, the promise is made that all problems can be solved in half an hour, an unrealistic expectation that must result in low tolerance to life and stress.

A permissive society has forced choices not only on young people but on adults as well, requiring that decisions be made in everyday life situations before individuals are knowledgeable, mature enough, or able to perceive the consequences of their choices. Failure to choose rightly leads to desperation, depression, and sometimes to suicide.

Societal imperatives

There are instances when there is a cultural imperative to suicide. In World War II, young Japanese men were pledged to join the Imperial Navy Air Corps as kamikaze pilots. On their suicidal missions, they were given only enough fuel to reach their military objective, usually American warships. The pilots then dove their planes directly onto the ships, inflicting significant damage, and themselves going to glory, destruction, and death.

The Samurai warriors of Japan traditionally were expected to commit hara-kiri or seppuku in disgrace. The warrior would drive a short sword into his left side, force it deep in the abdomen, then draw it across to the right, causing disembowelment. At the moment of dying, a companion cut off the head, concluding the ritual suicide.

Love-pact suicides occurred in Japan, as was the destruction of self and children by a mother shamed by her husband's infidelity or convinced she had failed her maternal duties. Although ritual suicides are fewer, the idea persists that death is an opportunity to free the self from ignorance and misery. In recent years, disgrace in battle or personal life, unrequited love,

33

or guilt for failure to please one's husband is less likely to cause suicide than is failure in educational performance.

The increase of suicide among young people in the United States and elsewhere in the world is especially evident in Japan among youth who fail examinations in that country's intensely competitive educational system.

Warriors promised the delights of paradise if they should die in battle were prepared for a suicidal effort in combat. In Judaic law, suicide was permissible to forestall death by torture. King Saul fell on his sword in battle, a death accepted as legitimate and irreproachable.

Martyrs who sacrifice their lives in suicidal acts are held in esteem in their societies. Terrorists who, chancing death, capture aircraft, take hostages, and blow up buses are considered heroes in their own communities if they succeed in their military objective, martyrs if they are killed. Their missions are understood to be "suicidal."

Spy movies accurately portrayed American espionage agents who carried cyanide pellets, ready to kill themselves if they should be caught. Their readiness to commit suicide was considered honorable.

When Sydney Carton in Dickens' *A Tale of Two Cities* went to his death, sacrificing his life on the guillotine for his beloved, he murmured, "It is a far, far better thing I do . . . than I have ever done; it is a far, far better rest that I go to, than I have ever known." According to the romantic tradition of our culture, we would agree.

CHAPTER 4

Categories of suicidal persons

It will be helpful to categorize persons at risk of suicide according to their ostensible reasons to die, setting aside the most flagrant, bizarre suicides whose act is generated from a severely disturbed sense of reality as is true for psychotic patients abused by hallucinations and delusions.

Manipulators. The person who demands, "I want something from you, and if I can't get it, I'll kill myself" is a blackmailer, not unlike a terrorist who, bomb in hand, demands "a million in gold and take me to Libya or I'll blow this plane to bits." All the following are menacing, gun-in-hand demands by a threatener holding hostages:

- "Marry me or . . ."
- "If you date another girl, I'll . . ."
- "If you flunk me in math, it'll be . . ."
- "Refuse me again tonight and . . ."
- "If you fire me . . ."
- "Give me a loan on my policy today or pay my widow the face value tomorrow."

All such manipulators say in effect, "You want me alive more than I care about my own life. Therefore, I can hold you hostage and demand that you give me what I want, at some loss to you. If you don't, you'll suffer even greater loss—my life." The manip- ulator is not always aware that he loses even when he wins. He may secure a temporary advantage, but he risks the eventual loss not only of what he extracted from his victim, but also of any hope of maintaining the relationship in the future. A woman who consents to marriage under her lover's threat that he'll kill himself if she refuses will sooner or later regret her capitulation, and the blackmailer eventually will, too.

The parent, intimidated to purchase a car by his teenage son—"or I'll kill myself"—will find ways to cut himself off emotionally as well as economically from further instances of bullying by the adolescent.

Suicidal attempts, sometimes called gestures, qualified by low lethality and by low intent or expectation to die, are fre- quent in this category. However, the manipulator who succeeds in his efforts to blackmail is forced to employ repeated threats of suicide, and each successive episode may escalate in lethality.

Angered by the seeming crass opportunism and selfishness of the manipulator, the family, friends, and physician may miss the essential point: The manipulator, a mentally disturbed, regressed person who has run out of options, is desperately crying out for help.

Hopeless. "My life is so miserable I wish for no more of it," wrote the wife of the poet Dante Gabriel Rossetti before ending her life. Persons who believe they are trapped in a situation with no possible solution and no resources to bear the mounting anguish are depressed. Suicidal preoccupation soon follows such a conviction. The expression of hopelessness is a sensitive indicator of suicidal intent.

Helpless. Persons used to being in command of themselves suffer badly when they are put into a dependency relationship. If symbolic representations of power, such as money, station, talent, or physical strength, are lost and if there is a terror of being in a passive state under the domination of others who may be perceived as malicious, the response may be suicide.

Guilty. Shame and humiliation derived from real or imagined incidents may give rise to guilty thoughts and fantasies. Some persons of high idealism and high standards of self-conduct live with rigid notions of propriety and morality. They writhe under self-imposed punishment for their supposed crimes: "Since I have done wrong and deserve punishment, I'd rather punish myself fittingly and take my life." The husband, faithful for many years, becomes involved in an opportunistic one-night stand with a pickup at the motel lounge. He's found dead the next morning, a cord around his neck, hanging from the shower-curtain rod.

The young sailor, months at sea and languishing for affection, is made drunk and seduced by an older, homosexual seamate. On awakening, teased by his companions, he throws himself into the ocean. There's no truce for the guilty who have no way to mitigate their loss of self-esteem. Suicide offers an end to pain. Many of the suicides among jail inmates, particularly first-time offenders, are examples of guilty suicide.

Sufferers of loss. Children who in their early lives are separated from an important person, such as a parent, by divorce, abandonment, rejection, or death are particularly susceptible to depression, psychiatric illness, and suicide under stress as they mature. Adolescents, confronted by the breakup of a love relationship, experience an unexpected sense of isolation. This occurs with a shocking intensity never before felt, which the youngster is quite unprepared to manage. Older persons who have grown close may follow each other in death in quick succession. When one dies, the other may suicide.

Deaths of famous persons are frequently followed by suicides in the community. This occurred with the passing of Marilyn Monroe, John Lennon, John Kennedy, and Mahatma Gandhi. Divorce, particularly for men, brings a sense of irreparable loss out of which suicide impulsions result.

Some suicides among alcoholics who have suffered loss, death-seeking behavior among intimates who have been close to a suicide, and acting-out in rage that results in multiple murders and suicide exemplify the reactions of those who suffer loss.

Isolates. Bright children who are ostracized by their classmates; retarded or physically handicapped youngsters who have been separated from their peers; shy, withdrawn, friendless youngsters playing by themselves are stigmatized at a

young age by social isolation. In high school, when peer acceptance is crucial for identity and belonging, the thoughtless
cruelty of the teenager for others who lack social and athletic
skills or who try to establish some independence in choice of
behavior may drive susceptibles to suicide.

From the earliest history, exile has been known as the worst
punishment a person can be made to suffer. Whether exiled,
isolated, alienated, or separated by accident or design, the alone
person is figuratively on an ice floe in the middle of an arctic
wasteland, drifting aimlessly. With no one to talk to and no one
to touch, he suffers unbearable loneliness. Death seems
preferable.

Exhibitionists. When Jack Ruby shot Lee Harvey Oswald, the
killer of John Kennedy, not the least of his complicated motives
was to hold a certain place in public notoriety. He was seen by
millions on television and will make a footnote in history. Mass
murderers and terrorists make a public declaration that they are
willing to die to make their political or philosophical point.

The man on the ledge needs to communicate his plea for help
to as many as possible, hoping for rescue but at the same time
demanding public recognition that his plight is poignant and
should be taken seriously. Buddhists in Saigon who poured
gasoline on themselves and died in self-immolation hurled a
reproof into the teeth of their oppressors.

On July 15, 1974, TV commentator Chris Chubbuck read the
news, announced she would shoot herself, then did so on
camera, in color. She later died.

Jumpers from the Golden Gate Bridge and those who go over
Niagara Falls may have such a poor self-image or feel so effaced
that they try to redeem themselves, seeking attention in an
instant of conspicuous dying.

Intimates. Exposure to suicide of an intimate—a relative,
friend, colleague, or lover—increases the suicide potential for
survivors. The spread of suicide after personalities have died by
their own hand makes the concept of suicide by identification
credible.

The process by which a person patterns himself after some
other person operates unconsciously. Development of personality is in considerable measure accomplished by identifying

with others. One's personality has traces of dozens, perhaps hundreds of persons, although major contributions, of course, come from parents and other intimates. How a person manages adversity, whether he anticipates good or misfortune, is generous or selfish, picks his teeth, how he laughs, or what makes him cry are pieced together by conscious role modeling or unconscious identification.

A suicide may teach his son how to handle failure: "See, my son, when confronted with difficult problems in everyday life, take my example. Get drunk and kill yourself." The lesson is powerful and not soon forgotten; it makes a deep and lasting impression, and in the survivor's future, when he is faced with a problem, that part of his father that the son chose to incorporate into his own identity may give rise to the same malignant solution.

At the age of 50, a menopausal woman was treated after a suicide attempt. She was still in the state of deep despondency. Her act occurred as consequence of her terminating a casual love affair. The woman associated her dreadful feeling of alienation and abandonment with an episode that had occurred when she was a young child, when her mother and father were breaking up the family.

There were five children, two older brothers who were then teenagers, a sister who was approximately 10 and a brother who was six, slightly older than the patient. The two oldest had already left the house several weeks before to live with other members of the family. The 10-year-old sister and the youngest child, the patient, were to remain with the mother. Social workers had come to take the six-year-old boy away and place him with a foster family.

When the social worker tried to reach the little boy, he squirmed and ran away from her. Screaming, "I won't go, I won't go!" he went under the big oak dining-room table. The patient remembered that she wept in terror and tried to go to her brother, but the mother prevented her from doing so. The little boy held on to the center post leg of the heavy table with his arms and legs. He was finally pried loose, pulled away from the table, and carried kicking and screaming under the arm of the social worker and out the door that slammed behind. The patient never saw her brother again, but never recovered from the separation.

Transcendental seekers. Some suicidal persons believe that they will die by suicide to be reborn into a better existence. In Zen, Confucian, and Buddhist philosophies, since nature is immutable, the only chance a man has for changing his fate is to escape present time and hope for reincarnation in a new and better life. The suicide sometimes expects that by killing himself he will enter the spirit world, united with God or the Eternal Presence. There may be the expectation of permanent reunion in death with a lost loved one. Such ideation isn't overtly psychotic, but is characteristic of a kind of repudiation of or inability to formulate logical thinking that occurs to suicides as their sense of reality constricts and despair deepens. Death itself becomes a ghostly pale light of hope promising a transformation.

Murder by suicide. The four brothers playing cards were mildly annoyed when they heard their sister screaming at them as she ran past the table to the door toward the attached garage, "You don't believe me? I will, I will!"

The four sighed in resigned disgust, shrugged their shoulders, and went on with the game. They had been through this before. The auto engine roared. One of the brothers got up, shut the door to the garage firmly and returned to the table. Hours later the brothers found their sister dead in the car, an example of murder by suicide.

Mark Hellinger wrote about a man who dealt sadistically with his wife. Any time she displeased him, he put a bullet in the chamber of his revolver, spun the cylinder, put the gun to his head, and pulled the trigger. His wife would faint. When she revived she would beg for his forgiveness and do whatever he wanted.

In the story, the police were called one day to the home to find the man dead with a bullet wound in his head. Puzzled by the wife's explanation, the officer wondered why a man bent on suicide would need to load all six chambers of his gun with live bullets.

An elderly lady, now dead, told me many years ago that whenever her husband found her playing around, he used to drink poison—"At least he said it was poison"—from a glass vial he carried in his vest pocket. She said he always quickly recovered from the alleged poisoning. One day, though, he did die from poison. With a self-pleased grin she whispered, "Somebody put real poison in that little bottle."

Murders have been accomplished by forcing the victim to commit suicide. Socrates was executed by mandatory suicide. He was sentenced to drink poison hemlock for his impious teaching and for corrupting the youth of Athens.

Suicide by murder. The youngster came out of the high school gym where a dance was in progress. Two of his buddies were squaring off to fight. One drew a large knife and threatened the other. The youth just emerging from the building flung himself on the boy with the knife and suffered a mortal wound in the chest. Later investigation determined that the boy who had been killed had been despondent and had talked about suicide. His behavior had surely been death-seeking.

A middle-aged male patient had lost his job, his wife, and alienated his children because of his drinking. He was profoundly depressed and confessed that he would kill himself if he had the courage. He was on a bus when a robber stood up suddenly, pointed a pistol at him and demanded his wallet. The patient lashed out with obscenities, provoking the robber, and dared him to shoot. He did. Victims of murder such as this who bring about their own killing are listed as homicides but properly belong in the statistics for suicide.

CHAPTER 5

Physicians
and suicide

Suicide, with all its associated philosophical, sociological, psychological, and, of course, medical problems involves physicians personally and professionally more than most realize. From his or her earliest aspirations to enter the career in medicine, suicide shadows the physician. First, it's perplexing for the physician to confront a patient, whose survival is the goal of his art, who wants to die. Second, the doctor himself is at higher risk for self-destruction than almost any other college graduate who has chosen engineering, accounting, sales, farming, or some other career.

Women who elect a career in medicine are even more vulnerable than men to emotional turmoil, morbid thinking about suicide, and acting out self-destructive impulses. This tendency follows them throughout their professional lifetimes. Not only are physicians marked for greater susceptibility, but so also are their spouses and children.

Few events in a physician's professional life are as upsetting to his equanimity and confidence in his knowledge and ability and few challenge his humanity as does his confrontation with a patient who has made a suicidal attempt or his learning that one has died of suicide. The majority of physicians who reflect on lethal attempts and successes among their patients are shocked at the event and usually admit they did not consider the probability of self-murder. Then, as a defense tactic, the doctor rationalizes to reduce the pain of guilt and the rue of a misdiagnosis that may have contributed to the injury or death of his patient.

Many patients have been seen by their family physicians within a few weeks of killing themselves. Most have been examined within a year of the self-destructive act, which prompts a search—in memory or a chart—for the enlightening clues that probably had been missed on the last visit to the office or clinic.

Just as do family and friends, the physician feels anger, grief, guilt, and, sometimes, the dread that suicide by an intimate can generate: "If he did it, would I?"

Physicians meet morbidity and death all their professional lives and manage their feelings during most of the occasions when a patient had "gone bad" despite their best efforts. But suicide can be particularly disturbing to the physician if he sees it as an unfair and treacherous trick played upon him for which he was unwarned. He can be quick with defensive self-exculpation:

- "He was out of his mind."
- "No one can prevent suicide."
- "He never told me. How could I be expected to know? I'm a doctor, not a mind reader."
- "He had a mind of his own, even if I would have tried to talk him out of it, I couldn't."
- "He had an absolute right to dispose of his life any way and any time he wanted to."
- "Anybody facing the troubles he had in his life would do the same."
- "I thought he was kidding."
- "I'm not a psychiatrist; it's out of my field of expertise."
- "It was up to his family to do something."
- "If he hadn't been drinking, this would never have happened."

Ignorance of what constitutes suicidal risk, the impression of the inevitability of suicide and its supposed inextricable and fatal power over its victims, the presumed uselessness of intervention, the belief that suicide is an esoteric condition reserved for treatment only by psychiatrists: All these are common among physicians.

Physicians were similarly baffled with tuberculosis before Koch's postulates and isoniazid, epilepsy before anticonvulsive drugs and the electroencephalogram, deficiency disease before the discovery of vitamins, sepsis before antibiotics, and mania before lithium. Ironically, there's a greater probability that competent medical intervention will save a patient endangered by suicide than is the case with almost any other potentially lethal condition.

The unrecognized disease will never be treated. By making a relatively small investment in time and effort, by sharpening awareness and mobilizing already existing skills, you can become adept in recognizing and adequately treating the would-be suicidal patient. Not only can you save others, but by applying newfound insights you may improve your own chances of surviving the seduction of suicide.

You can and should be taught to be a basic rescuer of potential suicides. Exactly for the same reasons as physicians are encouraged (even bullied) into learning cardiopulmonary resuscitation, doctors should learn to deal with the emergency of suicide. The argument becomes most compelling when we consider how few are the occasions for CPR compared with the much greater frequency of encountering a self-destructive patient. After all, how often in his professional lifetime will a doctor perform CPR at the curbside or at the beach, or the Heimlich maneuver in a restaurant?

From a public health point of view, suicide rightfully qualifies as a primary target of concern. It's a noxious process which causes morbidity and mortality, it can be epidemic, it may be transmissible from one generation to another or, by vectors poorly understood, contagiously spread within a community. We can learn a great deal about how suicide occurs and how it can be transmitted, identify who the susceptible persons are, and how to protect individuals and the community from its ravages.

There are also ethical and legal considerations that should encourage you to learn to manage the suicidal patient. Motivated by compassion and accepting appropriate responsibility, you may not only reduce morbidity and save lives but also avoid malpractice lawsuits by satisfying the reasonable expectations of the community that you practice according to good standards.

Not the least motive for being concerned about the suicidal patient is the distinct possibility that you, your family, or your staff may be injured or murdered. A desperate, depressed, psychotic patient may suddenly exteriorize the aggressive component of the impulse to suicide and shoot or stab his physician or those close to him whom the patient discerns as agents of his misery or a fitting object of vengeful feelings.

A middle-aged man, for example, had been drinking heavily. He suffered impotence and became depressed. He admitted self-destructive fantasies to his doctor, who put him on a program of withdrawal from alcohol, counseling, and treatment with disulfiram and vitamin injections. After a particularly humiliating failure at sexual intercourse, the patient telephoned the doctor late at night, weeping, threatening suicide, and begging for help. The physician was irritated and sarcastically reminded the patient that inability to effect an erection was not a fatal condition and that he could wait for regular office hours.

The next morning, the patient contradicted his physician's assurance that erectile impotence has no fatal consequences. When the doctor admitted the patient to his examining room, the man shot him dead.

Identification of the potential suicide

CHAPTER 6

Clues to suicide

$\mathbf{A}$ pathologist I know, advising physicians to be alert to clues that might point to violence as a cause of illness, injury, or death, says to them, "Think dirty."

A questioning attitude, an open mind, and reasonable acquaintance with the possibilities you may encounter are what you need to determine diagnosis and establish a treatment plan in the clinical setting. This—together with "thinking dirty"—is also true in dealing with the patient who may be contemplating suicide or who has presented with symptoms whose etiology is a self-destructive act. Examination of the patient in such a case proceeds in the usual manner. In addition, you need to be specially aware of techniques for evoking the facts, clues that may offer helpful direction, and sources to confirm and cross-check your suspicions. This review will sharpen your skills in identifying the patient at risk for suicide.

It's difficult for the pediatrician examining an unconscious seven-year-old with an empty bottle of pills by his side to consider that the child took the drug deliberately with intent to die. It's commonly assumed that the ingestion of poison by a child is accidental, so no one asks the right questions that could reveal that the youngster had been depressed and had talked about dying. Even if a flicker of suspicion should enter the doctor's consciousness, he's not likely to follow it. Even after the doctor has done all the right things to diagnose the condition and has begun medical care for poisoning, he still may make no attempt whatever to ascertain the motive of the child, and accident is assumed.

By fixing limits to what he wants to know, the examiner assumes the answers he wants to hear and makes it difficult for observers to tell him what he would rather not know. For instance, the doctor holds the bottle and the cap in his hands. Begging the question, he asks the parents, "Did he think this was a bottle of candy?" Or, fixing guilt by innuendo, he may demand, "Who left this open pill bottle where the child could get at it?"

The sullen adolescent who put his hand through a glass window on the way to the principal's office and is taken to the emergency room with a radial artery transection and a few tendons cut is considered a delinquent. All questions are based on the assumption that the boy was injured in an attempt to get away from the teacher escorting him or that he was in a blind rage and had to hit something. The notion that the youngster may have wanted to die might not surface at all unless you "think dirty."

The elderly asthmatic's wife complains, "He won't talk; he just sits and stares." The man may wheezingly tell the doctor, "Had a bad week. Can't breathe. The pills don't work. I'm so weak, Doc. Got anything else?" After the doctor checks his chest and finds bronchiolar spasm more a problem than usual may give the patient a vitamin B_1 injection as a placebo, change his prescription, and send him home with reassurances. At no time will the patient's depression become an object of the physician's attention, much less the probability that the patient is fighting obsessive suicidal thinking.

A diabetic, middle-aged woman who has left the hospital just the day before with her blood sugar in excellent balance turns up unconscious and in shock in the emergency room with a glucose of 30 mg/dl. In a case such as this, when the patient who has symptoms untypical for his condition or when previously reported symptoms occur in a peculiar context, a warning light should go on that says, "Check this for factitious etiology." In other words, "think dirty."

Missing or ignoring the fact that the patient suffers from self-inflicted illness or injury doesn't mean that he can't be saved or physically rehabilitated from his immediate acute infection, toxic reaction, or fractures, burns, or lacerations. The injured or diseased body will respond to good treatment expertly applied, no matter what caused the immediate insult. But failing to uncover that an injury was caused by suicide may ultimately mean the loss of the patient.

The patient, a truck driver, age 22, was overcome by fumes when he supposedly fell into his tanker through the top vent. He was found in respiratory arrest, and his condition was assumed to have been accidentally caused. An intensive-care team worked all night and successfully brought him out of danger. They stabilized his blood gases, fluids, and electrolytes and established cardiopulmonary integrity.

Late the next day, the patient regained consciousness. Shortly afterward, during a change of shift, he snatched a scalpel from a tray and cut his throat. No one had come forward with the information that the young man had been warned he was in danger of being fired for drinking on the job and had threatened suicide. No one passed along the information that he had been separated from the service two years before with a diagnosis of psychotic depression. No one had asked because no one was "thinking dirty." Any doctor competent to ask a patient if he now or ever has suffered night sweats, constipation, or shortness of breath can learn to ask, "Have you ever had suicidal thoughts or actually made an attempt on your life?"

By no means is the recognition of the depressed individual about to take his life a monopoly of the medical profession. Nurses, psychologists, ministers, teachers and school counselors, vocational advisers, medical technicians, even bartenders, police officers, cosmetologists, taxi drivers, caterers, and security personnel can learn. Anyone may become a basic rescuer for the suicidal person. It may indeed be possible for anyone of reasonable intelligence to learn the necessary skills. It would be especially valuable for high school and college students who live, study, and work in the midst of relatively high-risk populations to have instruction in suicide identification. But since health-care professionals, especially physicians, are those most likely to deal with suicidal persons, they should be well-versed in the clues to suicide.

Suicide does not announce its potential to destroy the patient any more obviously than does hepatitis, brain tumor, aneurysm of the circle of Willis, blood loss from duodenal ulcer, cardiomyopathy, or pancreatitis. The physician's assignment is to search out hazard to health and life and to rid the patient of his illness, according to the state of the art and his own skills.

The most successful approach is to throw the biggest net: to conduct a thorough history and order all appropriate laboratory tests, and then to examine the catch of information hauled in. Each of us, however, to suit our style and the demands of time, has learned through years of practice to dispense with sections of the textbook examination he learned in clerkship. It's just those components that many of us trim out of the classic routine, particularly in out-patient practice, that might alert us to a patient at risk for suicide.

History

Taking a good history is undoubtedly the most helpful means to an accurate diagnosis. It involves the patient's presenting complaints and psychologic affect and his personal, past, and family histories.

Presenting complaints

You may find that the potential suicide has been in good physical health until his present symptoms "suddenly" appeared. The most frequent physical complaints include sleep disturbances particularly early-morning awakening or hypersomnia. Anorexia is common, with or without nausea. The patient describes lack of interest in eating, a loss of relish rather than food intolerance. Loss of weight may be profound and rapid. It's not uncommon for a 150-lb man in a state of despondency to lose 20 lb in four or five weeks.

Low energy or asthenia may at first present as muscle weakness, but with close questioning you find the patient has a subjective impression of exhaustion and easy fatigability with no myopathy whatever. "I'm so weak, I spend most of the day in bed," the patient may say.

Constipation is a remarkably frequent complaint of the depressed patient. It occurs because of reduction in muscular effort due to immobilization and is aggravated by low fluid intake. The dysphoric person ignores basic sensations—hunger, thirst, pain, and physical discomfort, such as feverishness, chills, or the signal to urinate or defecate. Even the vital stimulus to breathe is circumvented to a certain degree. A deeply despondent person sighs heavily not only as a sign of hopelessness but because his shallow breathing fails to provide adequate ventilation. His cardiac reflexes then respond to relative hypoxia, and he is forced to sigh deeply to make up his oxygen deficit.

There may be an obvious discrepancy between the intensity of physical distress and objective signs of illness. "I have this terrible pain in my chest, as if my heart were about to split open" may be a symbolic statement by a man who checks out perfectly on physical and lab tests but who is indeed "heartbroken."

The patient may admit to symptoms caused by drug use or withdrawal. If not, ask explicit questions regarding the use of prescribed or street drugs and about drinking habits.

Overuse of medication raises a question of habituation. The patient's rationale for refusing to take prescribed drugs, on the other hand, may reveal that he fears side effects or does not want to admit he has a chronic illness. Either is an inappropriate · response to reality.

You need to know precisely how the patient uses drugs and alcohol. It is not sufficient to learn that he drinks "a few beers" every night. You must persist until you know, for instance, that within the previous six weeks your patient has increased his alcohol consumption from an occasional 12-ounce can of beer in the evening while watching TV to a six-pack or more, and that he drinks alone, avoiding the rest of the family. The patient who has escalated drug and alcohol use may already have put into effect a subintentional or even intentional suicide program at the time of his examination.

In addition, consider possible side effects themselves. For example, the cumulative depressant effect of up to a week's regular daily dosage with a slowly metabolized benzodiazepine tranquilizer may aggravate pre-existing depression.

Gastritis, nausea, vomiting, tremulousness, imprecision in gestures and gait, slowness in physical performance, sweating, headache, dizziness, imbalance, difficulty in swallowing, dryness of the throat, numbness of the extremities, blurred vision, burning of the eyes, intolerance of loud noises, and an exaggerated startle response—and many other signs and symptoms—

may signify conversion of deep emotional hurt, which the patient cannot admit to consciousness, to physical complaints, which he can.

Psychologic signs

The patient usually does not volunteer information about psychologic distress. He may, however, describe himself as sad, blue, or down in the mouth. He may tell you he is depressed. More likely, he may say he's nervous but can't explain why or even how his nervousness affects him. He may complain of irritability or be overemotional or apathetic and limp. Invited to describe how he thinks about himself, he may say, "I can't seem to care about anything." He admits to being indecisive. He's unkempt, not at all up to his usual standard of grooming.

Weeping in response to a routine question is a useful clue to strong affect but does not necessarily indicate depression. The patient may report, as if puzzled at himself, "I seem to cry for no reason." Until you ask, "You seem a bit weepy; can you tell me why?" you cannot presume the weeping is an irrelevant affective display. Its presence in the interview gives you an opportunity to impart kindly concern for the patient's feelings.

The potentially suicidal patient has low expectations of recovering from the illness he brings to you and is pessimistic that anyone can help him. He has lost interest in his family, children, job, and hobbies, in current events, reading, and socializing. He's apprehensive about his brain and complains something is wrong with his mind because he can't reason, concentrate, remember, calculate, argue, or tell or appreciate a joke. Sexual desire has been extinguished or has faded to a passive accommodation endured for the partner, devoid of erotic excitement and essentially nonorgasmic.

His self-image is remarkably deformed, and he describes himself as a burden to others, expressing personal worthlessness or guilt for his seeming failures, betrayals, and errors of omission or commission in the past. You may wonder at the extraordinary remorse he expresses for relatively ancient sins of minor significance. For example, a 61-year-old man said to me, "I was 21 years old, a sailor on a tanker. I got drunk one night, and my ship pulled out without me. It took me two weeks of chasing before I caught up with the boat. I just can't forget it."

Personal history

Check whether the patient has been caught in a stressful situation by asking about major recent changes in his life-style, living arrangements, and emotional relationships. In his personal history of the previous several months, look for loss due to separation or divorce, bankruptcy, loss of a job, injury or illness, robbery, religious conversion or loss of faith, arrest, incarceration, lawsuits, auto accidents, gambling or stockmarket reverses, eviction from his apartment, mortgage foreclosure, fire in the home, breakup of a romantic affiliation, betrayal by a friend or colleague, disgrace or humiliation leading to loss of prestige or status, and grief and bereavement due to severe illness or death of a loved person, particularly someone who has died by suicide.

Changes in the patient's usual sociability may be quickly evident on inquiry. He may say he feels isolated, lonely, friendless, or abandoned; he may admit that he has been avoiding friends and associates. Highly significant, of course, are expressions of suicidal ideas such as, "I'm tired of living—I'd be better off dead," "You'll all be better off when I'm dead," "I can't take it any longer," or "I'm not afraid to die."

Acting on the belief that he will soon be dead, the patient may call old friends he hasn't talked to for years; rearrange his personal affairs; rework his will; buy or contract for a gravesite; give power of attorney to a relative, friend, or business partner; sell out a business interest that he has possessed for many years; or give away precious mementos or possessions. Indulging in unaccustomed extravagance, he may gamble excessively, purchase recklessly, or make donations to causes and institutions to which he had never donated in the past.

In a seemingly cynical or despairing, self-denouncing manner, he may perform acts quite contrary to his usual moral code, cheating employees, acting out sexually, falsifying records, and lying overtly. It's as if he is declaring that he knows his reputation has been destroyed, so there's no further sense in being virtuous.

Past history

The patient's medical record may include prior psychosis or a previous suicide attempt. History of loss of a parent or a significant caretaker in childhood, early isolation from peers due to frequent moving or chronic illness or because the social climate was alien and rejecting may surface as your patient describes his early life.

Patients who have had encounters with serious injury or illness in childhood may have lost time from school, suffered loss of function, or cosmetic defect. Any such experience in childhood could result in sacrifice of normal interaction with peers and prejudice the patient from early life on toward being overdependent and alienated, carrying crippling social ineptitude into adult years.

Some children may be victimized by exploitative plans and ambitions of their parents. A junior high girl, for example, seemed to have talent as a singer. Her ambitious mother pressed her to learn voice. She was never permitted friends, social interaction with her peers, physical recreation, or dates with boys. Her time was taken up either with school or with voice instruction.

Her mother reacted to the girl's failure to win an important contest by berating her with accusations that she had failed to prepare herself adequately, concluding with: "I gave up my life for you, and this is the thanks I get." The girl died of injuries suffered when she jumped out of the window of the apartment house where she had lived with her mother.

Family history

Family members may have suffered illness that could have some degree of genetic or role-identification influence on the patient. You should ascertain if there is a parent who suffered manic-depressive illness (now called unipolar or bipolar affect disorder) or schizophrenia or who had other indications of chronic mental illness, such as alcoholism, psychiatric hospitalization, chronic depressive symptoms, or had made a suicide attempt. The patient may have suffered psychological trauma in early developmental years, not because of genetic defect, but because of parental instability. A child brought up in a chaotic family, living under severely deprived circumstances of poverty and nutritional deficiencies with abusive, alcoholic, or mentally ill parents, may suffer both constitutional and environmental handicaps.

Periods in family life in which one or both parents or siblings were not home may have seriously affected some chronically depressed suicidal persons. The father, for example, may have been absent because he could find work only in a distant town or had an extended tour of duty in the military service.

Marital friction, separation, divorce, desertion and death, mental illness, or legal intervention causing dissolution of the family and subsequent farming out of the children to foster families leaves emotional scars that later in life can figuratively be made to bleed if excoriated by rejection or the loss of love.

Other sources of information

You should actively seek data from anyone who knows the patient or has any information about his present illness or injury. There's a chance that members of the family or friends may be hesitant, suspicious, and even angry if you raise the question of suicide, so be prepared to deal with their feelings.

When the spouse, parent, or friend is available and you're trying to find out why your patient is so depressed and how to proceed, take advantage of any opportunity to meet with your informant privately. You may learn, for instance, how worried the family has been because Jill has collected a whole box of pills and has hidden it in the drawer with her blouses. Or that John suddenly has become interested in knives and guns and is spending his earnings and savings on a weapons collection. Perhaps Dad has called the insurance man, his lawyer, the funeral director, and the minister and won't tell the family what's on his mind. Or Sonny, who's careful with his motorcycle and has never had a serious accident, unaccountably swerved and struck a utility pole in perfect weather last month and is all banged up in the hospital. Rebecca has been acting strangely; she's been skipping school and just gave away her stereo, her favorite records, and her stamp collection.

If you turn up this kind of information, then, in the privacy of an interview, ask Jill gently but definitely whether the pills she's been hoarding have been put aside for use in case she wants to die by suicide. Ask John outright whether he's aware that his sudden fascination for weapons might be a step toward self-destruction. Tell Dad flatly that his preparations for his own demise can be interpreted as an expectation he will soon be dead by his own hand. Or remind Sonny that his accident is untypical of him, and ask him to confide whether an impulse to kill himself contributed to his crash. If you tell Rebecca that her inappropriate giving is consistent with what people who want to kill themselves sometimes do, she may be encouraged to be open with you.

Old medical records to which you have legal access, teachers, employees or employers, school chums or teammates, the spouse, children, parents and other family members, clergy, the ex-spouse, business partners, or neighbors may give valuable recent and past history that could be important, not just as aids to a correct diagnosis, but also to your care for the patient through his therapeutic course.

Examination of the patient

Although you're not expected to approach your patient with the level of suspicion that a forensic medical examiner has, you do have to conduct the physical examination with enough sophistication so that, after you've identified the problem and begun treatment, you'll be able to identify the cause as natural, accidental, or related to a suicide or homicide attempt.

If you find signs of illness and injury that are incongruous and unexpected for the age, personality, social position, circumstances, established life pattern, or previous medical history of the patient, think dirty. Could you be dealing with a suicide or a homicide?

Consider: An epileptic patient who cannot be roused from deep sleep may not be in a postictal, comatose state, but may have taken an overdose of anticonvulsive medication, especially barbiturates.

Almost any gunshot wound, allegedly made "while cleaning the gun," that could have been inflicted intentionally probably was deliberate.

The near-drowning of a nonswimmer who has fallen into waters when alone at dark or the rescue of a good swimmer from far out beyond the beach limits certainly raises the question of intent to die.

Fresh, single or multiple, surgically clean, transverse incised wounds of the volar aspects of the wrists or throat or feet are virtually always intentionally self-inflicted. Scars in those same areas may indicate previous suicide attempts and should warn you of the possibility of another attempt at self-destruction.

A well-dressed, middle-aged businessman is found unconscious and near-freezing in his car in the early morning hours. He parked in a lot he never uses in a part of town he normally doesn't drive through. He may have suffered a heart attack or stroke, but as likely has taken a drug overdose and hidden away to die.

Any patient, conscious or otherwise, who is at suicide risk should be carefully examined for self-inflicted injury. Examiners have missed incredibly severe wounds because the point of entry—for example, of a small caliber bullet—was covered by hair or concealed in skin folds.

I recall an elderly schizophrenic patient whom we called Mr. George. He was admitted one morning to the emergency room at Bellevue Hospital in New York City. He was well-known to us and to the police who had picked him up when they saw him stagger about on First Avenue.

Mr. George was hallucinating, saying, "They told me I was a letter." Ordinarily plethoric, he appeared quite pale. Apparently near shock, his blood pressure was extremely low, he was sweating heavily, and his pulse was thready. A ruptured viscus? Cardiac tamponade? Bleeding gastric ulcer or esophageal varix? By the merest luck, while trying to palpate the outline of the liver, I encountered a small, solid object just at skin level in the left hypochondrium. I attached a hemostat to this object and astonished withdrew, inch-by-inch, a thin, six-inch-long steel rod—a broken-off letter spike. The voices had told Mr. George he was a letter and, therefore, he "filed" himself by plunging the sharp spiked instrument into his abdomen. The base broke off and he threw it away.

The characteristic pink color of methemoglobinemia due to carbon monoxide poisoning or massive whole body burns caused by gasoline, propane, or other highly inflammable liquids on a victim, who did not seem to have any reason for conveying such substances, should lead you to suspect suicide.

Tracks on veins give witness that the patient has been a drug user and may be in a toxic state due to a combination of drugs taken by any route.

Inflamed, eroded nasal membranes suggest the use of insufflated drugs, such as cocaine. Stimulant drugs, such as

amphetamines, ritalin, cocaine, and even caffeine, aren't ordinarily employed for suicidal purposes. But the drug abuser
may inject them, seeking an ultimate high and hoping to die in
intoxicated ecstasy.

An agitated, belligerent, aggressive patient may seem to be
trying to protect himself, yet have strong suicide impulsions. He
may be hostile to attendants and staff because by their constant
attention they are preventing him from committing suicide.

An unexpected change for the worse in a patient whose
illness was considered relatively stable might arouse suspicion
that the crisis may have been factitious. On examining the
mouth, you may find evidences of recently ingested crystals,
fragments of capsules and pills, or burns from an ingested
corrosive. Look for edema of the pharynx. If, though conscious,
the patient is unable to speak, injury to the larynx may have
occurred. Look carefully at the neck for the impression from a
belt or cord. It may be many hours after trying unsuccessfully to
hang himself that a victim comes to the emergency room. By
then, the mark of the strangulating cord or belt may have faded.
Fracture of the larynx and airway obstructed by edema may
require prompt surgical intervention.

Runaway infections may have been caused by deliberate rejection of antibiotics or by contamination of wounds with food,
saliva, excreta, or any other object within reach. Dehiscence of a
surgical wound, particularly if it occurs repeatedly, may be
caused not by suture failure, but by the patient tearing open his
own wound. The patient who sabotages his own treatment is
intentionally or subintentionally committing an act of suicide.

Laboratory tests

There is both clinical urgency and legal reason for using the
laboratory to reinforce your examination when you suspect
suicide, homicide, or accident. Coroners' and medical examiners' offices in many parts of the country have toxicologists or
other forensic experts at telephone reach for consultation. In
some jurisdictions, the local health department or the police
laboratory may run tests on request.

Some or all of the following tests are used in routine examinations: complete blood count, differential, urinalysis, chemistry
profiles, chest X-ray, and electrocardiogram. If you suspect drug

overdose or poisoning by chemicals or by household gas, send samples of blood, urine, vomitus, and feces promptly for analysis with a request for Stat turnaround.

Find out the blood levels of any drug the patient was supposedly taking: anticonvulsives, cardiotonics, diuretics, sedatives, endocrine preparations, anticoagulants, antidepressants, lithium, and other psychotropic drugs, particularly tranquilizers. The presence of even small amounts of a drug that had not been prescribed and unusually high values of prescribed medications raises suspicion of deliberate or accidental overdose. A significantly low level of a vitally necessary drug, such as digoxin, may indicate a deliberate noncompliance, out of a wish to die.

In the days before computerized axial tomography, a medical resident stood with two consulting physicians at the bedside of an elderly man who had been found unconscious, near respiratory arrest, at home the previous day. All findings on examination were nonpathological and gave no hint of the reason for the patient's comatose state. The patient had not yet responded. There was some consideration that trephine ought to be done, on the chance that a subdural hematoma might be found.

The resident, reviewing the lab reports, quoted a note that stated, "Barbiturates: barely detectable." One of the physicians observed, "That level is insignificant. It isn't relevant to his condition." After a moment, the young doctor asked diffidently, "But sir, why should there have been any barbiturates in his blood? His doctor assured us he wasn't on any prescribed medications."

Treatment for acute barbiturate poisoning was immediately instituted, and the patient eventually recovered. Later he admitted that he had taken his brother's medication for the purpose of committing suicide.

X-rays of a suspected foreign body can help you judge whether the wound could have been self-inflicted. The CAT scan is especially valuable in head injuries in helping to determine the precise location of foreign body fragments. Ultrasound is also helpful in determining self-inflicted injuries or inclusions in abdominal organs.

The findings of hepatitis, hypoglycemia, uremia, marked anemia, and elevated enzymes do not by themselves point to attempts at self-destruction, but raise the question of a primary disease which caused the abnormal findings, such as alcoholism, diabetes, or chronic drug use. Noncompliance with prescribed treatment and general neglect of nutrition and fluid intake may expose a profound level of despondency in a patient who has given up his desire to live.

Speech-lag: Promising measure of depression

Depressive illness is frequently manifested by slow movement. The pace of speech is particularly affected. Although motor retardation has not been statistically linked with suicide, it's a valuable indication and can be rather accurately charted. With devices that may become widely available, one can objectively and sensitively measure the retardation of speech and get a record of a patient's depressive symptomatology.

Either directly or over the telephone, these devices measure the patient's speech—the actual length of phonation of each word, the pauses between the words, and the time between question and response. The motor retardation measured can be correlated with the degree of depression. Patients whose depression is lifting show less retardation and lag or pause time in their speech. Those who are having an exacerbation or exaggeration of their depression manifest a greater speech lag.

A doctor wishing to monitor a patient can arrange for his patient to come for a speech check every day at a certain time. The equipment allows for rapid analysis of the pause time, and a comparison with previous tests may give the physician valuable objective information in his overall estimation of the patient's mental status.

CHAPTER 7

Predictors of
suicidal risk

In the material in this chapter, you'll find a scale of hazard for nonlethal and lethal suicide. It doesn't matter that we can't accurately calculate absolute values for this scale: They are irrelevant to rule-of-thumb risk estimation. Keep in mind, too, that the number of suicide attempts may be anywhere from eight to 100 times the number of successes. This is important information for one who deals with a great many suicidal persons, but is not helpful in constructing the suicide potential for a specific patient.

Most models for estimating suicidal risk and rescue are intended for research and retrospective review of suicidal intention after the fact. Further, some are beyond practical clinical use, because of their mathematical sophistication, and most have problems with culling out false positives.

The suicide index in this chapter may also err on the side of false positives, but this should not create a burden on the doctor or a significant imposition on the patient. Our purpose is not to collect numbers but to save lives. In some instances, we may be overly concerned. The penalty for exercising a somewhat greater investment in clinical intervention to prevent suicide than is precisely indicated is minor. It's an insignificant consequence compared with the loss of life because of underestimating suicide hazard.

It's estimated that anywhere from 20 to 70 percent of suicides fail to give prior warning of intent to die. Whatever the figure, the more physicians and basic rescuers in the community are aware of the signs of suicidal danger, the fewer suicides there will be.

Information in the table is designed to enable you to quickly estimate the suicide potential of your patient. The index number you get has immediate relevance, alerting you to the relative degree of danger of suicide and to guide you in considering various options for case management.

The table is quite simple. Various demographic categories are assigned two numbers. The first indicates the relative probability of a nonlethal suicide attempt. The second indicates the likelihood of a lethal suicide attempt. The categories are ranked on a scale of one to 10. The higher the number, the higher the risk present.

Other relevant factors are also ranked. Some factors are broken down into several slightly different entries, permitting you to take into consideration the circumstances, which may differ widely, that incline the patient to the brink of self-destruction.

Building the suicide potential index requires consideration of several elements from both the demographic and the relevant factor lists.

This table has not been objectively validated. Its components are drawn from experience, not from statistical studies. It's been weighted to include a maximum number of high-risk suicidal patients, with the acceptable probability that low- and intermediate-risk patients may be "caught in the net" as well. The numbers from one to 10 do not suggest any more than a wet-finger-to-the-wind integration of a multitude of factors into a system that offers more discrimination than is possible on, say, a three-point scale such as "high-intermediate-low." In fact, after you've become familiar with the table, you may find it helpful to assign a different weight to a factor to suit a particular patient.

If the table is not precise, why bother to include it at all? We can't wait for scientific studies to validate clinical judgment as to when a patient may commit suicide any more than physicians refrained from dealing with infectious disease before the existence of bacteria was proven. We can't hold off an attempt to treat suicidal patients with the best inferences, intuition, and techniques we presently can mobilize, given the state of the art. We can't wait for double-blind studies and controlled experiments on a thousand suicides, half treated one way and half treated another, before we intervene and hospitalize an individual who has been taken from the ninth-floor ledge of a high-rise apartment.

The overly impatient practitioner may skim over the table in a search for specifics. The compulsive doctor may dally too long, puzzling over differences and weightings among variables which are of little significance. The clinician who wants his patients to survive will use the table as it is intended to be used: to get a fix on the operant probability that a patient, abused and buffeted by a variety of inimical vectors, may attempt to kill himself.

Factors listed in the table

Age and sex. In most instances, statistics have been collated according to groups of persons identified by age, race, and sex, such as "37-year-old white male."

Race. The race of the patient may carry a separate risk factor. If so, its number value is to be used instead of the age and sex index.

Marital status and sex. Usually sex and marriage are linked in identifying classes of persons at suicidal risk such as "male, widower."

Professions/religions. Certain groups with special social characteristics are estimated to have some suicide potential. Select whichever factor is significant for your patient.

Geography. You have to judge if the country of origin influences the patient. A recent immigrant from Denmark may have a higher suicide potential than a tourist from Great Britain might have.

Past personal history. Growth and development factors, school-related, psychologic, marital, socioeconomic, and chronic stress, military service.

Physical history. Childhood acute and chronic illnesses, injuries, surgery; hyperkinetic syndrome, epilepsy, allergies.

Family history. Physical and mental health of family members, stability of family.

Environment. Any immediate stress in the present life of the patient: job change, recent bereavement, loss of love object, significant social change.

Mental status. Appearance, mood, thought patterns, affect, psychomotor state, neurosis, personality disorder, or psychosis manifested by hallucinations, delusions, particularly paranoid thinking, agitated behavior.

Suicide rumination or recent attempt. Although it's easy to include many factors in the calculation, an attempt should be made to limit them to the most important influences. For example, a despondent woman may imagine that she has caused the death of her newborn infant because she failed to attend prenatal classes. Her guilt feelings, although they are certainly present, are probably not as important in estimating her suicide potential as are her agitated, psychotic, depressed state, her expressed sense of loss, and the overt expression of the wish to end her life.

Special categories. Descriptions of patients in special categories are elaborated in Chapter 4. They include manipulators, hopeless, helpless, guilty, sufferers of loss, isolates, exhibitionists, intimates, and transcendental seekers. These categories may identify certain patients better than any other descriptors.

After the factors have been judged and number values assigned to each are entered on the worksheet, the sets of numbers should be added up. There will be two sets. The first gives the predictable probability of a nonlethal suicide attempt; the second gives the chances for lethal outcome. The higher the number, the more the danger and the more urgent the need for timely, competent intervention. Recommendations for management in each range of indices can be found following the table and worksheet.

Table of demographic and relevant factors with nonlethal and lethal index markers

	INDICES	
	NONLETHAL	LETHAL
Age and Sex		
Adolescents to early adult, female 15 to 24	10	5
Adolescents to early adult, male 15 to 24	9	6
Adult males 75+	10	7
Adult females 50 to 54	8	5
Children, to age 10	2	1
Children 10 to 14	3	2
Adult males 25 to 30	3	2
Adult males 31 to 45	2	2
Adult males 46 to 74	4	4
Adult females 25 to 30	2	1
Adult females 31 to 49	4	3
Adult females 55+	2	1
Race		
Blacks, young females to age 17	6	4
Blacks, to age 14	2	1
Blacks, young males to age 25	4	2
Blacks, adult females 25+	2	1
Blacks, adult males 25+	3	2
American Indians and Eskimos, males to age 45	6	4
American Indians and Eskimos, females to age 45	3	2
American Indians and Eskimos, males 45+	5	3
American Indians and Eskimos, females 45 to 55	7	5
American Indians and Eskimos, females 55+	6	4

continued

Table of demographic factors *continued*

	INDICES	
	NONLETHAL	LETHAL
Marital status and sex		
Divorced men	9	6
Married men, separated	5	3
Single men	6	4
Married men	1	1
Single women	4	2
Married men and women under age 20	3	2
Divorced women	4	2
Widowers	4	2
Widows	2	1
Professions/religions		
Physicians, pharmacists, and business executives, male, early and late career	4	1
Physicians, pharmacists, and business executives, male, mid-career	9	5
Psychiatrists	9	6
Artists and actors, mid-career	8	6
Physicians, pharmacists, and business executives, female, early and late career	5	2
Physicians, pharmacists, and business executives, female, mid-career	9	5
Physicians in retirement	6	4
Artists and actors, male, early and late career	5	3
Protestant	4	2
Catholic	3	1
Jew	1	1
Buddhist	5	2
Hindu	5	2
Moslem	4	2
Confucian	4	1
Mohammedan	2	1

continued

Table of demographic factors   *continued*

	INDICES	
	NONLETHAL	LETHAL
Geography		
Austrian and Swiss	7	4
Vietnamese, Korean, Taiwanese, Indonesian, Danes, West Germans, Swedes	6	3
Indian, Arab, Chinese, Japanese, French, Belgian	5	3
Israeli, Africans—native born, central, west and north, Norwegian, Dutch, Italian, British	4	2
Native-born South Africans, Irish	3	1
Past personal history		
Sexual maladjustment, compulsive masturbation, sadomasochistic or homosexual relationships, extreme prudery, avoidance of dating, exhibitionism, sexual assault, pedophilia	9	3
School maladjustment marked by truancy, repeated lateness, defiance of teachers, destruction of school property, smoking, drinking, use of drugs on school property, fighting, failure to learn, reading disability, dyslexia, rejection by peers	8	3
Social maladjustment rife with conflicts with the law, vandalism, delinquency, violence against persons and property, disruptive conduct, acting out in public, maladaptive behavior, transient residence	7	3
History of previous suicide attempt (for each attempt)	10	8
Drug abusers, female	10	4
Alcoholics, male	10	4
Drug abusers, male	9	6
Alcoholics, female	6	3
Family members of substance abusers	4	2
Adopted, early childhood	5	3

continued

Table of demographic factors *continued*

	INDICES	
	NONLETHAL	LETHAL
Past personal history—Cont'd		
Separation in childhood from important caretaker	5	2
Military service, Vietnam	6	4
Military service other than Vietnam	4	1
Physical history		
Somatic complaints, hyperkinetic syndrome in childhood, chronic illness	8	4
Epileptics, male	8	3
Mutilative surgery, ostomy, coronary bypass, facial disfigurement, loss of function of extremity	7	4
Asthma, cardiac disease, impotence, orthopedic dysfunction, head injury	6	3
Other physical illness, chronic	4	2
Family history		
History of suicide by parent	9	8
Family life disorganized, broken; abusive parents, violence	8	5
Father chronically ill, unable to work	5	4
Mother chronically ill, unable to function	5	3
Father absent in early life	4	2
Mother absent in early life	5	3
Parents separated or divorced in childhood	6	4
Parents separated or divorced, adolescence or later	4	2
Siblings dead at early age	3	2
Recent death of a parent, in childhood	5	4
Recent death of a parent, in adolescence	7	5
Recent death of a parent, in adult life	4	3
History of suicide attempt by family member	6	5

continued

Table of demographic factors *continued*

	INDICES	
	NONLETHAL	LETHAL
Environment		
Availability of lethal means—guns, knives, ropes, poisons, caches of medication, access to closed garage, access to heights, such as windows, bridges, viaducts, stairwells	10	8
Recent separation from important intimate	10	6
Jailed inmates, male, first offender	8	6
Recent accidents, falls, burns, fractures, unusual clusters of injuries on job or at home	7	3
Normal grief or bereavement	3	1
Recent social trauma or humiliation, robbery, fire in household, theft of goods, physical fight, termination from job, out-of-wedlock pregnancy, gambling loss	6	3
Employment, poorly adjusted, male	6	2
Unemployed, male	7	4
Employment, poorly adjusted, female	3	1
Unemployed, female	3	1
Jailed inmates, male, multiple offender	5	3
Jailed inmates, female, first offender	3	2
Jailed inmates, female, multiple offender	2	1
Time of year—spring	6	4
Time of year—fall	3	1
Time of year—summer or winter	2	1
Holidays—Christmas, Easter, Thanksgiving	5	3
Anniversaries—wedding, birthday, important life event	3	2
Mental status		
Depressed, previously hospitalized	10	7
Manic-depressive illness (affective disorder), depressed	10	8

continued

Table of demographic factors *continued*

	INDICES	
	NONLETHAL	LETHAL
Mental status—Cont'd		
Depressed, suddenly euphoric, paradoxical depression or elation	10	10
Indication of high suicide preoccupation on psychological testing	8	4
History of post-partum confusional or psychotic reaction	10	6
Low IQ, maladaptive behavior, poor memory retention, frustration with learning	4	2
Loss of control of life	8	4
Loss of independence	8	4
Recent change of personality	8	4
Acute depression, untreated	7	5
Depressed, in out-patient treatment	8	5
Schizophrenia, chronic, with recent acute exacerbation	5	6
Schizophrenia, chronic	4	2
Schizophrenia, acute	6	4
Organic dementia, acute	6	3
Paranoid disorder	8	4
Anxiety and phobic disorders	4	1
Obsessive-compulsive disorder	3	1
Somatoform disorders	3	1
Dissociative disorders	3	1
Dependent personality	5	2
Passive-aggressive personality	5	3
Borderline personality	6	4
Suicide rumination or recent attempt		
Suicide attempt, recent, high lethality	10	10
Evidence of suicide plan	10	8
Statement of desire to die	10	8

72

continued

Table of demographic factors *continued*

	INDICES	
	NONLETHAL	LETHAL
Suicide rumination or recent attempt—Cont'd		
Assaulted in homicide attempt provoked by the victim	10	10
Suicide note	10	8
Hiding lethal instruments	10	8
Suicide attempt, recent, low lethality	8	4
Inquiry about measures and means to suicide	8	5
Reading and fascination with suicide	6	3
Vague or no denial of intent to die	5	4
Special categories		
Manipulator, adolescent female	10	3
Manipulator, adolescent male	10	5
Manipulator, elderly male	10	3
Manipulator, child or adolescent	5	1
Manipulator, adult male	5	2
Manipulator, adult female	8	2
Manipulator, elderly female	5	1
Hopeless	10	10
Helpless	5	3
Guilty	5	2
Recent loss of intimate	8	4
Isolate	7	8
Exhibitionist	4	2
Seeker of transcendental transformation	8	3

Worksheet for calculating suicide potential

DEMOGRAPHIC FACTORS	INDEX VALUE	
	Nonlethal	Lethal
Age and sex		
Race		
Marital status and sex		
Professions/religions		
Geography		
RELEVANT FACTORS		
Past personal history		
Physical history		
Family history		
Environment		
Mental status		
Suicidal rumination or recent attempt		
Special categories		
Totals		

Management recommendations

The following four approaches to management of the suicidal patient are general recommendations for various ranges of the suicide potential of index calculated on the worksheet. Specific steps, of course, have to be determined on the basis of the individual patient's needs.

Index of 10 to 20, low suicide risk. Express concern about patient's attitude. Recommend consultation with a psychiatrist or clinical psychologist or referral to a mental health clinic. If the patient refuses psychiatric help, see him yourself within several days for a brief visit or at least ask for a telephone report. A few may need hospitalization.

Index of 20 to 30, moderately serious risk for suicide. Gently but firmly advise the patient he needs specialized professional help. Do not let him leave the office without securing an appointment or insisting on speaking to a member of the family, a guardian, or a responsible intimate who should be advised that the referral is recommended. If the patient and family don't accept your recommendation to see another consultant and if you wish to continue to assume responsibility, consider proper use of an antidepressant or lithium. Advise removal of all weapons from the home. Consider hospitalization if there is legitimate medical/surgical reason for admission. Be prepared to request liaison psychiatric help and consultative management.

Index of 30 to 40, serious suicide risk. Insist on psychiatric or psychologic consultation. Notify family that the patient's illness is a threat to his life and he should be hospitalized, even if it's necessary to secure a court action to admit him as an involuntary patient.

Index of 40+, extremely serious suicide risk. The patient requires urgent and immediate suicide protection. The clinician's responsibility is to remain physically available to the patient, to secure professional consultation, to effect hospital care, to surround the patient with a protective enclave so long as the crisis exists, mobilizing medical resources, including psychiatrist, psychologists, psychiatric nursing staff, social worker, hospitalization, medications as may be useful in managing agitation, paranoid thinking, belligerency, violent acting out, withdrawal of the patient from site of danger. Members of the family, friends, employer, religious counselors may be sensibly utilized to distract the suicidal obsession. A patient in this category who refuses cooperation establishes by this very fact his lack of judgment and warrants prompt legal action to *require* hospitalization on a nonvoluntary basis.

Practice examples

Woman, age 35, black (race, 2–1), married and separated one year, husband an alcoholic, violent to patient and two preschool children (past personal history, 4–2). The patient is working (environment, 3–1), but depressed because of economic problems and the threat of her husband unexpectedly coming to visit. She has expressed the thought, "Sometimes I wish I were dead. But I never do anything about it" (mental status, 7–5). No history of personal or family psychiatric illness. Nonlethal index: 16; lethal index: 9; management category: relatively low.

High school student, white, female, age 15 (age and sex, 10–5) appears at physician's office weeping and highly histrionic (mental status, 8–4), brought by concerned parents with the complaint of abdominal pain. Examination demonstrates that she is in first trimester pregnancy (environment, 6–3). She and her boyfriend recently parted, at which time she dramatically "took some pills" (suicide attempt, 10–10) and was attended in the emergency room of the local hospital, given ipecac, had an emesis, and was sent home. She began to act out sexually to spite her boyfriend and doesn't know who the father could be. Overtly she threatens to kill herself (manipulator, 10–3) if the doctor refuses abortion. Nonlethal index: 44; lethal index: 25; management category: urgent protection from impulsive suicide attempt required, serious suicide risk suggested.

Black male, widower, age 65 (age and sex, 4–4; marital status, 4–2), hypertensive, overweight, deaf (physical history, 4–2), lives alone in rooming house on Social Security (isolate, 7–8), drinks heavily (past personal history, 10–4), recently fractured ankle in fall. Admits severe depression and thoughts of suicide (suicide rumination, 10–8). "I haven't a friend left in the world. My father was killed in a mining accident when I was a child" (family history, 4–2). A buddy who worked with him has also retired, left the city two months ago to live with his own family, and is no longer accessible to the patient (environment, 10–6). Has a revolver (environment, 10–8). Nonlethal index: 63; lethal index: 44; management category: urgent and imminent probability of lethal suicide attempt.

Married white male, age 45, (age and sex, 2–2; marital status, 1–1), executive of large electronics firm (profession, 9–5), recently promoted. At first exultant, but in a few weeks precipitiously became despondent (mental status, 7–5), overtly weeping, wringing his hands, expresses fear of his new responsibility (environment, 6–2), complains of sleep lack and early morning awakening. Compulsive gambler (environment, 6–3), has encountered recent high losses his raise in salary will not cover. Mother died six months before (family history, 4–3) of a coronary heart disease. She had been hospitalized for a suicide attempt (family history, 6–5) during menopausal depression. Nonlethal index: 41; lethal index: 26; management category: serious probability of nonlethal suicide attempt. Moderately serious probability of lethal suicide attempt.

Recently divorced (marital status, 9–6) black male, age 33 (race, 3–2), seen in jail, arrested for disturbing the peace in a barroom brawl (environment, 8–6). Suffered minor injuries. A Vietnam veteran. Admits use of heroin and alcohol while in Vietnam (past personal history, 6–4) and since. No steady employment (environment, 7–4). Seen in VA hospital out-patient department for drug abuse over the last four years (personal history, 9–6). Known as a noncompliant patient. Terrified of jail (mental status, 8–4). "Never been in jail before, I won't stay around here long." He laughs but does not answer when asked if he has been thinking of suicide (suicide rumination, 5–4). He sighs and admits his situation is "hopeless" (special category, 10–10). Nonlethal index: 65; lethal index: 46; management category: urgent and imminent risk of lethal suicide attempt.

Management of the suicidal patient

PART III

Management of the suicidal patient

CHAPTER 8

Factors affecting treatment

The survival of the patient who has been identified at special risk for suicide depends on how well you construct and implement an appropriate treatment plan. There are many factors that may facilitate or frustrate a successful intervention. Some are not within the power of the doctor to effect, others are.

Factors extrinsic to the physician

You don't practice in a vacuum. You and your patient are affected by conditions arising from the times in which you live and work. Physicians in Northern Ireland treat relatively few suicide attempters. The fact that Ulster is engaged in bitter conflict explains the low incidence of suicide. Apparently, when a society is engaged in hostilities, elements of aggression that might be turned upon the self are deflected to the enemy.

Societal factors

Relative economic stability, political disequilibrium, good times, bad times, natural calamities, peace or war, prosperity or depression all affect the probability curve that inclines people to suicide. Though you can't change these factors you ought to be aware of them. Management of suicidal patients in a war zone surely is different from what it is in a ghetto.

It's a fact that where guns, drugs, and alcohol are easily available there is greater chance of suicide. A rash of suicide may be set off by a noteworthy personality dying by violence. And the success of disenfranchised groups pressing to achieve social equality and civil rights is ironically plotted as an increase in the suicide rate.

For example, women, blacks, and others who have fought against discrimination in education, jobs, economic opportunity, and the law have won important gains since World War II in America. But along with equal rights has come equal sharing with the majority in vulnerability to suicide. Before the civil-rights gains, suicide rates for blacks, especially for black adult women, were much lower than for persons of equivalent age and sex among whites. Now they approach the rate for whites. Improvement in economic and social opportunity is dimmed by the penalty of increase in the black suicide rate, now 10 times what it was 25 years ago.

The women's liberation movement has taught women—and men—that women can do anything men can do. Rosie the Riveter of World War II has made successful entry into almost every area, appearing in jobs that were once considered a monopoly of male macho, such as meat cutters, stick men at the crap table, bus and truck drivers, and corporate leaders.

However, along with increased choice of careers and the option to avoid marriage and maternity, with the attendant susceptibility for exploitation by husbands and children, has come familiar penalties that go along with dominance and responsibility. The monkey who pushes the button gets the ulcer, whether male or female. Women elevated to eminence in the business hierarchy and who exercise power and decision making in the professions, in government, and in law are increasingly suffering psychosomatic illnesses. Their exalted status is also accompanied with an increase in the lethality as well as the incidence of suicide among women.

The vulnerability of women physicians to self-destruction, probably greater than among male physicians, is poignant reminder that confusion in role identity and conflicts regarding life priorities heighten the hazards of professional and executive life.

It's a morose probability that full membership in a society confers *all* the perquisites of membership, good and bad. In our society it bestows such advantages as a higher standard of living; it also threatens new members with a higher likelihood of death by suicide.

However much you may dislike it, you can have generally little effect on disturbed relationships and their ultimate deleterious effect on children in our culture. The rising divorce rate and the fact that parents are unwilling or unable to tolerate pleasure and excitement in their youngsters indicate a generation less pleased with their role as parents. Short of divorce, some parents close themselves off from close ties to spouse and child, a behavior that results in a kind of emotional paralysis on the part of their children which brings its own pathologies. Psychiatry, unfortunately, doesn't know how parents can learn to love their children and enjoy parenting.

Much as we might wish for the insight of hindsight we can't always know when patients may be affected by circumstances that might cause them to commit suicide. Just as a pulmonary embolism eight days after an uneventful gastrectomy is dismaying to the surgeon, so is the news shocking that a colleague seen at rounds this morning hanged himself in his office this afternoon. We can't always know all the vulnerabilities of our patients. We can, though, try to minimize the idiosyncratic effectors that might kill them.

Rules and regulations

The constitutional safeguards on civil rights and on individual liberty in America have created the freest society the world has yet seen. However, the guarantee of these rights to persons, who by reason of mental disorders can't know how to utilize their freedoms in the service of their own survival, establishes an unnecessarily exaggerated hazard to life itself.

The right to refuse treatment, commitment laws so stringent that a patient cannot be saved from suicide unless he's virtually in the act of killing himself, and legal strictures limiting the use of electroconvulsive therapy to a degree that almost removes this treatment as a medical option prejudice in some circumstances successful management of the depressed, potentially self-destructive patient.

The penalties patients suffer because of intrusion of law into the practice of medicine is poignantly illustrated by the fate of mentally ill patients who "die with their rights on." A patient resuscitated in the emergency room after a drug overdose who flatly refuses to accept voluntary hospitalization may leave against all sound medical advice, and may, on returning to his home, finish with a lethal dose what he had unsuccessfully attempted earlier.

Physicians learn to live with these justice-is-truly-blind legal glitches. Our problem is how to live within the rules so that our patients won't have to die with them.

Situational factors

The physician who practices in a rural area where there is no psychiatric backup readily available and the doctor who has no in-patient facility to sequester a violent, psychotic patient absolutely bent on killing himself may have to arrange with the sheriff to create the myth of a medical facility by declaring one of the cells in the town jail as a holding area.

No one has ever counted the outcome of high-risk suicidal patients who have had no access to trained mental health professionals as compared with those who have been managed by competent medical psychiatric or psychological help. "Outcome" research of this sort is not easily planned or supported, nor are claimed statistics reliable.

The physician who practices medicine in several different circumstances knows he may not always have the correct medication, instrument, staff, or laboratory he needs for most effective work. In the management of the suicidal patient, no matter where he may be encountered, however, a knowledgeable physician may offer effective intervention equipped with sensitivity, empathy, patience, affection, and awareness together with his good medical training and his humanity.

Physician reluctance to identify suicidal intent

The fact that the event of suicide is underreported should alert us to the distinct possibility that many suicidal patients are given emergency treatment and admitted to medical and surgical divisions of hospitals without ever having access to appropriate psychiatric evaluation and treatment. These lapses may include the immediate post-venture period at the hospital, after acts of self-injury, and later, while the patient recuperates from the effects of the suicidal attempt.

Self-inflicted injuries and poisonings may never be diagnosed or charted as such. The failure of physicians to recognize or acknowledge self-destructive acts results in patients with self-inflicted trauma receiving routine management with no reference to their suicidal intention. These patients are a hazard to themselves or others throughout their hospitalization. On discharge from the hospital, these patients leave no better protected against self-destructive impulsions and their primary psychiatric illness than when they had first been admitted.

Some physicians deliberately or carelessly fail to identify as suicidal patients known by them to have suffered self-inflicted injury as the presenting cause of hospitalization. Some doctors may entertain a strong presumption that suicide had been attempted, but ignore the facts, discourage the patient's discussion of suicidal intention, and decline to accept evidence or speculation by family and friends that injury or seeming accident had been intentionally caused.

Reasons given by the doctors to explain their reluctance to identify suicidal acts are ostensibly altruistic, but sometimes self-serving. Some physicians decline to chart a patient as suicidal to protect the patient's reputation, marriage, prestige, or job, feeling these would be imperiled if the patient were to be labeled as self-destructive or mentally ill. There is an impression that insurance companies billed for hospitalization and medical services or for disability and death benefits may refuse to meet claims if care was acknowledged to be related to deliberately self-inflicted disease or injury.

Physicians concerned with patients' rights hold the opinion that it's not relevant to treatment to identify suicidal impulsion and that it would intrude on the patient's privacy to ask. Unless the patient volunteers the information, they will not ask the question.

Fear of legal reprisals, not wanting to get involved, and reluctance to make moral judgments inhibit physicians from taking and charting an adequate history. Some few admit so great a bias against psychiatry that they never make a diagnosis or identify a problem that would require consulting a psychiatrist.

Physicians are reluctant to stigmatize patients by putting in writing anything that could be detrimental to them. They fear breaches of confidentiality and the difficulty of keeping secret the fact of a suicidal act once it has been entered into the medical record.

Beyond those who avoid the issue, some physicians actively and aggressively intervene and demand that their patients are not to be identified as suicidal. Nursing personnel may be rebuffed when they attempt to warn the attending doctor that his patient manifests suicidal preoccupation or behaves in ways that auger an imminent suicide act.

A nurse who has been chided for including apprehensions of suicide in nursing-care notes or after repeatedly offering relevant information concerning patients about whom she has anxieties will become discouraged when the doctor does not act upon the information or scolds her for harassing him with unwarranted observations.

Physician provocation or sanction of suicide

A suicidal gesture or act may be the result of an iatrogenic vector. The physician's attitude and his omissions and commissions professionally and personally in the doctor-patient relationship may make a difference between whether the patient takes his life or looks hopefully to healthier options. The culpability of physicians as a causal factor in suicide attempts, varies from honest unawareness of lethal intent to perplexity regarding management, then, more darkly, to negligence, and all the way to overt provocation of suicide.

If a doctor can't abide being disliked and has to play "good fellow," he may be unable to confront his patient with the observation he may be killing himself with substance abuse or habits that are inherently damaging. A cardiac patient who wants to jog may announce to his doctor a week after getting out of the coronary care unit that he is going right back to his two-mile-a-day run. The physician who cannot look the patient in the eye and with quiet and resolute firmness tell him he has to postpone his workouts is failing his profession and may be an accessory to self-murder.

In these days of polypharmacy, physicians ought to be aware of the possible toxic effects of drugs they may prescribe when combined with those prescribed by other doctors, particularly psychiatrists.

Continuing medical education courses emphasize the effects that psychotropic drugs can have. Yet, some physicians unthinkingly cease such medication when a patient is admitted to the hospital for a nonpsychiatric condition, which may provoke an overt psychotic crisis. For example, stopping a patient's lithium may precipitate an acute manic attack even within several days or, somewhat less frequently, a crushing dysphoria that could lead to suicide.

Tricyclic antidepressants and the monoamine oxidase inhibitors are potent and should not be ordered, discontinued, or combined with other drugs without consulting the psychiatrist who prescribed them. Antidepressant medications, which are, without exception, potentially toxic in even low doses, should be prescribed with caution. Such a prescription given to a despondent patient may be equivalent to offering him a loaded gun, hammer back, butt first.

A 59-year-old woman in cardiac failure had been seen by the psychiatrist because she had been depressed and talking peculiarly. Minutes later, while the psychiatrist was attempting to locate the referring physician to arrange for her immediate transfer to the psychiatric service, there was a loud crash. The patient had jumped through a window, landing in the courtyard four flights below. She succumbed to her injuries within several hours. In the suicide autopsy held subsequently, a nurse who had been at the bedside of the patient shortly before the psychiatrist visited, quoted the patient as asserting that she wasn't crazy and if the psychiatrist tried to make her go to a psychiatric ward, she would kill herself.

The psychiatric consultation had been urgently requested because the patient had made remarks that clearly indicated her suicidal rumination. Leaving the patient alone, even briefly, established a vacuum of medical control and supervision in which the patient acted.

There are instances when a chance or offhand remark made to another doctor or resident, a nurse, or even a relative has been misinterpreted by the patient and led to severe dysphoria and suicidal acting out. The doctor ought to prepare patients and families for the outcome of surgery, the side effects that go with use of potent drugs, the possibility of morbid outcome or complications. The patient should be encouraged to ask questions, even simplistic and naive ones. These questions should be answered straightforwardly, with no evasion on the part of the doctor. Not every physician can communicate easily with patients. Those who can't should engage a colleague to respond to their questions.

If a woman is going to lose a breast, a man a finger necessary in his work, a child a leg, not only should the facts be laid out, but opportunity taken to describe rehabilitation and substitutive therapies. As an example, an opthalmologist setting up a comprehensive treatment program should prepare the patient for the possibility that an operation to save his sight may fail. Frankly confronting possibilities with the patient before surgery can be a deterrent to suicide if the treatment is unsuccessful and the patient's expectations are realistic.

When a patient asks a doctor to call in a psychiatrist, the physician may take the request as a reproof or he may be insulted or surprised. Sometimes the doctor's response may be denial—for example, "Aw, I've known you for years. You don't need a psychiatrist. There's nothing wrong with you that a week's rest at home after you get out of the hospital won't cure." Or, "Feeling a little down? I'll give you some antidepressant medicine and fix you up."

There are physicians who don't refer to psychiatric consultation. In a survey of several thousand physicians requesting information concerning emotional disturbances in their patients, one obstetrician wrote across his questionnaire in big bold print, "I never have such problems with my patients."

The bias of the physician is not always his fault. It may have been formed on the basis of bad prior experience with psychiatric intervention. Access to good psychiatric practice is not universal. In some hospitals, there may be poorly established liaison between medicine and psychiatry. Many physicians are not aware of the strenuous and earnest effort organized psychiatry has made in the last few years to "remedicalize" the specialty. The effect has been a healthy rejoining of psychiatry to its origins in medical science.

The patient and the patient's condition, rather than the physician's idiosyncracies, are of primary concern. If a patient manifests psychiatric disorders beyond the competence of the physician, the physician's neglect or mistreatment, particularly in the case of a potentially self-destructive patient, may lead to loss of life. It may constitute malpractice on the same scale as would apply if the doctor attempted a surgical procedure beyond his capabilities and for which he was not accredited.

When Patti, an unmarried 17-year-old high school drop-out, received her brand new son in her arms in the delivery room of the municipal hospital, it was the only brief moment of warmth she had experienced in nearly a year of chaotic stress and bitter disappointment. Her 23-year-old boyfriend, a macho biker, had been despised and reviled by Patti's family. She had moved out of her own home into a miserable one-room apartment with David. As soon as they discovered she was pregnant, he took off on his Harley-Davidson, not to be seen again.

She responded weakly to the encouraging murmurs of congratulations and the assurance that the baby was altogether and healthy. Patti felt a tiny surge of hopefulness and optimism until the obstetrician stopped at the head of the delivery table. He took off his mask, stared down at the girl, and said with a sneer, "I don't think you whores should be having babies," then turned away, flinging his rubber gloves on the floor for emphasis. Several hours later, Patti grabbed a bottle of cleaning solution from a maintenance cart and drank the corrosive liquid.

The physician had passed judgment on the girl. He was indignant at what he considered her immoral behavior. In his arrogance, he considered himself the judge of what Patti should do with her life.

Not every physician who deals with patients whose lifestyles are different from his own is as vituperative as Patti's obstetrician was. But physicians who dislike a patient may betray their medical obligation and their Hippocratic oath by withholding from them their best treatment and an aura of comfort and support that any sick person has a right to expect from his or her doctor.

Physicians may provoke suicide by cutting an important tie to the real world for a patient whose sense of belonging and identity has already been compromised. It was after midnight, already New Year's Day, when the doctor shouted angrily, ". . . and don't call me again tonight!" to his middle-aged woman patient and slammed the receiver on the cradle. With an exasperated grimace he said to his wife, "It's that woman again. She keeps complaining about being alone on New Year's Eve, says she has nothing to live for and that unless I put her in the hospital, she's going to 'do something bad.' She's been making threats like that for months. She's like a kid demanding attention."

Shortly afterward, the phone rang again. The doctor pulled the plug out of the extension receptacle near the bedside. The ringing stopped.

On the afternoon of January 3, the police telephoned the physician in his office. The woman had been found dead of carbon monoxide poisoning in her garage. The police officer asked if the doctor would comment on whether he thought she had been depressed.

The physician who abandons, spurns, or rejects a patient who turns to him for a touch of human compassion or assurance that someone cares may deprive the patient of any hope of continuing the human connection to life itself.

In the emergency room of a large general hospital, a physician confronted his patient, an elderly male with arthritis, diabetes, and emphysema. The patient had been taken to the emergency room by the police after swallowing a handful of pills with declared intent to kill himself, "Because I'll never get well."

It was the third such episode within the year. The physician glared at his elderly patient. It was early in the morning. The doctor had been roused out of bed and was deeply annoyed at the imposition. With cold sarcasm he said, "This is the third time that I've had to come down to tend to your hysterics and pump out your stomach. You're the most inefficient man I ever saw. Next time use a gun."

Still retching from the effects of the emetic and the gastric lavage, the patient stared at the doctor and whispered, "OK, Doc." Several days later the patient was taken to the morgue from his home. He had followed the doctor's prescription, prn.

For a complex of reasons, physicians may threaten, browbeat, and even abandon their patients. However, apart from the infamous offenses committed by doctors in Nazi concentration camps during World War II, can we identify physicians who actively, deliberately, and purposefully assist and induce their patients to kill themselves? Such an instance in recent history can be cited: Doctor Lawrence Schacht portioned out cyanide punch to hundreds of persons in Guyana at the time of *Götterdämmerung* of the People's Temple Commune.

Physicians consider themselves overtrained, overworked, overzealous, hyperconscientious, imposed upon, undercompensated, conspired against, browbeaten, intimidated, unjustly criticized, and held to impossible standards. At times, the doctor feels as if he had fallen down in a muddy backyard patch and is being pecked to death by a flock of screaming chickens. Whatever confusion, however irascibility and tempestuousness of mood and temper may affect the doctor, he can't avoid the somber and awful responsibility that passes into his hand the moment he accepts the diploma with his graduating class from medical school. It is a bifurcated responsibility. First, to save and preserve life. Second, *non nocere*, "cause no harm."

Finally, the physician who may provoke suicide among his patients is the doctor who kills himself. The risk of suicide increases for a person who is the intimate of a suicide. Not only does intimate include family members and friends, it also may include one's physician. When the doctor kills himself, the event may have a catastrophic effect for those among his patients, not to mention his family, who have cast him in the role of parent, sibling, or friend or have otherwise deified him. He may, by his act, provide an example to his patients, an identifiable reference, suggesting the morose solution: "When life seems difficult, kill yourself."

Physician's personal bias and attitude

Death by suicide of a patient evokes a broad spectrum of responses in physicians, ranging from deep mourning to overt hatred, and touches disbelief, shock, anguish, terror, guilt, depression, pain, and loss. A physician may interpret his patient's suicide as a rebuke, as if accusing the doctor: "You aren't what you're supposed to be. You're not competent."

The physician may defend his ego with one or another of the classical psychological mechanisms available to anyone who needs to cope with a powerful assault on his personality. Examples are: "I'll attend the funeral and make a contribution to his family" (compensation). "This whole mess is going to bring back my ulcer" (conversion). "It doesn't mean a damn thing to me" (denial). "Suicide is proof of his courage" (idealization). "I could do exactly what he did" (identification). "After all, it was a good death. He suffered no pain" (rationalization). "In a way, I think it's kind of a big joke that he played on all of us" (reaction formation).

Guilt etches at the doctor's self-worth and sense of competence. As is true in all experience in medicine, the physician learns from failure as much or more than he does from success. After all, we do speak of the experimental model as one of trial and error. Reviewing the case of the patient who has died by suicide or caring for the suicide attempter who had not been recognized at risk is a hard way to learn, but for those who are open to instruction it can teach a great deal about the signs that point toward suicide.

If a physician is compassionate and ethically involved with his patient, recognizing a patient at suicide risk or treating a suicide attempter will mobilize his best efforts. Appreciating his own anxiety, he may convey his projection of caring to the patient. On the other hand, some physicians may disdain, reject, or even revile the patient for a host of reasons derived from their own psychological bias and prejudices. For example, they may believe that suicidal patients do not deserve consideration. Other professionals fear suicide and react with self-saving revulsion; they avoid dealing with a suicidal patient as they might try to avoid any acute personal crisis or violence in their lives.

In management of the suicidal patient, it's necessary for the physician to know what his feelings about suicide are. If the doctor understands that he may lose his objectivity or even emotional control when dealing with a suicidal patient he should request another professional to tend the patient. This is exactly what would happen if a surgeon who just scrubbed felt on the verge of syncope. He'd leave the operation to another surgeon.

No physician can care for all patients. Some cannot abide snotty-nose babies; others hope never to see plethoric, wheezing, middle-aged women or elderly, confused men who clack their dentures; still others abhor and avoid alcoholics, drug addicts, long-haired, black-jacketed adolescents. If a physician is trying to cope with his own suicidal impulses he may dread close contact with suicidal patients.

Physician's training and experience

Medical school and residency programs for physicians and postgraduate studies for psychologists and social workers include virtually no course of study and instruction in "suicide medicine." What doctors know about suicide risk is passed along in corridor exchanges, across cafeteria tables, and in occasional death-round presentations.

There are excellent seminars on suicide presented now and then around the country, usually well-subscribed, and a significant literature is accumulating in our medical libraries. But nearly all serious formal teaching is directed to psychiatrists, with opportunities for voluntary participation by psychiatric nurses, clinical psychologists, social workers, and pastoral counselors. Nearly all the papers in suicidology intended for physicians are concerned with statistical changes, crisis intervention, discussions of depression, and on how the event of suicide may involve the physician's legal accountability.

Emergency-ward physicians who have practiced in hospitals for the last 20 years or more, particularly in urban centers, well appreciate that their facilities have attended more suicide victims each year, an overall increase of approximately 1,000 percent. Some of those patients are refugees from state psychiatric hospitals whose population since 1955 has been reduced by about 350 percent.

Patients who had felt secure in the hospital setting are now denied admission. The reasons are diverse. Over the last 20 years the courts have created stringent legal criteria for holding patients. Next, there is an illusion that psychotropic drugs reliably protect patient and society from the gross evidence of psychotic acting out. Further, the lack of interest of state legislators in the adequate care of the mentally ill and inflation's devouring of what funds have been set aside have created for psychiatric facilities a budgetary austerity that can result in economic marasmus.

The emergency-room physician knows a great deal about the crisis of suicide and is quite good at reducing morbidity and mortality for patients transported by the police, fire department, or paramedic transport or patients who walk in with self-inflicted injuries and poisonings. In fact, up to 95 percent of suicide attempters who come to reasonably well-staffed emergency rooms are kept alive at least for this attempt. However, in many hospitals there is no opportunity—or perhaps no inclination—to prevent suicide in the community or to enhance the possibility of survival of the patient once he leaves the hospital parking lot.

It's not that physicians don't want to know how to improve their craft. Most doctors are sensitive to and welcome new facts, are eager to learn how to diagnose and treat diseases of the flesh and, yes, of the mind as well.

Medical professionals and paraprofessionals are quite accepting of new and promising approaches in suicidology. Methodical, well-planned protocol and techniques correlated with everyday clinical experience and formal inclusion in medical school curricula might be a reasonable prescription for a continuum of education for professionals who meet and treat suicidal individuals.

CHAPTER **9**

Principles of suicide management

The unrecognized problem will obviously never be solved; unsuspected diagnoses will not be made; unidentified suicide impulses will not be blocked. The orientation of the doctor and his acceptance of responsibility to improve his skills in recognizing the presuicidal patient, evaluating risks, and implementing appropriate intervention strategies are the first considerations in a coordinated, integrated approach to suicide prevention. But physicians and most clinical professional and paramedical personnel become involved either just at the moment of crisis or after, doing little to prevent suicide in the community.

Revising values

Consider the kind of commitment required for a major sustained attack on epidemic suicide. Prevention requires sober and philosophical address to the disquieting *anomie* of our times. There are sufficient traces of it: the deterioration of affectional ties, the abandonment of or by the family, the ready resort to violent solution in conflicts between and among individuals and nation, and the widespread after-me, you-first egocentrism. Passion, kindness, and love have become first victims to competition. There's prevailing mistrust of leadership. There's a glut of information with no adequate enzyme of collective intelligence available to help digest it. Humanity is desensitized to pain and despair in its own corpus. And the neutralization of idealism makes expressions of lofty hopes for human progress seem absurd.

The surrender of individual identity to purveyors of false religions, irrelevant solutions, easy shibboleths, hysteria, and hatred has made it difficult for individuals to develop sturdy self-reliance. The cult of mediocrity and the compulsivity to succeed are opposite ends of the same dirty stick that punishes the genuine achiever whether he succeeds or fails and denies the gratification of self-enhancement.

There are a multitude of influences in our culture that make it difficult to achieve and sustain self-actualization or even joy. In some women, especially young women, the feminist movement has created a revulsion against longstanding culturally produced patterns of behavior, many of them related to motherhood. Sexual experience no longer requires associated lovingness. There is pursuit of instant sensory gratification and the acceptance of the illusion that chemically induced pleasureful states, readily and swiftly available from alcohol and drugs, are as good or better than the natural highs achieved through personal creativity.

Society does not trust its leaders and institutions, is contemptuous of inspiration, unwilling to attribute the experience of loss, disappointment, and failure to the nature of the human condition, and insecure in its affections. Success is measured by the size of the lettering on the door, the number of Kruggerands in the vault, and the number of orgasmic experiences notched on the belt.

Individuals cannot be happy alone because of unsatisfied dependency yearnings or with others because of refusal to make concessions to the needs of another. Collectively and individually this 20-century civilization is not well defended against corrupting insinuations of the demon at the shoulder who preaches the valuelessness of life and the insignificance of the individual.

Despite amazing progress in the scientific understanding of natural phenomena and in constructing and fabricating all manner of wonderful contrivances from what we scratch, dig, scrape, and skim from the surface of this world, we cannot prevent vast hosts of people from starving to death, and we uproot and kill even more in the name of politics.

Suicide prevention begins with revising our priorities and definitions as to what constitutes the good life on earth. It also arises from the obvious and essential doctrine that each of us is in fact our brother's keeper.

Community participation and involvement

By no means is suicide prevention and management the exclusive domain of professionals in health care. Since self-destruction can affect any person at any age, teaching good health and self-care requires that education be directed from childhood on to enhancing the ability of each individual to cope with self-murderous impulses. Along with learning to brush teeth and massage the gums, eating nutritious food, getting adequate exercise, rest, and recreation, general hygiene ought also include procedures for what to do when suicidal thoughts surface in the mind.

The impulse to kill one's self is treated as though it were an extraordinary occurrence and not the commonplace hazard to health and life it truly is. Educational institutions from kindergarten on ought to include suicide prevention along with general hygiene, sex education, and fire drills.

Labor unions and corporate management may include in bargaining at contract negotiations adequate provisions to care for emotionally disturbed employees to save life rather than compensate survivors for death. Executives in management positions are specially vulnerable to suicide. They owe family and company an opportunity to explore options for life before a crisis happens. Professional and social organizations perhaps might give thought to how they can collectively protect their memberships from tragic and premature demise by suicide.

The media can certainly do more to expose the manner in which self-destructive ideas and acts steal hope and logic from the community. For example, there have been cleverly produced educational TV shows in the form of participatory quiz programs on various health topics, such as the hazards of smoking, fires in the homes, heart disease, and death on the highway. Demystifying suicide by discussing it and showing it as a human phenomenon just as are abortion, crime, influenza, and assassination will help many persons attacked by frightening fantasies to ask for help before their psychological awareness has been badly compromised by emotional perturbation. The telephone is light years away from the reach of a person who wants to die, wants to live, wants rescue, wants peace, and is exhausted in lonely struggle.

Like headache or indigestion, the urge to suicide is autogenous, and usually relief or rescue is effected by private remedies. Few self-destructive scenarios are shared with intimates. But the outward evidence of intense interior struggle is sometimes apparent to the observant and the concerned.

The first line of defense is to teach self-defense against suicidal ideation and impulsion. Next, each person must become his brother's keeper, alert to the suffering and sadness of others, ready to ask, "You seem really down. Are you fighting bad thoughts—like hurting yourself?"

Honest self-reflection requires frank responses to such questions as "Under what circumstances in your life have you felt, even momentarily, driven to consider killing yourself?" When an individual looks into his own eyes in the mirror, taking inventory of his competence to run his life and reviewing significant weaknesses and strengths, susceptibility to self-destruction is a legitimate and necessary item on the agenda.

Women who have had suicidal or infanticidal urges in one childbirth may likely experience those same terrifying impulses with successive pregnancies. A man who has barely saved himself from jumping off the bell tower the night of his high school prom when his date danced too often and too close with other boys may find himself years later on the same brink when his wife threatens divorce.

Exactly the same psychological processes that thrust suicidal persons into combat with the compulsion to take their lives make it seem virtually impossible for them to reach out from dreadful isolation for help in a time of extreme distress. The same chaotic flood of fear, anger, and hopelessness puts the mind into confusion, thus making sensible, rational, self-saving decisions almost unattainable. As a dazed boxer hit too often can't raise his arms to defend himself against the next blow, so the personality, abused by trauma to self-esteem and confidence, may pass the point of no return and be unable to respond to the instinctual mandate to live.

Learning suicide prevention

Military and police personnel, persons involved in high-risk sports such as parachuting, flying, scuba diving, and rock-climbing spend a considerable amount of time in training how to save themselves if threats to their safety occur. How to disarm an attacker, how to free-fall from a disintegrating aircraft to avoid being hit by debris, how to ditch equipment and rise to the surface in an underwater emergency, how to rappel down a cliffside and break a fall absolutely must be taught. Knowledge of these techniques and rehearsal of them serve a number of purposes essential for survival.

First, the trainee is made familiar with the grave risks that attend the activity. Next, he is put in touch with the anxiety and panic he may feel in a crisis. Then, he is made to understand that there are ways to save himself even if the dangerous event should occur. Last, he is put through contrived instances of the expected hazards and learns through practice that parachutes do open when rip cords are pulled, lungs don't burst nor does one suffer embolism if one breathes out slowly on free ascent from the dive beneath the sea, that the yell "Delay!" can save a climber from a fall.

Similarly, suicide prevention requires a major effort to awaken society to the danger of it and the development of training techniques by which people can recognize themselves at risk, learn the symptoms of increasing hazard, and be taught and rehearsed in self-rescue.

Children are taught fire-drill disciplines, water safety in their swim classes, and how to refuse candy and a ride home from strangers. They may also be warned that they will experience "sad thoughts" about dying and that these thoughts should be resisted and shared with a particular adult in the school setting, the parent in the home, or minister or rabbi in the church or synagogue.

Squeamish notions that such training "will just give them the idea" are as nonsensical as assuming children have no sexual thoughts and feelings until someone talks to them about sex and "puts dirty ideas into their innocent minds." Children do think about suicide, do make suicidal attempts, and do kill themselves with the more-than-sufficient cuing their everyday environment provides.

Anyone in a structured situation, such as school, college, factory, union, military base, retirement home, hospital, or jail ought to be provided with the name of a specific staff person who is accessible any time fantasies and obsessional thoughts occur on the theme of violence to self or others.

Whoever is designated to accept responsibility for receiving the appeals of residents, guests, or inmates of the institution or the group carries a somber burden. He needs special training and should know a variety of strategems to employ. These may include simply offering reassurance, giving a telephone number to call, requesting professional consultation, or even arranging hospitalization.

The petitioner ought to be given generous latitude with regard to confidentiality, but the counselor can't give unrealistic assurance that nothing will be divulged "under any circumstances." Rather it should be clearly appreciated that if the adviser discerns a significant threat he'll consider his duty to save life more compelling than the obligation to keep secrets.

Emphasis in the early stage of prevention is on developing self-awareness, fostering acceptance by the community that suicidal urges are common, understanding the special risk factors, for example those that affect prior attempters or substance abusers, establishing and publicizing rescue resources, and helping individuals to reduce the types of stress that may push them into self-destructive acts.

There are many suicidal persons who never threaten, never give warning, seemingly give no clue and no opportunity for intervention. These may become fewer if awareness and self-understanding were taught and if intervention by concerned others were more readily available.

When there is public acknowledgment of the dangers of suicide and help from the community can be enlisted, then there can be specific teaching on how to recognize persons at risk. When regular courses of instruction for would-be "basic rescuers" is established, there may be a rededication to a philosophy that it's good social protocol to reach out in compassion to help another who is desperate. Not only should family members, friends, supervisors on the job, nurses on wards, teachers in the classrooms, bartenders in the pubs, and officers in the military know what positive things they may do to encourage certain co-workers, colleagues, or intimates to accept the helping care offered, but at the least it should come to be socially unbecoming—to put it mildly—to provoke another to self-destruct.

In high schools and colleges, student leaders as well as teachers and counselors may be mobilized to identify the shy, "queer" kids who may be unhappy isolates. Too often, there's a rigid caste system that brutally excommunicates certain youngsters from group acceptance. Sometimes they are excluded because they lack social grace, don't participate in sports, dress inappropriately, are too dumb or too smart, come from families that are too rich or too poor, have physical or mental disabilities, or are stubborn nonconformists.

Adolescence is a time for group identification. The boy or girl who does not feel a part of the whole is likely to be wretchedly unhappy. Teasing, mocking, and outright harassment is not unusual in the school corridor, gym, and cafeteria. It's the way things are unless someone in authority stops it. Humiliation is not a way of improving character through trial by fire, but rather an unmitigated, corrupt, and corrupting cruelty.

The victims of many adolescent suicides are described by their peers as friendless, creepy, odd-ball, and freaky. There are exceptions. The totally unexpected suicide of the class valedictorian, pageant queen, or Big Man on Campus may shock the school or college community. Investigation generally shows not only that the overt projection of success was flawed, but that many friends who attached to the young person who took his or her life were, in a sense, accomplices: They had abundant warning of the impending death and did nothing about it.

The same counselor or student adviser who is available for private talks with youngsters who are "sick unto death" may also receive anxious inquiry and information from anyone about others in the school who are subjects of concern.

Ministers have provided significant refuge in faith for persons in states of emotional and mental turmoil. The comfort of relating to and borrowing strength from a compassionate person who is detached from the terror and pain yet empathetic can be a greatly helpful resource for many potentially suicidal persons. For the believer in prayer, appeal to God in a time of affliction is inspirational to the point where vengeful, angry, destructive persons, committed to self-punishment, may be deflected from self-execution for alleged crimes by the promise of forgiveness.

Chaplains in the military services perform many important duties. Not only do they intercede with heaven but also act as caring intercessors with commanding officers. They are the unofficial basic rescuers for the soldier.

Many religious persons recognize that when a parishioner refuses to accept the comfort offered or twists it into rationalization, he reinforces the compulsion to die. At this point, the priest, minister, or rabbi sophisticated in psychological theory can become directive and initiate suitable interventions.

Suicide-prevention centers

The formal establishment of a defensive line against suicide is the community suicide-prevention or crisis-intervention centers that set up "hot lines." This tactic has spread around the world out of the notable success of the Good Samaritan movement in Great Britain, which was established in 1953 as a resource that people in distress could call for counseling. The centers are staffed by volunteers on a 24-hour basis. Analysis of the project indicates reduction in the number of suicides where the groups operate.

In America, the results of suicide-prevention centers are not well correlated with reduction in suicide attempt rates. Funding agencies complain that, since suicide hot lines cannot demonstrate that they have reduced the rate of self-destructive incidents, they ought to be discarded or their activity curtailed. The conclusion to abandon the centers is no more justified than ceasing influenza vaccine injections because they protect against only 60 to 70 percent of infectious viruses abroad in an epidemic.

The centers don't pick up the most strongly determined suicidal individuals who are too far committed on their melancholy course to attempt self-rescue, which calling a hot-line number would begin. However, the centers offer an important social service, that of case finding, and for that reason alone more than justify their existence and their cost.

The parent who calls the crisis-intervention number to ask for help for a teenaged drug-addicted daughter may receive advice today that may prevent a call tomorrow asking for help for that same daughter who in a state of frenzy is threatening to slit her wrists.

The very existence of the hot line tells the would-be suicide that the community cares, that it approves of the individual's search for an alternative to death. Calling a hot-line number defuses the danger in a particular crisis. It offers a potential victim an engagement that he himself has initiated and is a move to a psychological place of safety. It also involves the community in a lifesaving activity. Interestingly, persons who themselves have made suicide attempts have been found to be as effective as professional social workers in applying preventive techniques.

Despite a good public effort, many crisis-intervention centers and suicide hot lines are not equipped, nor are their personnel trained, to give service to young children who suffer acute psychological crisis. Recognition of psychological dysfunction and assessment of suicidal risk in children is somewhat different from what it is in adolescents and adults. Child psychiatric emergency services have in some places been instituted, usually as adjuncts to child psychiatric hospitals or welfare organizations that have established telephone receptors for cases of child abuse, delinquency, and disturbed families. Enlarging facilities for individual and family treatment can help to identify those families whose children are in need of specialized care for mental disorders or who definitely require skilled care when they threaten or act out in a violent or self-destructive manner.

Suicide screening

A bold but effective method of identifying potential suicide is the voluntary screening interview. The executives of a corporation or school, college, hospital, or professional organization agree that all members will have the opportunity for a brief, confidential interview with a trained person engaged as a mental expert. The agenda for these sessions is entirely open-ended, and the interviewer has the opportunity to help the interviewees express whatever doubts, fears, and difficulties concern them.

If the interviewer inspires confidence, is independent of the hierarchy of the sponsoring organization and—a sine qua non—if confidentiality is absolutely assured, a substantial number of interviewees, many of whom could not themselves have initiated a search for therapy, do admit they need help. A typical exchange might be:

"Have you been wrestling with suicidal notions?"

"Yes, I guess I have."

"Have you ever told anybody about them?"

"No. I've never had such a chance as this to talk about it."

This technique has had unexpected success. Although a few may resist the voluntary program when it's first announced, a surprising number of grumblers do attend the private sessions. The experience is almost universally gratefully received. The knowledge that a visit by a neutral, impartial, empathetic person has been scheduled makes it possible for some persons at risk to hold out long enough for their sessions with the counselor.

Aside from the direct screening interview, there are ways for the community to make self-rescue available to the solitary, drifting victim of despondency. For example, a self-assessment questionnaire, especially tailored for a particular group, industry, or organization. can be distributed to the entire group. Periodically—say, twice a year—individuals can discover by objective standards that they suffer derangements and dysfunctions in their mental lives of such dimensions that they are well-advised to seek professional help.

Psychological tests that can be quickly graded by a computer, such as the Minnesota Multiphasic Personality Inventory, are relatively inexpensive and give valuable readouts of personality defects and strengths. The MMPI or similar tests should be made part of a regular medical examination, which then more appropriately could be called a physical and *mental* examination.

Signaling for help

Most industrial plants and large corporations encourage employees to submit ideas for innovative improvements in the operation of the business and use suggestion boxes to receive them. Those who can express themselves best in writing could use similar boxes, designated to receive notes from employees who feel ill, depressed, aggrieved, or suicidal. Such initiative would invite confidential correspondence. Workers who can't muster the assertiveness sufficient to speak directly to a foreman or call the plant infirmary would be able to make a minimal gesture to receive help. Any correspondence in the "help, please" box would, of course, be confidential and only the designated ombudsman or the plant physician would read the notes, and they would never become part of the employee's personnel record.

There are clever devices by which persons engaged in hazardous occupations are automatically prevented from self-injury. In the event that they are rendered helpless in an emergency, the devices summon help by setting off an alarm or signal that alerts others to their peril. Industrial machines such as punch presses, cutters, and grinders are equipped with safety gadgets that automatically stop the machines and sweep away the hand of the worker who inadvertently placed it in danger.

Boaters and scuba divers carry high-intensity blinking lights which automatically activate when wet. Lifeboats are equipped with radio beacons that beam a repetitive signal that can be triangulated so the lost craft can be found or have metal-foil sails that reflect radar signals to ships cruising in range whose observers could not possibly see a lost boat low in the water in a rough sea. Similarly, victims of personal catastrophe, adrift in a tumultuous sea of despair and psychologically so enfeebled that they are unable to help themselves or petition for rescue, need to be equipped to signal for rescue with minimum effort.

The nonverbal communications of the depressed patient are dramatically expressive of distress for those attuned to receive the message. Flat facial expression, down-turned corners of the mouth, weeping, deep sighing, unkempt clothing, and slow body movements are vivid indications of hopelessness and helplessness. Many more are described in Chapter 6 and are S.O.S. signals from a person in mortal danger. But there is no limit on how a group might set up a signal system that could encourage deeply troubled people to signal for help. For example, posted instructions might suggest: "In case of serious personal distress, please indicate your need for help by dropping your identification card into the 'personal emergency' box nearest your section," or ". . . by pressing the red personal alarm signal button nearest your job station. This is connected to the infirmary and will signal an aide to meet with you at once."

The communication industry, including newspapers, magazines, TV and radio stations, may be approached to maintain emergency telephone lines to receive calls from people who are frightened by their impulse to violence. Paranoid personalities, those who are antiestablishment, desperate persons who are exhibitionistic may call a media personality sooner than a health professional when they have a grievance or a threat against themselves or another.

Such calls are received frequently, especially by hosts of talk shows, but few publishers, columnists, TV or radio station managers, or commentators have a sensible protocol for dealing with distressed persons. Psychiatrists, psychologists, psychiatric nurses, and social workers who are experienced in suicidology may profitably be employed to establish basic training or at least be equipped to give on-the-scene advice for the communications agent who is puzzled yet willing to offer an important preventive service in the public interest.

Courses in basic rescue might be established for personnel in various social pursuits who inevitably are brought into contact with suicidal persons. High on this list are, of course, physicians and psychologists, nurses, educators, policemen and firemen, other law enforcement officers, and also persons in the field of entertainment. Vocational advisers, bartenders, barbers and beauty shop operators, restaurateurs, cab drivers and other public transportation workers also may be invited to refine their shrewd intuition to a functional as well as observant sensitivity.

Not only may the cabbie on the way to the hotel with his silent fare be able to say, "Hey, it may be none of my business, but you really look beat;" he may then add, "We have a good thing going in this town. Anybody who needs somebody to talk to, about anything, can call this number." Then the cab driver would hand the passenger a card with the crisis-intervention telephone number.

Those trained in mental health science have as much work to do as they have time, energy, and devotion to invest in community education at many levels. They may devise and participate in lectures, seminars, workshops, the preparation of booklets, questionnaires, tapes, brief spot messages for TV and radio, talk shows, formal and informal presentations in schools, colleges, union halls, sports arenas, hospitals, shopping centers, and police academies to carry the message: *Suicide is an avoidable hazard to health and life. It can be prevented. Save yourself. Save another.*

106

Despite the best efforts of all our counselors and therapists, self-help books and programs, lectures, sermonizers and healers of all description, people need to talk to people. There are never enough listeners.

CHAPTER 10

The crisis

Patients who already have been defined as being at risk may be subject to a sudden storm of distress which, if adequately treated, may pass quickly. If the episode is carefully monitored and the patient safeguarded, the probability of reactivation of suicidal hazard can be lessened. But the chronically depressed patient who teeters constantly on the edge of self-destruction may also present the would-be rescuer with acute aggravation of his morbid state and needs close observation and care through an extended period of increasing impulsion to die. He requires different management because of the likelihood of a continuing high level of vulnerability to relapse even after the acute episode.

A suicide note may be discovered by the family or sent to friends or even to the therapist. It may be found after an attempt, but frequently may signify an appeal for help before the event. There is a range of dangerousness that suicide notes may suggest. To the extent that the message is relevant, internally consistent, attempts to grapple with facts as they truly are, and considers the possibility of a future for the sufferer, the note does not forebode an imminent highly lethal suicide attempt.

If a note is full of irrelevancies and displays fallacious reasoning, if the writer betrays a constricted point of view without alternatives and refuses to admit any other description of his condition but that which he conceptualizes, if he is explicit about how suicide will be accomplished, the note is an alarming indication of imminent peril. "I have had enough of life. It's no use anymore. . ." in a suicide note of a chronically depressed person who has had previous history of suicide attempts warrants mobilization for crisis.

You may note indications of deterioration of your patient's morale either during office visits or from information volunteered by members of the family. If, despite therapy for his dysphoria, your patient's despondency worsens and his withdrawal intensifies, and if he manifests restlessness, loss of appetite, sleeplessness, and constipation, and if he overtly weeps and expresses self-blame, uselessness, and hopelessness, then a crisis may be at hand.

The patient who actually makes a suicide attempt, even a half-hearted, low-lethal, ineffectual gesture, is sending up a rocket from a limbo in which he cannot retrieve his will to live without outside intervention. Just as significant are statements that reveal that the patient has a precarious hold on life. He may tell you, "You've done all you can for me. It's no use," or, "I'm exhausted with thinking. I need a rest from my thinking."

A man contesting a divorce action has just received a subpoena to appear for a hearing "in this cause"; a homosexual schoolteacher, despondent over the loss of a lover, has just been arrested on charges filed by parents of one of his students "for contributing to the delinquency of a minor"; a middle-aged woman, who has threatened to kill herself if her son should marry the "slut" he's been dating, suddenly receives a telegram saying "We are married!"—each has suffered a significant new aggravation to an already depressed state. Such new blows are likely to escalate the patient's despair to the verge of acting out.

Patients who have been compliant with treatment and seem to be making slow progress may suddenly become resistant to a therapeutic program. They may rationalize either that they now know the answer to their problems and don't need the doctor, or they simply admit that they have given up. In either case, crisis is apparent.

One of the most dramatic death threats is done by the patient on the verge of jumping from a building, bridge, or other high structure. He ambivalently exhibits a confusion of motives: "Save me before I die" and "I hope you're all satisfied. You've finally driven me to this place of no return." The patient on the ledge requires skillful and immediate intervention.

An employee in a plant, a member of an organization, a client of a counselor, a student, a physician, or any patient who has previously been identified at risk may enter into a communication agreement with the therapist. The rescuer agrees to periodically make contact with the supervised person at risk. The patient agrees not to kill himself between calls. It would be further understood that failing to communicate at the appointed time would automatically set in motion an intervention process. "I'll call you at this number, at this time. If you don't answer, I'll send the rescue squad to investigate."

The fact that a link is established between the suicidal person and his rescuer reduces the sense of abandonment and painful solitude the patient feels. It shows that at least one person cares, and gives the patient a reason to continue to live from one call to the next.

Involvement of the rescuer

Whenever circumstances bring the victim into crisis, they force the rescuer into crisis too. As the diner who struggles to his feet soundlessly clutching at his throat needs someone to free up a bolus of food caught in his larynx, so the suicidal person in crisis needs someone to take responsibility to save his life. The designation of rescuer carries with it responsibility to promptly, decisively, and effectively do something. The unconscionable act is to do nothing. If, for any reason, the rescuer can't fulfill the need for correct and prompt intervention, the responsibility should pass to someone who can.

The rescuer who accepts the assignment of saving the patient ought to be *empathetic,* but not *sympathetic.* That is, he should maintain his own professional poise and understand the patient's perturbation and pain. He shouldn't allow his objectivity or judgment to be clouded by overidentifying with the confused distortions of the patient's perception.

"The whole world wants me dead!" is an obviously fanciful delusion the rescuer does not believe. The physician can empathize with the dismay of the sufferer whose paranoia may drive him to death, but the rescuer should not accept the false belief, or he would be as helpless as the patient.

The rescuer should be nonjudgmental, abundantly patient, respectful, should convey his acceptance of responsibility for the patient, and indicate his total attention to the cause. The crucial message from the therapist to the patient is, "We are engaged in an alliance to save your life. We will confront together whatever we need to know to effect this rescue." The availability of the therapist must be assured throughout the crisis, and the terms of the intervention should be stated. The patient ought not be lied to or given false assurances or guarantees.

The question of confidentiality inevitably will arise. The patient can be told that the particulars of his case will not be shared with anyone. However, to the extent necessary to assure his safety, that there is a risk of suicide will be divulged to whoever needs to know it in order to save the patient's life. Whenever possible, interview and examination must be conducted in private to avoid the humiliation of the patient by exposing him to the scrutiny of relatives, friends, or colleagues when he is in a state of psychological or physical dishevelment. It's highly unlikely that the patient will confide in a doctor who allows third parties to be present. Protocol is well-defined for the physician who would discourage intimate confessions. The doctor who does not want to hear the details of the love life of a 15-year-old junior high school student who has threatened suicide unless her boyfriend is allowed to take her to the movies can insulate himself by inviting the girl's parents into the room while he interviews the girl.

An elderly psychotic nun who suffered bipolar affect disorder was in a depressed phase of her illness and wrestled with suicidal thoughts. The physician who interviewed her misguidedly allowed her mother superior to be present during the initial interview. He learned nothing from this interview and found an uncommunicative, weeping, obviously distressed woman before him who could only shake her head in response to his questions.

Months later, when she recovered from a serious suicide attempt, she had an opportunity to speak privately to the physician who had initially examined her. She spoke bitterly of the distress she had suffered. She had not been able to tell the doctor how desperate she was because she had felt the mother superior could not appreciate how sick she was.

The therapist has to establish open communication with the patient. The dictum "When the talking stops, the shooting starts" applies to suicide as it does to war. By inquiring about the thoughts and feelings of the patient, the therapist creates an ambiance of acceptance of the patient's pain as believable and deserving of his thoughtful care.

Suicidal ideation

"Thoughts about suicide are sometimes scary. Have you visualized in your mind how you might destroy yourself?" Discussing suicide in such a conversational yet dispassionate way links the patient with the doctor in a therapeutic bond. It detoxifies the concept of some of its awful mystique and reduces the feeling of isolation that the patient has had to endure.

Conversation with the patient may proceed, with the therapist encouraging a detailed exposition of all the factors that have brought matters to their present dismal state. "However did you come to this situation?" may encourage confidences that the therapist carefully notes for reasonableness, logic, and factuality. Later, the doctor can propose alternatives to the morbid conclusion that the only way out is suicide.

Reintegration of the personality, restoration or compensation for what was lost, and reasonable concessions for the manipulative threateners are what the therapist works for. These concrete missions are inspired at all times by the proposition that life is precious and that the ultimate vandalism is the taking of life, one's own or another's.

Strategies and techniques

The threatening suicidal person is not attractive. He's likely to be stubborn, egoistic, petulant, hysterical, selfish, illogical, inconsiderate, childish, and arrogant. Not infrequently, he elicits feelings of shock and anger even from well-intentioned, would-be rescuers. A self-serving reaction to him may be to shut off the flow of complaint, the self-pitying apostrophes, the whining excesses of inappropriate emotion. The doctor may respond curtly, "Get to the point. What do you expect me to do about it?" or "It just isn't as bad as all that," or he may attempt to arouse guilt: "Do you realize how frightened and unhappy you're making your family with these threats?" Since the suicidal impulsion may be fired up by unresolved guilt feelings, aggravating them will certainly not reduce the tension and may well increase it.

"Won't you be a pretty sight in the morgue with a bloody hole in your head and the few brains you have leaking out" or "Go ahead and jump; who cares" or "You don't have the guts to pull the trigger" constitutes validation of the patient's sense of abandonment, his humiliation, and the contempt in which he feels he is held. Added rejection reduces his chances and choices to only one, to destroy himself.

Out of common experience, suicidologists advise that the important elements in meeting a crisis are *talk* and *time*. The first necessity is to form a relationship, whether dealing with a teenager who has locked himself in the bathroom, the menopausal woman who holds a razor to her wrist, or the agitated young man who has doused himself with gasoline and is trying to light a match.

The rescuer needs to say what he must say and do whatever he has to do to keep the connection intact, however tenuous it may be. Most often it will be through dialogue, either directly or by telephone. A remarkable example that reinforces the point occurred in the early spring of 1981 in Marina Del Ray, California. Deputy Sheriff Teresa Hamilton, using sign language, "talked" a death-seeking 18-year-old suicidal youth off a sixth-story ledge to safety.

The conversation perhaps should not begin with reference to the obvious—that the patient is threatening to kill himself and is the self-placed center of a cyclone of anxiety—rather, it should begin by orienting the person at risk. If previously unknown to each other, the rescuer may introduce himself by name and briefly explain his presence. The rescuer may then state how he as health helper wants to be of service in any way possible and ask the victim how he thinks he can be assisted in his obvious predicament. If the suicidal person draws back and refuses to respond or otherwise indicates hopelessness, the rescuer must persist in offering a variety of conversational gambits in hope of winning an acknowledgment.

"Can I get you a blanket? That cement ledge must be awfully hard" or "Are you hungry? Can I get you something to eat?" or "Do you smoke? Would you like a cigarette?" or "Is there anyone you want to see? Can we get in touch with your parents or friends?" Such easy overtures establish the benign purpose of the rescuer and his defined role as helper.

Whether on the ledge or in the doctor's office, the patient will be encouraged to express his feelings, assured that it is legitimate and right to air his hurt and grievances. Once the patient has, even in the smallest way, returned an appeal or suggestion of the rescuer, he is engaged. The part of his psyche that wants to be saved has begun to accept the possibility that a way back can be found. The longer dialogue continues, the more offering of services, favors, and accommodations the suicidal person allows, the less the likelihood of sudden morbid resolution and the greater the enhancement of eventual successful intervention.

Police departments have certain sensitive, trained, experienced officers who are specialists in the delicate skill of imparting trust without intimidation, impatience, or threats to would-be exhibitionistic suicidal persons. The task of "talking down" the suicide on the ledge may best be done by them, unless the patient himself insists that the rescuer or other health helper who made the initial contact remain with him.

A search for alternatives to suicide is begun when the victim can speak of his pain. The rescuer does not have the constricted view of the suicidal person. He can suggest that living is worth trying, that, for example, the loss of a loved and loving wife who has unexpectedly died is a terrible blow, but the worth of those who die lives on in the lives and work of the survivors. Hope in the possibilities of the future is a most important concept to convey, since the suicidal person thinks narrowly only of a tiny spectrum of time in the present.

A therapist had a telephone discussion with a jealous teenage patient who vowed he'd kill himself now that he knew for certain that his girlfriend had once spent the night in a motel with a boy the year before the patient had even known her. The youngster was alone in the house and had a gun. He clicked the safety on and off several times and spun the cylinder near the telephone to be sure the therapist could hear. He was subliminally appealing for help to find a way out of his dilemma.

The therapist recalled that the patient had an interest in football. After an hour of discussion, he reminded the boy that his obsessive concern about his girlfriend's virginity might cost him his life, a terrible penalty for indulging an aberrant prejudice he needed to understand better. But even worse, if he died, he'd never know the outcome of the last game of the National Football League playoffs!

He began to laugh, challenged the therapist to bet on the game, then conceded he would put the gun down. The therapist lost the football bet but won the bigger gamble.

The manipulative suicidal person may bargain and demand extraordinary concessions as a condition for giving up suicide. Insofar as possible, those demands should be conceded, but guarantees that are unreasonable shouldn't be offered nor should promises be made that cannot be honored.

Whatever the would-be suicide may disclose, however bizarre or contrary to usual moral principles, encourage him to express his feelings and his confidences. Ask him to speculate why he has become so upset in circumstances which admittedly would be unhappy for anyone but have brought him to the edge of his life.

As the doctor gives fluids to the dehydrated, vitamin B_{12} and folic acid to the anemic, and whole blood to the exsanguinated, so, too, the suicidal person, bled white by despair, needs the infusion of hope. If he identifies with a lost love such as a dead parent or girlfriend grown cold, suggest the possibility of new and better bondings. If the overachiever has just suffered failure, talk about the relativism of failure.

As an appeal to the right of the person at risk to consider himself not unlike other persons, remind him that the suicide he proposes as a solution to his problem is, in a sense, unfair. If he would enforce a death sentence on himself for failing to make his quota in life, then, by the application of simple justice, every salesman who fails to make quota should be subject to execution. Only the most delusional patient will miss the manifest absurdity.

In an attempt to reintroduce a concept of worth to a person whose self-image is damaged, it's essential that proffered assurances be modest, within the realm of reasonable probability, and consistent with the patient's own values. For example, an elderly diabetic woman who had been supporting herself with meager earnings developed gangrene and required a below-the-knee amputation. She turned on the gas and put her head in the oven. The custodian was able to reach her and summoned the rescue squad before she had inhaled a sufficient amount of household gas to cause unconsciousness.

This patient would clearly be at high risk for another suicide and a strong candidate for psychiatric hospitalization. If her physician should tell her, "You'll be up on your feet in no time," if he assures her that she can get back her job when she gets used to her new artificial leg, or that her son who has ignored her for years will come to visit her in the psychiatric hospital, he will have broken faith, not only with the patient, but with his own professional ethics.

More realistically, someone in the community in which this lady lives—a neighbor, a friend, distant relative, social worker, or minister—might be summoned to assure her that she is not abandoned, that social welfare agencies that offer support services to families may find a place for her if her present residence is too expensive and to draw on whatever financial resources there may be in the community to help the elderly, sick, and disabled.

If the physician is comfortable in his role he may with concern and affection offer his best professional wisdom to maximize her return to optimal function. By doing so, he in effect compliments the distressed patient by convincing her that she's "worth" his professional attention as a physician and his concern as a friend. However dilapidated a view of self may be, something positive and good results from enhanced self-worth.

The self-punishing person perhaps can't believe he can ever again take responsibility or be trustworthy because of some error or failure—even one that he could not avert. Gustav V. Akerlund, the Mayor of Annapolis, shot himself to death when he became frustrated by his inability to balance the city budget. The intimates, including the physician, of an obsessional, perfectionistic person who is put to the rack in a no-win situation have a lifesaving responsibility. Though he defines himself as a failure, by reasonable criteria applied to anyone else he would be considered responsible and accomplished. Their intervention should be aimed at countering the forces of self-contempt and their likely summation in the abolition of the hated object, the failed self.

When the physician or other professional health helper is aware of impending suicidal crisis, he should take certain precautions. The degree of risk, the rapidity with which events flow toward the critical mass, so to speak, mandates not only the sequence but what the details of rescue should be. A patient who has been putting himself into life-threatening situations and has suffered a series of accidents or a patient with cirrhosis of the liver and esophageal varices who has ignored the doctor's order to stop drinking present a different kind of crisis from the patient who threatens to take "every damn pill in the medicine cabinet."

The protocol for the patient who arrives at crisis via the route of slow chronicity is not too much different from that for the patient who reaches the crisis acutely. The timing and order of priorities is elected as a matter of professional judgment.

An adult son and his wife visited his father in an attempt to console him several days after the parents' divorce was final. The son found the door open. He and his wife went into the father's home and found him sitting in a darkened room, weeping. There was no food in the house. The father seemed dazed and did not respond to his son and daughter-in-law. The young couple were alarmed at the father's gaunt appearance. They assured him they would go out, bring back some food. "We'll be back in just a few minutes," they said. In doing so, they broke the communication bond. When they returned, they found the man slumped over the couch, dead, shot under the chin. His foot was bare, the big toe caught in the trigger guard of a rifle. *Do not leave the patient in suicidal crisis alone.*

Confront the patient with the probability he has been planning suicide with the lethal means at hand. Request that he voluntarily turn over his guns, car keys, knives, beer and liquor, and his cache of pills to a trusted relative or friend. Encourage him to confide his fantasy of attaining his death. The patient who lives in an apartment on the sixth floor who describes fighting the urge to open the window and jump requires different management and restriction from what the teenage girl requires who warns that she has mentally rehearsed getting into the family car and driving off a pier into the lake. *Remove lethal means and opportunities from the patient or the patient from lethal means and opportunities.*

Consider whether another person or other persons must be engaged. The 15-year-old girl who has taken an overdose of drugs calls the doctor, but says, "Please don't tell my parents." In such a case, the physician must immediately and urgently request that whoever is in the house with her—friend, sibling, or parent—must speak to him so he can instruct that she be moved at once to the nearest emergency facility.

The middle-aged man who has just lost his children in a custody fight may telephone the physician, threatening suicide. In conversation the physician learns that a priest from a nearby parish has been a comforting friend to the patient. If the doctor is alone and cannot give a message to an aide to call the priest, he must decide at some point in the dialogue when the patient can tolerate a one-minute suspension of the talk so that the doctor can call the priest.

If the suicidal person persists in his intention to kill himself and if the rescuer on the telephone senses the situation is deteriorating, it may be possible for him to signal someone in his office or household while he is still conversing with the suicidal patient. By note or sign, an aide can be instructed to summon the rescue squad, police, paramedic service, or some significant other to go to the patient to effect rescue, by physical intervention if necessary. If the patient cannot be protected against impulse in an outpatient setting, the least restrictive, therapeutically necessary facility may be a psychiatric hospital.

The rules are the same if the patient calls from a distant place. A widowed patient had been treated several years before by modified mastectomy for breast cancer. Recovery had been uncomplicated. The patient moved out of town. Unexpectedly, she called the physician, thanked him for his good services in the past, then told him she had detected lumps in the other breast and could not bear to go through "all that" again. She then told the doctor that she was about to kill herself. "I wouldn't want you to think, when you read about my dying, that I blamed you in any way."

With good presence of mind, the doctor signaled his receptionist and, while he continued to commiserate with his patient, scribbled a note to her: "GERALDINE SMITH. SUICIDAL! GET CHART. CALL DAUGHTER ON OTHER LINE. *NOW!!!* While the physician talked to the distracted patient, the nurse located the daughter, advised her to reach her mother at once, and successfully managed timely intervention.

An important caveat: Whatever contacts are made with the patient or third parties should be jotted down, together with the precise time when events occurred. Such documentation is important in later reconstruction of the sequence of steps that built up either to safe resolution or to injury or death. Such data in your private file may be helpful in later conferences with the surviving patient who may have only a hazy or distorted memory of the occasion, or of considerable value in "suicide autopsies" that can help you to assess your performance for future encounters. They may also be of substantial help in case of lawsuits for malpractice.

Action taken in crisis must be decisive, directed as circumstances permit, and performed with measured and appropriate alacrity. As plans emerge out of the professional judgment of the rescuer's experience and ingenuity, they should be shared with the patient. In any event, they are clearly his responsibility to carry forth with no vacancy of his presence until the patient is transferred to another, equally well-qualified rescuer in the chain of intervention.

Suicide is a frequent and sometimes lethal complication of depressive illness. Emergency intervention by psychiatric consultation or direct hospitalization should be sought if the depressed patient worsens, if he continues suicide rumination or threats of self-destruction, if the means of suicide are explicitly stated, if there is psychotic disorganization and an impression that the patient has lost his judgment to a point that his hallucinations and delusions rule his destiny, if there is an obvious, even weak, nonlethal suicide attempt, and if his support system of family and friends are weak or unavailable.

CHAPTER 11

Problems in the hospital

Superior care and protection for potentially suicidal patients are provided in hospitals, but serious hazards for survival exist there, too.

Expert personnel and technology make it possible to support the patient therapeutically on a 24-hour basis through a variety of treatment modalities. This is especially true for the patient in crisis or immediately post-venture, after an unsuccessful suicide attempt. However, the hospital itself may create stresses that, even in providing good medical and surgical care for a patient, may create circumstances provocative of suicide.

How therapeutic the hospital may be to the mentally disturbed patient at risk depends on how well qualified the staff is to recognize the risk and how it provides good care for his psychological deficiencies as well as physical dysfunctions and to what level of commitment the staff may be devoted to assure effective treatment not only from admission to discharge, but after discharge as well.

Emergency room and intensive care

Medical and surgical skills available in modern hospitals, especially urban institutions, offer the probability that 90 to 95 percent of patients brought to the emergency room and intensive-care units will survive suicidal attempts by whatever means. This probably coincides with the recovery from acute injury from all causes, accidental or intentionally self-inflicted. Reinstituting autonomous breathing in respiratory arrest caused by opiates, establishing normal rhythm in a heart abused by tricyclic overdose, elevating blood pressure to levels compatible with sustained body and brain functions by giving blood transfusions for the patient exsanguinated by reason of self-induced injuries—these are only the beginning of successful rehabilitation.

Admittedly, emergency-room personnel are frequently over their heads in the demands that circumstances force on their professional skill and coolness. The principle to first take care of the sickest patient or the most seriously injured generally applies. Time and energy are concentrated on saving lives. The patient who has injured himself should receive the necessary care to offset life-threatening trauma on an equal basis with other patients, but after the critical phase is over a special attitude should prevail.

The suicidal patient's attempts to thwart the efforts of the physician and staff or even to actively resist lifesaving treatment becomes a resented and onerous burden to them. At times, such a patient forbids the emergency-room physician and nurses to administer to him or warns them that their efforts are "of no use." In contrast with most patients who are grateful to receive treatment for illness and physical injury, the would-be suicide is sometimes reproachful or even hostile to his rescuers. He requires time-consuming, excessively detailed administrations and participation in his care by a variety of officials, specialists, and others, including psychiatrists, psychologists, social workers, attorneys, hospital administrators, police, and court officials. Because he may even be combative, he puts the hospital personnel not only in legal but also in physical jeopardy as well.

The entirely logical and reasonable assumption by physicians is that the patient has, by his suicidal act, temporarily suspended his civil right to full autonomy. The emergency-room team will not usually allow themselves to be cozened into becoming accessory to self-murder. However, months later in a court room, the emergency-room physician may be pressed to justify his treatment of a patient who was not willing to receive treatment, and was vengefully seeking financial reward for the doctor's allegedly unwarranted intrusion into the patient's privacy and assault on his person. This, the doctor did by forcing a rubber tube down his throat and a needle into his veins to save his life.

Another scenario, even sadder, takes place when the family of the suicidal person calls the doctor and the hospital to task for having failed to recognize that the injuries of the patient were self-induced and, following his emergency treatment, for improperly denying him examination by a mental-health specialist. Supposedly a psychiatric consultation would have protected the patient better than the emergency-room staff did who discharged him after suturing his wounds and giving him an injection of penicillin. As the story goes, on returning home he killed himself.

Even if there is a psychiatric consultation and the psychiatrist advises continued institutional care, the patient can successfully force his discharge if the protocol for involuntary hospitalization was not properly pursued. Here again, the survivors of the suicide may seek redress in a malpractice lawsuit.

The frustration and personal risk involved in the care of a suicidal patient are not the only problems. Often the circumstances of injury are not known or even discoverable by emergency-room personnel. The fatally injured victim of a single-car accident may not be identified for days, if ever, as having been a suicide attempter. Patients who have neglected their life-sustaining medications, such as insulin, thyroid, steroids, cardiotonic drugs, or antibiotics, and others who have suffered injuries in falls, fires, and explosions may have been victims of deliberate, self-induced injuries and illnesses.

Sometimes police, ambulance rescue crews, and paramedics have training to look for and report clues that may be useful to the emergency-room staff. They can advise the treating physicians that the patient's injury may have been suicidally caused.

The most frequent offender in failing to inform is the referring physician. Physicians may send the patient or advise the family to convey a patient to the hospital without ever specifically informing the hospital personnel either that the patient has a history of psychiatric illness, depression, or suicidal acting out or that he has reason to believe that the illness or injury for which he is advising transport to the hospital was self-induced.

Physicians who fail to specify patients as suicidal or intentionally withhold their conviction or suspicion from the hospital personnel cause a void in information that can be most troublesome. The quality of care given to the patient may be adequate for the immediate needs for crisis but are by no means sufficient for his ultimate well-being.

It's entirely possible for a patient who has entered the hospital with fractures of skull, pelvis, and tibia due to an "accidental" fall from an apartment-house window to be picked up at the scene of injury, transported unconscious to the hospital, properly and expertly treated in the emergency room, sent to the intensive-care unit, transferred to the neurosurgical or the orthopedic services, then eventually discharged with no opportunity to have been adequately and correctly treated for the *cause* of his injury: depression and lethal suicide act.

Residents and emergency-room physicians agree that if a patient is known to be suicidal he should not be discharged without psychiatric evaluation. They would like a psychiatrist or psychiatric resident on call to advise them and, in any event, they believe the patient should be kept in the hospital with protection against suicide at least overnight, preferably for up to 72 hours.

Some emergency-room physicians believe that if the treatment of the suicidal patient is made unpleasant, the distressing nature of the experience may act as a deterrent against future self-destructive acts. The assumption is usually a glib rationalization of an angry, annoyed, or threatened doctor who needs an excuse to punish a patient perceived as a nuisance or even as disposable.

In fact, the more painful the recollection of the patient of his emergency-room experience, the more convinced he may be that his suicide attempt obtained the desired results: helped to expiate his guilt and called attention to his unhappiness. Further, inflicting punishment may alienate the patient even more and destroy any trust or belief that the medical profession has any interest in him other than as a mechanical problem.

The closing of state mental facilities has put many patients with psychiatric illness on the street or housed them with mercenary caretakers in poorly kept, cheap, rundown hotels or inner-city residences. Since the state facilities cannot accept them, they now enter the emergency rooms of various city hospitals seeking admission. A not-infrequent tactic to gain hospitalization is a relatively low lethal suicide attempt. Patients who resort to this ruse are frequently on welfare, may become habitués of the emergency room, and cycle in and out after receiving perfunctory care.

There are many problem-patients with suicide on their minds who must be assessed swiftly and accurately by emergency-room personnel. But the chronically suicidal patient requires expert assessment, whether he's evaluated by a physician, a psychiatrist, or a psychologist. Patients frequently do not really wish to die in their apparent life-threatening attempt, but may use means that create greater hazard than they intend. Other suicide victims have a serious wish to die but do not know how to kill themselves efficiently and take self-destructive means that are not particularly lethal and therefore do not give true indication of the seriousness of their intent to die. Some patients who are deeply serious about committing suicide and do have an accurate knowledge of the lethality of the means available are at the highest risk. They, of course, include persons in the health professions such as dentists, pharmacists, and physicians.

Psychiatric or psychological consultation should be obtained as soon as possible following the patient's restoration to consciousness. The longer the patient remains in the emergency room or in the intensive-care unit, the more anxious he may become regarding psychiatric attention and the probability of his being transferred to a psychiatric unit. Also, as time passes, the patient may begin to mobilize increasing leverage against whoever he believes must be made to feel guilty.

In some communities, where hospitals do not have psychiatric or psychological consultation available on the premises, arrangements can be made with a local community mental-health center or a suicide-prevention center to furnish personnel, sometimes on a 24-hour availability basis, to serve the emergency room in offering expert evaluation and begin treatment for suicidal patients.

A clear and simple exposition of the precise technique of obtaining legal authority to hold a patient involuntarily should be conspicuously available. The exact protocol and the names and telephone numbers of responsible persons who should be approached at any hour to effect involuntary admission to the hospital should be established by the medical staff, reviewed by the executive committee, and examined for legal compliance with existing statutes by the hospital attorney.

Accurate recordkeeping is critical not only for medical documentation but also for legal and administrative requirements. Because so little time is available for it, emergency-room records are likely to be epigrammatic and brief to a fault.

Doctors unwilling to label a patient as a "probable suicide" laconically describe the overt lesion as cause for emergency-room admission. Seldom is there any attempt to amplify the specific description of "wrist, lac." or note that the injury was possibly suicidal. Not only is there need to identify the patient's suicidal potential for his emergency care, but subsequently when he is transferred elsewhere in the hospital. Nursing personnel and other physicians need to be alerted wherever the patient may go to prepare for the possibility of acting out.

There are various devices by which this can be done. The first is the tried-and-true "hospital grapevine." Even when the notes do not go on the chart warning that the patient has potential for violence, experienced nurse-administrators may receive and pass along appropriate warnings to the receiving wards to which patients may be transferred after receiving emergency care. For example: "Male patient you are getting from ICU has been in the hospital a couple of days. He claims to have been shot in a robbery. We think the wound was intentionally self-inflicted. The family tells us that he has been depressed and warned that he might kill himself. Keep an eye on him and inform the resident and the attending doctor if he tries anything funny."

Another useful technique is attaching some signal to the chart that can be understood by all personnel as identifying a patient at risk for violence, either suicidal or homicidal. The sticker does not have to be defended or even charted. However, its removal should be authorized only by a physician.

Patients at risk

Suicidal patients are often transferred from the emergency room or intensive-care unit after resuscitation and critical care directly to medical and surgical floors. Even if there is a psychiatric service in a hospital, admissions are restricted.

Psychiatric wards in general hospitals have a heterogeneous population, men and women of all ages, representing virtually the entire range of psychiatric disorders. However, the psychiatric service may refuse such patients as court-ordered involuntary admissions, those who are physically powerful and constitute a hazard to other patients and staff because of their potential for severe combative behavior, drug addicts, or patients who have severe surgical and medical illness that takes precedence over their mental illness. Not infrequently, psychiatric wards are completely full, and "no psychiatric beds" is one of the unpleasant facts of life that the hospital staff must learn to accept.

In some private hospitals, indigent or welfare patients may not be accepted or will receive emergency care only for several days until transfer can be effected, usually to a public institution.

Most general hospitals in the United States do not have any designated psychiatric beds. It's inevitable that a substantial number of depressed and potentially suicidal persons will be treated in the hospital setting without the medical and architectural specifics designed for the protected treatment of psychiatric patients. For instance, there are no security screens on windows, locked doors, closed-circuit video viewers, one-way mirrors, seclusion rooms, protected electrical outlets, shielded lamps, and—most importantly—no trained psychiatric personnel.

With no tools, talent, or education to care for suicidal patients, it's not surprising that 10 times the number of deaths by suicide in general hospitals occur on nonpsychiatric services as compared with those that occur on psychiatric wards or in psychiatric hospitals.

The experience of being hospitalized is special. It's a time when a sick person needs the best expertise, applied effectively with his full cooperation. It's a time of total dependency, isolation, depersonalization, humiliating violation of privacy, disturbed and contradictory communications, prolonged discomfort, intense pain, and seemingly unnecessary restrictions of basic human rights. It's a time when events and relationships with staff and with their own families may provoke patients to feel helpless, worthless, and hopeless to a degree never previously experienced in their lives.

Acute illness can destroy a sense of internal cohesion and push a person to the limits of his or her endurance. This is especially true for those unaccustomed to stress, unprepared for pain, asthenia, paralysis, hemorrhage, mutilation, and loss of control over bodily functions such as speech, respiration, voluntary movement of the extremities, swallowing, and toileting. The result may be a stress reaction manifested by dissociation, confusion, easy startling, numbing of responsivity to the real world, loss of cognitive skills and judgment, and mental deterioration progressing to overt psychotic decompensation.

Chronically ill patients, particularly those who believe that their condition has gradually worsened and whose symptoms are increasingly debilitating, proceed to the point where they feel their dignity as human beings has been lost as they slip into a state of virtual infantile dependency.

The hospital is designed to relieve pain, correct system failure, and rehabilitate function. But patients sometimes feel as if they have been reduced to passive objects, powerless to change the course of events and subject to the decisions of others whom they may not trust.

Institutionalization severs normal connections with supportive persons who, even if they wish to, cannot reach out to the ailing patient. Gestures of affection, lovingness, concern, or even interest shrivel in the artificial, sanitized atmosphere of hospital visiting hours.

Patients who manifest inappropriate social responses or bizarre attitudes to staff, are obviously depressed, express feelings of apprehension, speak pessimistically of imminent death, and who are also severely debilitated by their medical or surgical illness may be in danger of attempting suicide. All the signs of depression previously discussed in Chapter 6 apply to the hospitalized patient.

A suicidal attempt in the hospital is likely to be carefully planned. For example, a woman patient awaiting a breast biopsy died by drinking cleaning fluid grabbed from a tray of a maintenance worker. She had previously inquired, "When will the cleaning lady be coming?" A middle-aged emphysematous patient jumped from a window during a change in shifts when there was a short break in supervision. A young boy scheduled for a CAT scan of his head, whose boyfriend died in the same auto accident that caused his lacerated scalp, hanged himself from the shower-curtain rod with his bathrobe tie. He did so while the nursing staff was busy admitting a new patient.

Patients not recognized as potentially suicidal may take advantage of a transfer. On leaving a relatively protected ward for laboratory tests, physical therapy, or special examination, they may break away from attendants and jump down a stairwell.

Inadequate and unavailable information about a suicide patient may make it likely that he may self-destruct because staff members who may have picked up clues failed to chart them or orally pass them on to other members of the treatment team.

Information about a patient does not always keep up with him as he is moved from one unit of the hospital to the other. The admitting physician who knows that the patient was brought to the emergency room for self-inflicted wounds may fail to advise the staff on the receiving surgical ward that the patient was, and probably still is, suicidal, enhancing the potential for violent acting out for which the receiving ward staff may be completely unprepared.

The fact that a significant number of suicides occur shortly after patients are released from the hospital indicates that there is a vacuum of information and instruction. When the patient returns home, neither he nor his family are forewarned how to manage intense depression or self-destructive impulses.

Reactions of staff

Nursing personnel have moment-by-moment responsibilities in the basic care of patients and are under immediate stress when a patient manifests psychiatric symptoms. Unsure of the significance of episodic disorientation, hallucinations, agitation, despondency, belligerence, shouting, absurd demands, vituperation, seemingly excessive or inappropriate complaints of pain, and threats of violence, it is not surprising that the nurse may respond by aversion.

It's taxing enough to meet the needs of patients who are cooperative, grateful, or at least compliant. However, when confronted by patients who actively sabotage their own treatment and then defy the best efforts of nurses to keep them alive, it's perhaps inevitable that defensive emotional reactions will be engendered. These may vary widely, depending not only upon the circumstances but also on the personality and the experience of the nurse. Some nurses expect that a particular patient may manifest emotional disequilibrium as a reaction to the compound effects of separation from family, uncertainty as to the future, unexpected and unfamiliar pain of an intensity never before encountered, abhorrent dependency feelings, and uneasy mistrust of the environment and everyone in it.

Some nurses may respond to the challenge of a difficult patient by becoming more attentive, finding more effort and time in their busy schedule for a special expression of reassurance. Others, protecting themselves, may withdraw. Still others, meeting a sense of mounting frustration and anger because of the obnoxious manner in which the patient behaves, may subtly or even verbally counterattack. As a result, the demanding, hypercritical, nasty patient will receive less understanding, poor quality basic care, and less emotional support than "good" patients who reassure the nursing staff of their appreciation and affection.

Patients who commit suicide in hospitals are often precisely those who are the least manageable, most provocative, most intolerant of every aspect of care in the hospital environment, and most dissatisfied with what is done for them. The staff's withholding emotional support increases the propensity to suicide.

The primary therapist, the physician in charge, is as vulnerable as the nursing personnel to the same sense of indignation and abhorrence aroused by the querulous, perpetually complaining patient. However, it's generally easier for the doctor to walk away from a patient than for nurses to do so. The physician who backs away from the patient may then compensate for his rejection by ordering that more attention and services be administered by the nursing staff, reinforcing their feeling of being unappreciated and imposed upon.

The result is likely to further alienate the staff from the patient. Physicians inconsiderate of the nursing staff write orders and assume they will be carried out. They never ask if there are sufficient nurses on duty or if equipment or drugs are available. If the physician tells his nurse, "Put this patient on suicide precautions," and turns on his heel and walks away, he may then throw the entire service into consternation because, what with illness, vacations, and below-complement staffing, there just aren't sufficient nurses to fulfill that order properly.

Disunity among staff members may occur because patients are seen from different perspectives by personnel who have overlapping, even contradictory, objectives in their treatment program. The oncologist consultant may insist on liver biopsy and order the surgical procedure scheduled to determine if the agitated, depressed patient with a long history of alcoholism has a fatty liver, cirrhosis, or neoplastic disease. The psychiatrist may suggest that the procedure be postponed because the patient does not understand the implications of the biopsy, is despondent, and is likely to misinterpret the recommendation as a final blow to his tenuous hope for recovery.

The attending physician, wary because the patient has threatened to sue him because of the blotches on his arms where venipunctures leaked, would like to find a way to resign from the case. In any event, he's reluctant to expose the patient to diagnostic tests or therapies that have a high incidence of undesirable side effects.

Nurses, caught in a flurry of orders and counterorders, communicate their dismay and confusion to the patient, who predictably reacts by becoming overtly irate and tries to cope with his helplessness and apprehension by a display of anger.

Having little confidence in their ability to manage the suicidal patient, nursing staff and the attending physician may then overreact, demonstrate overt anxiety, institute repressive measures, or take an avoidant, denying attitude and do nothing.

Many hospitals have no published procedures or guidelines for the staff. Neither administration nor the medical hierarchy seems to appreciate that violent patients on the doorstep who may commit suicide or lash out aggressively are a medical, administrative, legal, ethical, and philosophical problem much easier to plan for in anticipation than to rue after the fact.

CHAPTER 12

Suicide prevention in the hospital

All persons in the hospital who have any contact with patients, including business, maintenance, security, kitchen, administration, secretarial, and communication personnel, should be taught the rudiments of basic rescue of the suicidal patient.

A hospital photographer who was asked to take pictures of an interesting port-wine nevus on the scalp of an elderly man later diffidently mentioned that the patient had casually mentioned to him, "Make this a good one, it's going to be my last. . . ." The clue was picked up by an alert nurse who insisted that the visiting surgeon see the patient at once and flatly told the doctor that the patient was probably suicidal. A psychiatric consultant verified that the patient was despondent and planned to kill himself at the first opportunity.

The techniques of education are not as important as the willingness of the staff, especially physicians, to recognize suicidal risks and to manage them. Inspiration must come from the top, from the executive committee of the medical staff in collaboration with nursing, social service, and administration.

Instruction is best handled by the psychiatric department, if there is one. Otherwise, experts from the community crisis center and consultants in psychiatry, psychology, and psychiatric nursing and psychiatric social workers should be enlisted to prepare courses in suicide recognition and prevention. Seminars and symposia with didactic approaches and even isolated workshops and lectures are helpful, but one-shot approaches to learning will not serve the ultimate needs of the staff to look after their suicidal patients.

The medical library should keep a shelf of reading matter for staff members who wish access to the subject. The American Association of Suicidology has produced excellent teaching material for all levels of professional use and for laypersons as well. The bibliographic material in the appendix may be a guide for individuals and committees who have been given the responsibility for planning educational programs.

The objectives of education are not only to teach how to identify suicidal patients but also how to develop a confident demeanor from which staff members can inculcate hopefulness and convince the patient that the therapeutic environment of the hospital can indeed be trusted.

Recognition and identification

From the first inquiry regarding an available bed to the time of discharge, the possibility that a patient may be suicide risk should be anticipated. Whether by emergency or routine admission, information concerning a patient's present and past mental state and, in particular, his propensity for violence against others and himself ought to be routinely sought along with his name, address, age, sex, social security number, and third-party insurer. Ideally, it should be volunteered by the admitting physician, but family, intimates, employers, and rescue personnel as well as the patient may have relevant information and should be asked for it orally or by written questionnaire completed as soon as possible after admission.

Prior history of self-destructive attempts, suicidal rumination, patterns of behavior indicating the possibility the patient has or is suicidally inclined should be solicited by previously agreed-upon procedure. Information that identifies the patient as one who may self-destruct should accompany him as he moves from place to place within the hospital.

The responsibility for identification of a patient who may die by his own hand belongs to everyone in the hospital, but most often falls to the nursing staff. As part of their education and training, they should be encouraged and authorized to raise the question with the attending physician, their nursing supervisor, and with the chief of staff directly if their warnings have been passively received or ignored. If the situation warrants, the nurse should be quick to place a conspicuous note or sticker on the front of the chart, signifying that there is heightened risk attached to this particular patient.

As a matter of routine, patients who have been identified as suicidal, have been threatening suicide, or who have made abortive attempts to destroy themselves should be subject to special surveillance. The frequency and intensity of nursing observation and curtailment of ordinary privileges will vary with the level of hazard judged by the physician in charge, preferably in consultation with a psychiatrist.

Consultation

For the advantages of staff training and case discovery and management, it's helpful to invite a psychiatrist to go on rounds with the medical and surgical residents and attending physicians. In any event, rules and regulations of the hospital should mandate psychiatric consultation for any admission whose illness or injury has been the result of a suicidal act or in instances when there is severe depression, peculiar behavior, agitation, overt psychosis, or suicidal threats.

Patients suffering from organic brain syndromes with delirium, alcoholics and other substance abusers, and prior suicide attempters should be carefully observed for signs of mental decompensation and in most instances should be seen by the psychiatrist. There should be as short a time lag as possible between the request for consultation and its completion. Then, after the psychiatrist has seen the patient, advice and orders ought to be *promptly* communicated to the visiting doctor and implemented. If the request for psychiatric consultation is written on Thursday, the psychiatrist leaves the note warning "possibly suicidal" on Friday, and the attending physician reads the consultation on Saturday, the patient may jump out of the window and be found dead in the parking lot on Sunday.

The attending doctor requesting psychiatric consultation should expect as a minimum that the consultant will read the clinical chart, interview nursing personnel, and examine the patient. His note should include highlights of the history, the specifics of the mental status review, and appropriate psychiatric diagnoses according to the American Psychiatric Association's *Diagnostic and Statistical Manual of Mental Disorders,* third edition. Even a terse note should separate organic from psychological diagnoses and offer an opinion regarding the interplay of the physical illness with the psychiatric. Finally, the consultation note ought to state specifically what should be done for the patient in terms of medical, psychological, and situational management. If the psychiatrist believes that the patient is suicidal or homicidal, not only should he say so, but he should also state to what degree. Explicit directions should be given regarding the use of restraints, sitters, transfer to another facility, or involvement of other services or consultants such as social workers, religious counselors, finance administrators, attorneys, or court officials. The psychiatrist should further advise if he will remain on the case and be available to see the patient again or recommend another consultant if he cannot continue.

In a teaching hospital where psychiatric residents are available, the time delay is likely to be less. But in other hospitals, particularly those that don't have psychiatrists available on call, other mental health specialists—psychologists, psychiatric nurses, and psychiatric social workers—may be helpful in evaluating the degree of mental impairment and establishing a collaborative therapeutic relationship with the patient.

Nursing personnel from the psychiatric division may perform effective advisory functions in the management of psychiatric patients all over the hospital. Delegated by the psychiatrist, who may not physically be able to make an immediate bedside consultation, they may make appropriate observations and greatly shorten the response time to a request for an examination of a patient who has created an aura of unease. They may continue to monitor certain patients already seen by the psychiatrist, determined to be mentally ill but delayed in transfer to the psychiatric ward or to a psychiatric hospital either because they are too ill physically or for administrative reasons.

Nurses from the division of psychiatry can frequently help the staff on nonpsychiatric services to adapt general hospital policies to their particular needs. In addition, nurses can consult and participate in case finding, be an informal resource for case management, and help the nursing staff deal with their own feelings and attitudes regarding psychiatric patients.

Some physicians refrain from calling psychiatric consultations out of a cynical conviction that they have no use for the entire subject or become immobilized because of fear of their own feelings. In such cases, nurses offer a special and important service. They can, for the benefit of the patient, nag the doctor into action.

Advice should be sought not only from in-house or an outside mental-health specialist, but from anyone who can give information about the presence of risk and preventive measures appropriate to the patient. Members of the family, friends, intimates, employers, and colleagues of the patient may relate valuable facts, such as "He squirrels away matches and razor blades." "She once ate the thermometer in a hospital." "Don't let her have her perfume bottle. She'll drink the perfume, break the bottle, and cut her wrists with the pieces of glass." "Better not give him Thorazine. Last time he got it, he turned yellow with some kind of liver trouble." "He asked to see his lawyer because he wants to rewrite his will."

For legal as well as ethical reasons, consultation with colleagues, even nonpsychiatrists, is always desirable, not only to minimize the risk of error in management but to indicate that the attending doctor tried to act correctly within the limits of his own expertise. When the primary caretaker therapist is uncertain, he should not hesitate to ask another colleague to combine their experience and knowledge in order to arrive at the best possible therapeutic measures that meet the standards of professional practice recognized as competent in the community.

Protective strategies

The design of new hospitals, with or without psychiatric wards, ought to accommodate acutely ill patients who offer medical, surgical, and psychiatric illnesses or a combination of all three. Few hospitals have designated a team-approach, intensive-care unit of this kind. The personnel would be especially trained intensive-care nursing staff with particular interest and appreciation for psychiatry, presided over by a physician, perhaps with his boards in medicine or surgery and with extra qualifications in psychiatry, or, alternatively, a psychiatrist with good background in clinical medicine.

This section would be a locked ward with screened windows. The patients would remain under constant observation and, for safety, would be separated from each other by walls rather than curtains. As with any intensive-care unit, admissions would be made in acute need and would last until the crisis was concluded, after which the patient would be either transferred to a medical, surgical, or psychiatric unit.

Each clinical floor or hospital section in a general hospital ought to have at least one security room that is relatively suicide-proof. Screened unbreakable windows, shielded electrical outlets, locked doors with observation ports, covered pipes and ventilation grilles, light plastic hangers and open closets would be unremarkable to the patients but would be of inestimable value if the need arose to manage a violent patient.

Windows must be secured so they can't be opened widely enough for patients to squeeze through, stairwells should be protected so that patients can't jump from towers, roofs, or observation points. Ventilating ducts and elevator shafts ought to be made impossible for patient access.

Horizontal rods and structures over which a patient can throw a noose of some kind in an attempt to hang himself ought to be made of material that can't suspend the weight of a person or will break away from supporting walls. For example, clothes hooks may be attached to walls with glue rather than screws.

Restricted items to be kept from suicidal patients include drinking glasses or other glass items, vases, nail files, nail clippers, nail polish, nail polish remover, perfume, picture frames, spray containers, mirrors, hooks (both crochet and knitting), electrical equipment except battery-powered radios, cigarette lighters, matches, scissors, needles, knives, guns, tweezers, electric razors, razor blades, alcoholic beverages, gargles and mouth washes containing alcohol, pins, pop cans, hangers, and plastic bags.

The greater the hazard, the less time the patient should be left alone unobserved and the more safeguards are required for his protection. In any consideration of their level of dangerousness, patients may be controlled by any of the means that are described here.

Physical restraints

These include leather or canvas wrist and ankle cuffs, Posey belts, twisted sheets, ties holding the hands, feet, shoulders and mid-body to the bed or a camisole. *Such restraints must be used minimally, only when absolutely necessary, and for the shortest time necessary.* A patient bound by any physical restraint should be checked as often as every 10 minutes to be certain he has not injured himself, cut circulation, or become exhausted fighting his bonds.

Physically restraining a patient often may agitate him even more. Each limb that has been secured should be released periodically, inspected for injury, massaged, and exercised passively before reapplying the restraint. In every instance, the order for restraints must be specifically written by the attending physician, and the time for discontinuing them should be made an essential part of the signed orders. Security persons at bedside may be hospital employees or sitters conscripted from the family or friends or off-duty nurses willing to help.

Psychopharmacological restraints

Physicians who wish to use psychotropic drugs in their practice ought to spend time learning how to use a select few medications competently. Drug therapy for psychiatric emergencies has inestimable lifesaving potential, but such drugs have serious limitations, exceptions, and short- and long-term side effects that make their prescription hazardous. Overutilization and misuse of drugs is a significant cause of confusional toxic reactions as well as exaggeration of depressive syndromes out of which iatrogenic cause for violent acting out can emerge. A good example is benztropine (Cogentin), a frequently employed antiparkinson drug. Even in small doses, benztropine can cause severe mental confusion, agitation, restlessness, and visual hallucinations—in short, toxic psychosis. Benztropine may also exaggerate existing psychiatric pathology.

Generally, the more people there are confronting an agitated, combative patient, the less chance is there that the patient or any of the team effecting control will be hurt and the shorter the time of danger in the period of confrontation. Similarly, the use of an adequate priming dose of any drug employed for the control of the violent patient intent on homicide or suicide is usually prudent procedure. If the physician and one nurse are attempting to subdue a muscular adolescent intent on smashing a window with a chair intending to jump out, their tactics are likely to be different from what they'd do in disarming an elderly amputee in a wheelchair sawing at his wrists with a plastic knife.

There are some general principles to keep in mind when using drugs. The use of so-called slow-release capsules is illogical and has no place in emergency treatment. Liquid doses taken orally are not particularly effective and attain their effect slowly because of poor absorption from the gastrointestinal tract. The old state-hospital procedure of inserting a stomach tube, then delivering drugs into the stomach requires that the patient be totally controlled by restraints. This may excite terror and aversion and cause nausea and vomiting. It seldom has a place in the contemporary treatment of the acute psychiatric emergency patient.

The depressed, apathetic, weeping, akinetic, anergic patient who vaguely threatens suicide, refuses food and water, and is passively resistant constitutes a problem in case management, but does not constitute an acute emergency and should not be treated as though he were.

It's almost never necessary or indicated to use more than one major drug at a time to control symptoms of acute psychiatric illness. Indeed, the cumulative effects of drugs are likely to cause serious side effects such as respiratory and cardiac arrest. An example of such a hazard is the instance when intravenous barbiturates are used to control an agitated patient such as one suffering from head injury or delirium tremens. Periods of unusual thrashing about, despite the barbiturate, are sometimes reinforced with the intramuscular use of psychotropic medications such as chlorpromazine (Thorazine) or haloperidol (Haldol). Often, respiratory arrest and death may ensue.

If major tranquilizers are used in emergency situations, it's inadvisable to use antiextrapyramidal symptom drugs in a routine fashion. They are probably not particularly effective prophylactically and they definitely increase the possibility of long-term side effects.

In treating elderly patients, avoid enteric-coated tablets, use smaller doses more frequently, and avoid anticholinergic drugs.

Elderly people are more susceptible to confusional toxic reactions with the use of benztropine-like drugs.

Before psychotropic drugs are even considered, the agitated patient suffering from medical and surgical illness ought to have his primary disease state treated as effectively as possible with due consideration given to the relief of intolerable symptoms and good nursing care. The patient who is agitated and frightened because he is suffering respiratory distress due to emphysema, bronchial asthma, or advanced pulmonary fibrosis may be approaching panic, and his total attention is focused on his next breath. Before such a patient seeks death for relief, the administration of oxygen or bronchodilators or just sitting at the patient's bedside and holding his hand will benefit this person a great deal more than injections of diazepam (Valium) or chlorpromazine.

Lithium and antidepressant agents are valuable in the treatment of mania and severe primary depressive disorders of the endogenous type. However, since they take from seven days to three weeks before they are effective, they have no place in the treatment of the acutely agitated patient.

Sometimes the best medical judgment regarding drug therapy is not to prescribe a drug but to discontinue one or change its dosage. Circulatory and metabolic complications of heart disease may cause neuropsychiatric pathology such as delirium, which is exacerbated by digitalis toxicity. Hydrocortisone may cause a variety of psychiatric complications, including increasing suicide potential and decreasing cognitive skills such as information processing.

Antihypertensive drugs precipitate and exaggerate depression if a history or tendency to endogenous dysphoria exists. Organic brain syndrome with visual hallucinations may also be precipitated with reserpine-like antihypertensive drugs.

Levodopa's side effects are common, with unexpected and fairly sudden incidence of acute organic brain syndrome, psychosis, or mania.

Isoniazid in the treatment of tuberculosis can cause a paranoid psychosis and catatonic-like symptoms. The disorientation may subtly convert into an organic brain syndrome that may last for weeks after discontinuation of treatment.

Patients with a prior history of psychosis, depression, severe phobias, and dissociative symptoms who are placed on various endocrine preparations such as estrogen and progesterone may suffer from exacerbation of depressive and psychotic symptoms.

Treatment of selected emergency states

Alert, aware, depressed, and deliberate in his insistence that he will die by suicide—such a patient, after his primary medical and surgical conditions are treated, is at high risk for suicide. If he's calm, in good control, and has warned you that he will kill himself at the first opportunity he is not subject to emergency pharmaceutical intervention. Psychiatric consultation and someone at bedside to talk and keep company with the patient is indicated.

Consciousness intact, severe dysphoria, psychomotor agitation, and no evidence of thought disorder—such a patient may already be a menace to himself. If the patient is resistive, consider the benzodiazepine drugs first. Use 5 to 20 mg diazepam intravenously or up to 100 mg chlordiazepoxide (Librium) intramuscularly. It may be necessary to have either sitters by the bedside or restraints or both.

Conscious, confused, dissociated, depressed, agitated, hostile, and fighting—haloperidol 10 to 20 mg IM immediately, then 5 to 10 mg IM every half-hour until the patient is sleepy. Alternatively, use perphenazine (Trilafon) 5 to 10 mg IM. You may repeat once or twice in three to four hours. Perphenazine and haloperidol are less likely to produce sedation and hypertensive reactions than are other psychotropic drugs.

Chlorpromazine causes fairly severe hypotensive effects and the injections are painful and frequently cause sterile abscesses at the injection site, particularly when it seeps into fat, as when given by intramuscular route. Some psychopharmacologists say that chlorpromazine once had an honored place in psychopharmacology, but now it is a relic and should be considered a museum piece.

Confused, agitated, belligerent, diaphoretic, alcoholic probably either on the verge or in delirium tremens—this patient constitutes a suicidal risk of considerable severity. Patients have suffered injury, even death, in the agitated state, either intentionally or accidentally, while trying to fight off or avoid hallucinated terrors. High doses of diazepam, 5 to 10 mg IV, or 50 to 100 mg chlordiazepoxide are effective and should be given to maintain sedation as necessary. Haloperidol and perphenazine are not contraindicated and may be useful in specific instances.

Rapid-acting barbiturates, such as amobarbital sodium (Amytal) still have a place in the treatment of alcoholic, agitated patients, particularly those who cannot tolerate neuroleptic drugs. The patient is given the intravenous injection of a 5% solution of amobarbital and will, over a period of three to five minutes, fall asleep. At that time, the intravenous medication is set in 500 to 1000 cc of distilled water so that 1000 mg of amobarbital is given by slow drip over a period of three to four hours, maintaining sedation. Simultaneously some practitioners may give such supplemental vitamin therapy as 1000 mg thiamine hydrochloride and B complex, perhaps in the form of 10 cc Betalin Complex or Solu-B, Sterile, added to the sterile solution.

Agitated, senile, combative—chlordiazepoxide 25 to 50 mg IM every three to five hours or diazepam 5 to 10 mg IM every three to five hours. The benzodiazepine drugs are preferred because they do not manifest an anticholinergic effect that may cause cardiac arrhythmia and exaggerate confusion in elderly patients. Although diazepam is not absorbed very well intramuscularly, it's probably preferable to give it that route because a possibly unexpected and exaggerated inhibitory effect on the respiratory center or on cardiac action can occur if given IV in adequate doses to control agitation.

A secondary choice may be the administration of haloperidol, 5 to 10 mg IM for two or three doses every one-half to one hour. The patient should be carefully watched for hypersedation or the development of extrapyramidal symptoms, which then would be treated with 50 mg diphenhydramine HCl IM every six hours. In more severe cases, it may be necessary to use 2 mg benztropine IM every three to six hours.

Here the anticholinergic effects, manifested by flushed facies, tachycardia, disorientation or confusion, agitation, auditory or visual hallucinations, dysarthria, or elevation of temperature would be treated with physostigmine (Antilirium), 1 to 4 mg IV every one to two hours or intravenous benzodiazepines such as 5 to 10 mg diazepam.

Conscious, severely depressed, threatening suicide, complaining of severe pain—patients who have low tolerance for pain require more frequent anodynes. Individual differences vary widely. An assumption that the patient ought to accept pain more philosophically may be prejudicial and abusive. Patients who are suffering from irreversible disease states may have pain medication withheld from them on the ridiculous rationalization that the opiates may be addictive.

It's honorable and consistent with the traditions of good medical practice for the physician who cannot cure his patient at least to give him surcease from pain. This should be done unhesitatingly, with whatever dosage, and as often as required. Sometimes placing the patient on an ad lib dosage of an analgesic, opiate drug may reduce the overall amount of drugs the patient will take.

Psychological measures

The projection of optimistic and hopeful attitudes is basic for whoever deals with the ill patient. By encouraging the patient to set his own limits by promise or by less formal understanding regarding suicidal behavior, the patient is made to appreciate that he has worth, is cared for, has his feelings respected and his anxiety shared.

Anything that can be done to help orient the confused patient will reduce anxiety and fear. A calendar on the wall, simple conversation, bringing the sound of a human voice to the patient are sometimes effective remedies for loneliness and mitigate the depersonalization of the hospital environment. TV and radio are minimally helpful, since so much of what is transmitted has no relationship to his interest and needs. Some programs, in fact, may further confound and depress him with inane irrelevancies and aural stimuli that may do more harm than good.

Music that is well-recognized and loved by the patient has particular value, but eventually may become tiring and degenerate to become part of background noise if left on interminally.

Visitors are vitally important, should be encouraged to come, but should be screened. Some visitors may be confronted by the patient in a hostile or rancorous manner. They may actually precipitate agitated behavior. One mother became annoyed when her drug-habituated son threatened suicide. She dared him to jump from the roof. Shortly after her visit, he did.

Administrative considerations

The governing bodies in the hospital hierarchy are usually the board of trustees selected from the community and the executive committee, which represents the medical staff. A chief administrative officer is employed. He has powers and presence linking the trustees and the physicians. The problem of the violent patient surfaces from time to time and the chief of staff, the administrative officer, and the trustees have to deal with it.

Incidents can be embarrassing, as when a suicidal patient has been turned away by the emergency-room staff because the primary finding was overt psychosis and the patient had insufficient medical or surgical injury to warrant hospitalization. Later the patient was picked up by the police for bizarre behavior. The family complained and the media told the story: "Sick man refused by hospital, put in jail. Lawsuit considered by family."

There are tragic incidents, too, as when a staff physician is found dead on a litter in an anteroom with a 20-cc hypodermic syringe, a tourniquet on the floor, and a bottle of potassium chloride nearby. Incidents can be costly, as when angry family survivors of a suicide sue the hospital, the attending physician, and everyone in sight for failure to have more effectively protected a patient who hanged himself from a washroom fixture with his belt. At meetings of the executive committee with the administrator, the question is eventually raised: "Was there any way we could have prevented this suicide?"

A determined person absolutely intent on killing himself eventually will succeed, despite the best efforts of the hospital staff. However, there are strategies that can be devised by administrative, medical, and nursing staffs working together to reduce the danger of suicide to an irreducible minimun.

There should be a standing committee on violence and unexplained death. The membership should include psychiatrists, psychologists, social workers, nurses, and representatives from the executive committee, administration, the emergency room, intensive-care units, nursing supervision, the hospital record department, and the hospital attorney.

The charge of this committee should be to meet regularly to discuss incident reports regarding violence or threats of violence as they affect or surface from among the patient complement or the staff. The agenda would include any event resulting in injury caused by any person to himself or another; suicide proofing areas of the hospital; updating relevant regulations and advisements; consideration, analysis, and eventually notification of the staff of new statutes and laws that may affect the status of patients; curtailing or making more flexible the tactics of the staff in dealing with suicidal or homicidal patients; to explicitly advise the manner in which records, data, and statistics about acts of violence are to be kept; to seek the best counsel available, by inviting knowledgeable experts to attend meetings; to advise and approve courses of instruction for the staff regarding the subject of recognition and treatment of violent patients; to review and advise the staff regarding the management of the dying patient, euthanasia, and termination of life-support systems.

The bylaws of the hospital, as a minimum, should contain provisions requiring physicians who admit patients or who authorize transfer between services to alert personnel to the risk of violence; to require psychiatric consultation and social service investigation in every instance in which suicide propensity is suspected or known; to require minimum standards in documentation of all instances in which illness or injury is related to suicide; to refer sensitive cases for investigation and review either to an ad hoc committee on suicide or to a standing committee on violence and unexplained death.

Further assignments for this committee might be to establish better criteria for documentation of self-inflicted injuries and illnesses; to distribute questionnaires and to arrange for interviews of members of the medical and nursing staff in order to establish confidential opinions regarding their own, their colleagues', and patients' propensity to homicide and suicide; to establish a protocol for the investigation and ultimate reporting to the executive committee of violent acts, either homicidal or suicidal (psychological autopsy); and to consider demands for euthanasia or the insistence of the family or the patient that the provisions of a living will should be honored.

Certain hospitals may take a leadership role in the community in organizing teaching at the medical association level for the entire staff in the hospital and reaching out into the community. A speaker's bureau may be registered and advertised, offering informative and authoritative approaches to suicide prevention. Speakers who deal with the community in public forum may speak at parent-teacher meetings within the schools and before groups such as the Elks, Lions, Shriners, and Rotary clubs. Hospital staff members who have prepared papers and audiovisual aids and tapes may create a library from which the community may borrow.

The administration is responsible for hospital security. The uniformed force of men and women who keep peace and order within the hospital, direct traffic, and generally keep things running smoothly in the interface between the hospital and the outside community should be a responsible, intelligent, well-educated corps. The members should be specially trained to help in critical situations in which patients may become threatening to others or place themselves in jeopardy.

Techniques of subduing a belligerent, confused, frightened patient who constitutes a danger to the hospital community as well as to himself are to be taught in such a way as to minimize the possibility of injury to the patient or to the staff. A set of signals and rehearsed protocol for rushing with measured haste when trouble arises will require cooperation from the medical, nursing, administrative, and communications staff as well as security staff members.

The highly sensitive concern for legal liability within the hospital is more fully discussed in Chapter 16. Courts appreciate that hospitals must have freedom to achieve therapeutic goals and cannot maintain constant supervision and totally curtail freedom. Such a restrictive environment is incompatible with a therapeutic program. In general, the principle presently exists that a degree of freedom is allowed to a patient, decided by the patient's physician.

The law demands reasonable care in foreseeable situations. Administration, working closely with nursing staff and physicians, should continue to refine policies and procedures to maximize the therapeutic benefit to all patients with the minimum curtailment of human rights.

CHAPTER 13

Physicians at risk for suicide

The management of the suicidal physician is explored here not because it's a pet subject—a physician writing about a physician's affliction—but because learning how to manage physician suicide contains lessons that can effectively be applied to almost every other population at high risk, including alcoholics and drug addicts, the elderly sick, menopausal women, the psychotic, the depressed, and prior attempters. With a little stretching, observations and strategies for management appropriately made about the physician at risk may apply to adolescents in turmoil as well.

Medical school applicants

Understanding suicide by physicians begins with appreciation that something is wrong with the manner in which the medical profession treats its own. The fault begins with unsatisfactory criteria in choosing candidates for admission to medical school. The ineptitudes escalate during the time of intensive education of the medical student and resident. Finally, the profession fails completely to help the mature physician in the course of his or her medical career.

"I haven't heard classical music in six months"; "My friends don't believe it when I tell them I was on duty for twenty-four straight hours"; "It's becoming a habit to counter fatigue by dipping into my stock of amphetamines"; "The idealism I took into medical school is being ground to bits by the crass materialism infesting medicine"; "They make us memorize weird and improbable biochemical reactions that not only have no relation to clinical practice but will be declared incorrect and invalid before the year is out"; "The professors lack compassion, not only for the students but for the patients as well"; "Why do you look at me as if I were some sort of a freak? I'm a woman and I want to be a doctor. What's wrong with that?"

Applicants to medical schools are chosen from top academic achievers. Insufficient attention is paid to obtaining applicants' psychological profiles, and what the role stresses will be for the medical student are not revealed to candidates.

Some would-be physicians are drawn to the profession because they have had bouts with physical and mental illness and want to beat their opponent on his own ground. It's not a correct inference that persons who have suffered illness ought to be ruled out of consideration for medicine, but the establishment does not identify or adequately protect the high-quality human talent shoveled into the maws of the medical school monster, especially those at unusual risk.

The following would help reduce the incidence of psychiatric casualties:

- improved liaison with colleges from which the students graduate;
- universal criteria for health reporting;
- more accessible mental-health services at colleges;
- specific attention to identify suicide-prone college students;
- development of new instruments for psychological testing of stress tolerance and adequate psychiatric review of protracted stress for medical school applicants; and
- less poetry and more realistic briefing regarding the consequences of acceptance to graduate education in medicine.

Students and residents

Perhaps it's a perseveration of some primitive tribal ritual that justifies the medical profession in stubbornly insisting that candidates for full membership must pass an initiation replete with suffering, pain, and deprivation. It's not long after classes and laboratories begin in the first year that the demands of the profession are encountered. The imposing intellectual achievements of their past careers as students have accustomed them to working and delivering successfully in a high-expectation setting. However, the medical student finds out quickly that the sheer volume of what he is expected to learn and the time-bind that forever puts him behind the scheduled curriculum place him in a potential fail situation for perhaps the first time in his life.

His quickness in understanding, ability in memory, intuition at judging what professors really want and therefore what and how to study, and his willingness to beat all competition by investing "however long it takes" into the task are not sufficient. The spectre of incompetence becomes haunting, and the idea grows malignantly that no matter how hard he tries, he may never really please his surrogate parents, the teaching staff. Even more difficult to bear is the sad appreciation that, despite lofty ideals and commitment to become a splendid doctor, there is not now, and never will be, a way to learn it all, to truly master medicine.

As the educational experience continues, the fantasy changes. Early on, it was fleet-footed Mercury leading the host, caduceus thrust forward in a gesture of victory. Then it changes to the grimy prisoner, chained to the treadmill set to go faster and faster, exhorted to give more effort by heartless jailers in white coats, clipboard in hand.

Gone for most are opportunities for play, socializing, hobbies, and the gentle arts. Three-times-a-week tennis, membership at the skating or swimming club, and romantic alliances are either canceled or drastically curtailed. Married and live-in student couples with one or both in medical school or residents suffer lonely separations and physical and mental exhaustion. They continually readjust and compromise their values and judgments as to what is more important, learning or loving.

Personality characteristics the medical establishment looks for in its medical school applicants are self-reliance, autonomy, devotion to self-mastery, and obsessive-compulsive ritualistic approaches to work. These traits make the student particularly vulnerable to the consequences of unending role strain. Experiencing lower than expected gratification, students experience frustration in their personal lives, and these would-be doctors are likely to fall into depression and suicidal rumination.

The health care of the medical student and resident can be improved. A reasonable program would include psychological surveys, frequent mental self-assessment testing, routine psychiatric interviews with every medical student and resident at least once each year, devising and publicizing protocols for requesting help, encouraging student leaders to identify and aid class members showing signs of despondency, and educating the teaching staff to become alert and responsible to the emotional needs and stresses of the students.

Some medical schools have introduced courses in self-awareness and in coping with personal stress and have established formal programs in which upperclassmen are assigned as student advisers to students who need a mentor and a friend.

It will require basic changes in the curriculum of the medical school and a revolution in the way the medical profession treats its students and its entire membership before the unnecessarily high social and medical casualty rates among doctors are significantly reduced.

Medical knowledge increases exponentially, and improvements in teaching techniques increase arithmetically, but available time to learn has not increased at all. Curriculum designers concede that they cannot expose the learner to all the concepts in medicine he theoretically should see, let alone expect him to absorb and integrate what is put before him.

Instead of insisting that the medical student demonstrate his powers of memorizing huge deposits of data he'll never use in practice, the accent might be placed on the development of the compassionate healer, effective because of the suitability of his knowledge base, congruent to clinical need, but enriched by the unabashed development of sensitivity and humanistic virtue.

Aside from research, practical bedside experiences seem best adapted to teach clinical medicine. Less trial-by-fire and more benign supervision may not only produce good physicians but dissolve the myth that becoming a doctor requires the surrender of idealism and the adoption of a bizarre life-style essentially inimical to sound mental and physical health and, for some, incompatible with survival.

It's not impossible for the profession of medicine to change, and when it does, it will have to begin at the top. The inspiration will come from the well-established physicians who, at the height of their careers, kill themselves, from chairmen of departments in medical schools who burn out in fatigue and leave vacancies no one wants to take to doctors whose use of time is so totally identified with their daily professional endeavors they completely lose their identities as parents, citizens, or spouses.

The profession must be candid with its applicants so that they may know much more than they do about the attributes and demands of a medical career. Conflict is especially keen in medicine. Helping students obtain gratification in work and encouraging and expecting them to attain satisfaction in their personal lives will make better students with fewer wasted and lost to psychosomatic illness and suicide. Medical students cannot be promised a rose garden, but neither should their education be an extermination camp.

Suicide and the career physician

Probably most physicians who die by suicide are prospectively and retrospectively identified by their colleagues as being at risk. The protracted stress under which physicians live and work is chronically self-imposed and unremitting. A summating melange of pressures from professional and societal sources causes psychosomatic impairment. The physical toll includes exhaustion, headaches, variable appetite and sleep problems, gastrointestinal symptoms, shortness of breath, and palpitations. The mental consequences are low frustration tolerance, labile mood, inappropriate emotional attachments, hypersensitivity to criticism, hostile reaction sometimes tinged with paranoid thinking, ineffectiveness in completing work, loss of empathy for patients, and excessive demand for time.

The impaired physician is unlikely to seek help for his mental aberrations, trying to cope with feelings of slippage by denial, other-blaming, falling into drug and alcohol abuse, and even more overwork.

The last car on the parking lot, the uneaten lunch tray, the tape received late at night at the typing pool may belong to the doctor who needs to feel needed but may be retreating into overwork as a refuge from overwhelming conflicts in his professional and personal life. Drug abuse, alcoholism, despondency, sexual intimacy with patients, and suicidal thinking and acting are common reactions to the stress syndrome.

Physicians specializing in such areas as oncology and hemodialysis who have a powerful need to help people may be frustrated by the low success rate built into their specialties. Others who need to establish dominance, evoke respect or even awe are nonplused by the demands of patients, the requirements of governmental regulations, the independent attitude of nursing staffs, and the impossibility of pursuing research, writing papers, teaching, conducting a practice, and being a visible and participating spouse and parent.

Drug and alcohol use by physicians is difficult to detect until its effects have severely debilitated the physician. Doctors do not generally overdose, do not associate with other chronic users, have poor insight into the nature of their problems, and seldom voluntarily seek help.

Women physicians, at higher risk for self-destruction than male doctors, suffer affective disorders that lead to loss of appetite and weight. They also encounter sleep difficulties, including hypersomnia, insomnia, loss of energy, agitation or retardation, loss of interest in usual activities, decrease in sexual drive, feelings of self-reproach and guilt, inability to think and concentrate, and recurrent thoughts of death and suicide.

The identification of the impaired physician on his way to suicide is done with a sidelong glance. Colleagues are reluctant to confront one of their fellows about to self-destruct—possibly to avoid a reaction of resentment, possibly because it's consistent with the tradition of social relationships in medicine, which can be epitomized in Cain's words: "Am I my brother's keeper?"

Although physicians believe they know each other, close friendships are not usual, even in partnerships and clinical group associations. Doctors know more about the drugs their colleagues prescribe, the tests they order, how to read their handwriting, and their golf handicaps than they know their hurts, fears, disappointments, bewilderments, and personal and family dilemmas. It would not come as a great surprise to most staff members in a large municipal hospital if one of their colleagues were arrested for widespread sale of illicit drugs or, on the other hand, was awarded recognition for a major breakthrough discovery in his specialty. They might say at lunch, "I just knew Charlie was up to something. He's always been so secretive" or "Quiet fella, that Charlie, but you can tell that he has good stuff going for him."

When a colleague suffers a great loss, is ill, divorced, or loses a spouse or child, it's not enough for the executive committee to vote to send him a book and a card with a brief pep-up sentiment. When the quality of the doctor's professional work is compromised, if he displays self-doubt, neglect of his appearance, change in behavior, if he seems indecisive, uncharacteristically irritable or despondent, someone ought to take notice and intervene constructively.

Intrusion into a doctor's private misery is qualified by the same concern and humanistic compassion as describes the lifeguard who saves the drowning swimmer, or the fireman at the top of the extended ladder ready to carry the smoke-poisoned victim to safety. It's not an imposition on an isolated, frightened colleague to offer understanding, acceptance, and encouragement, nor is it overprotective nor patronizing to tell him or her that you are worried about him and why. Exactly as any presuicidal patient must be confronted and engaged, the mirror of truth should be held before the colleague at risk: "This is how you look to us. Please let us help you."

Self-rescue ought to be taught first. Depressed physicians must see themselves and acknowledge their need for help. They ought to be educated to override their phobic distrust of fellow physicians, particularly psychiatrists. Next, they ought to reduce protracted stress by a variety of tactics: taking on a new colleague, reducing office hours, learning to say No to extra assignments, and spending more leisure hours in rest and recreation.

Admitting that they are not adequately coping with emotional demands in their lives and that they have been fighting suicidal thoughts, a clear and simple "Get professional help" must be impressed on them. It has been well-demonstrated that a high percentage of mentally-disturbed physicians, even those who are psychotic, can be successfully treated in an out-patient setting. Once a good therapeutic relationship is established, the physician has a somewhat better prognosis in the result of his treatment for depression, psychosis, drug- and alcohol-related disabilities, and neurotic disorders than persons in his or her own age group in the general population.

There are deterrents to the establishment of effective treatment for the mentally ill physician. Having to be all things to all persons, it's exceedingly difficult for the doctor who is ill to accept the role of dependent patient. The medical degree gets in the way of the treatment plan. The effect is that the doctor who needs treatment neither seeks it nor receives it and experiences hands-off neglect. Colleagues of the disturbed physician are avoidant and isolate him, avert their eyes, and just hope he will go away. Sometimes he gets the message and does leave—by suicide.

The physician who treats a doctor for mental distress must remember that his friend, colleague, or referral is now a *patient*. His medical degree is irrelevant to that status. When the history and physical review are completed and the suicidal risk is assessed, the examining doctor should candidly share conclusions and outline treatment with the patient. It's an exquisite exercise in diplomacy to maintain the pose of physician when treating the doctor-patient. This is evolved out of the independent wisdom and objectivity of the examiner, without his being supercilious or overbearing on one hand or obsequiously apologetic and deferential to the patient on the other.

The lies, distortions, denials, excuses, and rationalizations put forth by the patient need to be robustly challenged, not so much regarding their content, but because of what self-deception means in the context of the present illness and the probable consequence that persistence in error may block healthy resolution.

"Doctor, in reviewing your work in the clinic last month, you lost more than half the days you were supposed to be on duty. You stood up many patients and those you did see you turned over to the resident before you completed your examination. Now you recall nausea, vomiting, gripping abdominal pain, and mucous diarrhea. You also were drinking a hell of a lot.

"The problem you must settle is not whether the director of the clinic has a prejudice against you and, therefore, reduced your schedule; it's why you need to find someone to blame other than yourself and your illness for submarginal professional performance far below what you and your colleagues know you can do when you are not drunk."

The patient is informed that his behavior and his performance are under scrutiny, but that the medical establishment wants to help him survive and get back to an effective personal and professional life. Lightly he may be reminded when he waves his M.D. degree, expecting privileges, "Look, being a physician does not confer immunity from foolish, self-defeating behavior. It only increases the range of variety of the kinds of mistakes one can make."

The physician treated for depression must agree that he will not prescribe drugs for himself, change, quit, or modify the kind and dosage prescribed. If the doctor is musing about suicide, he ought to be reminded that impulse is a dreadful enemy and to protect himself he should surrender lethal devices. Other persons, a spouse, children, and friends may be solicited, with the permission and prior agreement of the physician, to give their support, comfort, and physical presence.

Since the psychiatric illness of doctors, as with patients generally, may relate to childhood experiences and formative learning, referral to out-patient medical or psychological psychotherapy is logically indicated. Noncompliance of the doctor-patient and unavailability of psychiatric or psychological talent may preclude the full and adequate treatment the patient requires.

If hospitalized, the doctor as a patient may disdain to go through the usual routines required of other patients. "I have no respect for anyone who isn't wiser and more knowledgeable than myself," reflects an inhibiting attitude. In dealing with it, whether the patient is physically or mentally ill, he needs the assurance that his compliance is not a demotion and that he is entitled to all considerations and services any other patient receives.

If other patients are not allowed to smoke in their rooms, neither is he. Refusing him exceptional privileges is not demeaning, but indicates he has an equal right, as any other patient does, to expect his physician and the nursing staff to safeguard and limit the degree of self-poisoning and pollution his smoking will cause.

A high-visibility staff person named as ombudsman who will accept direct appeals from the impaired doctor or anxious inquiries from associates or even family members is a good step. Annual mental health testing and a self-assessment questionnaire help, too. The impaired physicians' programs now operating in most states help to rehabilitate the ailing physicians and

aid in restoring them to good health and professional effectiveness. However, the essential strategy for successful intervention
still must come from an educated fellowship among physicians
who willingly will be their brothers' and their sisters' keepers
and are willing to confront and engage the suicidal doctor in
their midst with affection and professionalism.

Therapy with the physician suicide

Signals, even weak ones, are set up by persons at risk for self-
destruction which the observer may pick up or miss entirely. At
one of the first staff dinners I attended, I sat next to an eminent
physician. The older man relished talking and drank freely as
the excellent wine was poured into his cup for several refills. He
became reminiscent and nostalgically described the woods and
streams where he had hunted and fished as a boy. He mentioned
a lodge he had built in the woods, and regretted that he hadn't
been back to it for over a year. He sighed, shaking his head
sorrowfully, disappointed that those days were over. The trees
had been cut down to make room for high-rise apartments and
the fish were gone, poisoned by pollution.

As he spoke he looked at his hands. His voice became hoarse,
and he seemed almost maudlin. I had an uneasy feeling that
something was wrong. He didn't seem to have had that much to
drink. My dinner companion was clearly depressed. Within the
week, at the peak of his career and creativity, he killed himself
with a shotgun in that same lodge that he had mentioned in our
conversation. Later, I learned that his first wife had committed
suicide some years before in the lodge with the same gun he
used. The day of his death was the anniversary of her suicide.

Had my dinner companion consciously exposed his deep
dysphoria to me, hoping that I might pick up his slight clues
and rescue him? Or was he just doing his bit to make a young,
newly arrived member of the hospital staff feel comfortable?

Because the suicidal physician is likely to reject formal psychiatric consultation, his treatment frequently becomes the responsibility of his nonpsychiatric colleagues. Out of
squeamishness, misplaced identification, impatient or even
hostile repudiation, or avoidance of what may be a monumen-
tally complex task for which the physician does not feel confident, the patient may not receive the care he requires.

Just as hazardous is the tendency of friends, partners, family, and colleagues to enter into a conspiracy with the patient to block psychiatric care. Mistakenly they assume that, since the patient is a physician, he must know himself better than anyone else could and has the insight to cure himself. They may share in defenses against the admission of his illness or even actively and militantly set up barriers to his obtaining psychiatric treatment.

Therapy, such as it is, may then mainly consist of reinforcing the rationalizations and denials of the patient as if acceptance of the myth—"You're really not sick," "You can tough it out," "You don't need a shrink to tell you how to enjoy life and get back to work"—will contradict the fact.

Physicians and their families are a deprived minority. They receive relatively poor care for physical and mental ailments exactly because of the prevailing fallacy that physicians have the wisdom and the will to recognize and treat illness in themselves and their families. Confrontation with the grim fact that the patient is about to kill himself, is thinking of doing so, or has already made an attempt on his life is not only a necessary minimal concession for the physician at risk but for intimates who may help or hinder his chances for survival. The therapeutic process may be planned to involve not only the primary patient, but his family and colleagues as well.

It's neither invariably nor absolutely true that effective management of the suicidal patient can be done only by a trained psychotherapist. Essential qualities for the rescuer/therapist are compassion, special concern and affection, objective empathy, and uncompromising commitment of sufficient patience and time. The therapist must be identified and formally accepted as such by all parties, including himself. However treatment is managed, insisting on a schedule of regular visits is not the patient's responsibility but the therapist's. Not "Call me up when you feel rotten and need a shoulder to cry on," but "Until we both agree that you're out of danger, you and I will have regular sessions at my office, every Tuesday and Friday at 5:00 o'clock."

It's the therapist's responsibility to set limits, such as "No driving or long trips alone; no prescribing medicines for yourself; no drinking at all; no sky diving, rock climbing, or scuba diving; no handling of guns for any reason."

The therapist should respect the patient-physician's basic freedoms and not oppose a peculiar life-style, unless the indulgence threatens the patient. All transactions with the patient must be honorable and frank. There must not be collusive and whispering exchanges between the therapist and others.

When members of the family offer information, "Don't tell I called, but he is into the pills again," or demand to know what's going on, the caller must be reminded that the essential necessity for successful treatment is the maintenance of the therapeutic relationship. This depends upon the trust of the patient, which would be compromised if the therapist conducted secret alliances with persons in the patient's orbit or otherwise violated confidences.

Genuine concern can be kindly acknowledged. "As soon as I know how you can help, I certainly will advise you. Tell Joe you did call me and that you intend to inform me of any behavior on his part that worries you."

The therapist will help the potentially suicidal doctor to see his position as it really is and not as he fears it to be. Loss of hope is offset by the suggestion of positive and creative alternatives and the expectation of successful resolution that the therapist holds forth in what he says and conveys by his manner.

Despair emerging from the feeling of loss requires an accurate audit of strengths, virtues, and resources to the patient, which the patient has ignored or forgotten. The patient who may have a distorted sense of time must learn to use time properly so it can function as a healing resource. For example, since his divorce the depressed physician has slid downhill physically and emotionally and now thinks only of death. But time, now and in the future, can be invested in building up hope and new security, in learning how to cope with loneliness and how to find new friendships and perhaps new love.

Restoring what has been lost, or finding substitutes, may require the involvement of the therapist with the world outside the exclusive, tight therapeutic bond. If the physician has been required by the bylaws of his hospital to give up his department chairmanship because he has turned 65, alternative work can be suggested. The therapist may seek concrete assurances by asking the executive council of the patient's hospital whether, even if Joe must step down, he can be assured that he still has a secure place working with his colleagues in the hospital milieu.

If a parent, spouse, or child has died, members of the patient's family may be brought to therapy sessions, with his agreement, to assure the suicidal doctor that he's not alone in his grief and that he has others with whom to share his bereavement.

There are always new activities and new people in the community of medicine for a physician to substitute for what or whom he has lost. But the therapist must realize that merely pointing his patient in a new direction or furnishing lists may not be enough. The sick doctor's energy level and motivation are low because of his depression. It may take a few telephone calls to the executive secretary of the local medical society, a consultation with the chief of staff at the hospital, or a suggestion to the minister and to colleagues that "Joe needs companionship. Spend some time with him."

It may happen that the patient belongs to social groups, clubs, or hobby or alumni associations whose members would be delighted and relieved to know they can actively contribute to the restoration of good health to an unfortunate friend.

The clear view offered by a therapist includes truthful probabilities: Suicide will be devastating to the survivors; may ruin the spouse's chance of continuing at an accustomed standard of living; will cause psychological harm to children and greatly increase the chances that survivors someday may themselves suicide; the doctor's death will constitute unethical abandonment of his patients who correctly will interpret his suicide as selfish; suicide constitutes a waste of talent, education, and training, not to mention a total loss of an enormous amount of money that had been invested in the medical career.

The positive aspects of survival also must be presented: the reconstituting of hope; the many patients yet to be treated; students taught; research continued; papers published; friendships to be enjoyed; new pursuits, hobbies, associations to be joined; and family relationships rehabilitated.

Since protracted stress so often constitutes a major cause of impairment, the doctor may have to be taught not only how to pare down unrealistic expectations for his own productivity and ability to cure, but also how to avoid becoming bankrupt in time and energy. His escalating frustration, trying somehow to keep up with demands for continuing education, teaching, research, conducting his practice, and sharing with his family, has to be turned about.

The therapist may need to give license to the overworked, obsessed physician to reduce his workload and play a little. If work is haven, a rat hole into which he runs to get away from human relationships, the unconscious motivation must be confronted and rationalizations abandoned.

Women physicians need the opportunity to ventilate their special conflicts and doubts. They have to hear someone say they are not queer or unfeminine to follow a career in medicine. Their altruism, sensitivity to the values of others, desire for autonomy, and special nurturant skills will naturally surface, and the therapist must remind women doctors how important it is that they conspicuously offer these traits for the enhancement of the profession.

There is legitimate use of medication in the treatment of the potentially suicidal patient. Major psychotropic drugs to alleviate delusional thinking, agitation, and bellicose behavior are more appropriately used in a hospital setting where their myriad and complex side effects can be quickly identified. The tricyclic antidepressants are valuable, especially useful in the treatment of endogenous depression, less so in the case of reactive, situational, or chronic depression. The use of sedatives and minor tranquilizers such as the benzodiazepine drugs offset anxiety, apprehension, and many somatic symptoms; the authorization of "a little wine before dinner" is hazardous and may create alcoholic dependency.

Physician-patients do not have a good track record for compliance with drug therapy. They abandon and change dosages without discussing the issue with their attending physicians. They may sometimes assume that if drug therapy is prescribed, the medications are the principal means for their recovery. If they feel no better in a relatively short time or suffer undesirable side effects, they assume treatment has failed. Often drugs prescribed for averting suicide are used to accomplish it.

Once past the acute stage, the patient who has seemingly regained his composure and confidence may enter another crisis. With restored energy, the suicidal physician who was melancholy and anergic may now be able to mobilize forces within himself to take his life when the therapist is deceived into believing the danger has passed.

Psychotherapy should continue, and family and milieu therapies introduced. The physician should be encouraged to go back to work as his sense of competence is restored. Medications may have to be continued for several months, well into the period of successful rehabilitation.

There were eight suicides in 13 months among physicians placed on probation by the state medical board in Oregon. The physicians were marked by their peers as having erred in some significant way that warranted their having their licenses suspended. But the stresses were exaggerated, because the doctors did not know for how long a time they would not be allowed to practice. They were not informed of the explicit terms under which they could expiate their offenses and once more be restored to good professional standing. They were left in a state of limbo regarding licensure and, therefore, their right to practice.

The overt disgrace, the formal condemnation by the medical board, and the suspension of the privilege of practicing medicine created a powerful, emotional stress. The added punishment of procrastination and indefiniteness was intolerable for the eight physicians who killed themselves. That two of the eight were under psychiatric care emphasizes that psychiatric out-patient care does not always protect the patient. It further affirms the need for gathering much more information than we presently have to improve our sensitivity regarding suicide risks that affect the physician placed in such a specific stress situation as being put on probation.

Treatment and rehabilitation programs need to be critically studied, and new approaches suggested and taught that offer hope of success in the medical management of the physician at risk for self-destruction.

PART IV

Ethics, the law, and suicide

CHAPTER 14

The right to suicide

The right of any person to end his life at his private discretion has been a debated ethical and religious issue throughout history. Polarization of opinion has occurred with regard to the following questions:

- Does the individual owe his highest allegiance to God, the state, the community, or to himself?
- Is there an inherent, inalienable right of every human being to do with life whatever he wishes, provided he does not substantially interfere with the rights of others?
- Does the sanctity of life take precedence over any other competing value in our society?

Most mental-health-care providers, especially physicians, giving offhand response to a query about suicide might say it's almost never a rational response to stress, almost always to be deplored, and anyone who attempts suicide is probably insane and should be prevented from carrying out his morose project. Sentiment regarding suicide is definitely changing. There is emerging sympathy for the suicidal person and sometimes even tacit acceptance that the act of suicide is sanctioned, appropriate, and consistent with special virtue.

Advocates of the right to suicide propose arguments that range from the wildest meanderings of the psychotic mind to carefully reasoned, heuristically consistent dialectics, such as the following:

Die a martyr. The sacrifice of one's life for another or in a noble cause has always mitigated condemnation of suicide by society. Even when the act of self-destruction was termed an "abomination" by church leaders in the Middle Ages, the martyr was exempted from calumny. The spy who swallows a cyanide capsule rather than run the risk of betraying his comrades, his mission, and his country under torture is considered courageous and praiseworthy if not heroic in his act of suicide.

Die with dignity. The writing of a living will is an act of anticipatory suicide in which a person signs a document long before the fact, which states that no life-support system should be continued after meaningful existence ceases. The document attempts to exempt anyone from liability, civil or criminal, for carrying out the dictates of the testator. When quality of life has been debased by intractable pain, is definitely prolonged with no real hope of surcease, the option to be allowed to die by passive euthanasia is invoked.

Dr. and Mrs. Henry T. Van Dusen, two adult, literate, sensible, by no means psychotic persons faced with long suffering preliminary to painful death, died together in a suicide pact. Dr. Van Dusen was a prominent theological leader, president of Union Theological Seminary. Norman Cousins editorialized about their death. He said, "Death is not the greatest loss in life. The unbearable tragedy is to live without dignity or sensitivity."

A number of organizations have been formed for the purpose of instructing people suffering incurable illness who want to kill themselves to do so efficiently. The British group called "Exit, the Society for the Right to Die with Dignity" planned to publish a detailed booklet, which would be a guide for people who want to know how to kill themselves. General distribution of the pamphlet was canceled under the threat that its authors might be held guilty as accessories to murder, should anyone utilize the instructions. Another group called "Hemlock," based in Los Angeles, has proposed a similar manual.

The patient expecting to die miserably, who contracts with an intimate to help him find the means to terminate life quickly and painlessly or employs someone to actually kill him, is committing suicide by murder even if it is called active euthanasia.

The right to die and to die with dignity is insisted as a human good by individuals who believe that they should have the right to control their own life at least to the extent of ending it when they wish to terminate futile suffering.

Exact vengeance. The ferocious anger and hatred that inspires many suicides accompanies an expectation that, by the act of self-murder, those who have withheld love, privilege, or favor or have otherwise offended the victim will be overwhelmed by grief and guilt. Since suicides are frequently murders turned inward, the act of self-destruction is carried out as if the flesh of the perpetrator, torn by knife or bullet, poisoned, crushed, or burned, is the flesh of the enemy.

In an ultimate extension of narcissism, the vengeful suicide may believe his body incorporates all life, not only on earth but in the entire universe, and that at the instant of his death, doomsday will have come and all life everywhere will cease.

The Biblical example of Samson bringing down the temple on the heads of the Philistines at the willing cost of his own life is a poetic example from antiquity of a vengeance-seeking suicide.

Assume ghostly powers. Most cultures, sophisticated or primitive, have within them extensive mythology and belief systems that assert that suicides may become malignant, angry, restless spirits who can do harm to the living by directly harassing them or through intercession with gods or the devil.

The suicide is inspired to die by the expectation that he will be transformed in death into a spirit invested with somber and sinister powers that he had been denied in life. He embraces death as a means of infinitely increasing his ability to punish and wreak vengeance on his enemies.

Demonstrate immortality. In many people there is an abiding conviction of immortality. Some suicidal persons extend the idea of immortality to a point where the notions of invincibility, omnipotence, and immunity to death are so embellished that the act of suicide is bleached of its terror. "Don't interfere with my suicide, I won't really die. . ." is the fantastical assurance imposed on would-be rescuers.

165

Achieve transcendental unity. Human beings are probably the only species whose members explore their environment and try to reach beyond it for a motive other than to seek food, shelter, sex or to flee peril—namely, out of curiosity. The desire to know one's origins and one's ultimate fate and, if possible, to control life from conception to death and everything in between is uniquely human. But there is also a compelling desire to become omnipotent, omniscient, and to prolong life forever, to be godlike.

This is envisioned as possible by homogenizing the self with a being or beings of infinite power, or to coalesce into an identity that may require the surrender of self-identity in return for which there is given a sense of commonality with the absolutes of the universe. The process of reaching out requires transcendence beyond human limits to become one with such ultimate perfection.

Some accomplish the transcendental link through religious belief, others in meditation, still others by day-to-day attempt at self-betterment. Some seek mystical union by scarifying and denying the flesh, as did those ancient mystics who, seeking purification ran into the desert, and starved and flagellated themselves to rid themselves of evil thoughts and mundane concerns to become worthy of the transformation. Some seek transcendence through drugs, hypnosis, and identification with cult leaders. The prime example in recent times is the Reverend Jim Jones who promised his followers in Guyana that if they totally accepted his teaching they absolutely would become part of something greater than themselves. Still others seek transcendental realization through suicide.

For the seeker of the transcendental state, there is a belief and a promise of perfection in the afterlife never possible in this life; an opportunity to join forever in loving unity with those who may have been lost by death; an opportunity to learn the answers to all questions; to exist forever with no concern for earthly limits, pains, and denials; to float effortlessly in a state of infinitely prolonged ecstasy; to be reborn; to have life everlasting.

Conquer fear of death. Thanatophobia, an abnormal fear of death, may be opposed by counterphobic measures. One is to do that which challenges death, defies the fear, and asserts the denial as a means of conquering it. Not infrequently, persons engaged in the riskiest professions and hobbies are actually involved in a lifelong struggle with thanatophobia. In extreme instances, the persons so afflicted may actually suicide. Refusing to be further intimidated, the phobic person copes by confronting his fear of death head on.

Exercise choice. The dying person or one who feels helpless and has lost control of all aspects of his life may reach for some actual or symbolic sign of effectiveness and residual strength. Weak and immobilized by pain, disease, or despondency as he may be, some small gesture still is possible. Even the tiniest residue of demonstrated power is welcome to the powerless. Suicide may be that choice when all other options seemingly have been canceled.

Produce an artistic triumph. Artists and poets, such as Sylvia Plath, Vincent Van Gogh, Jo Roman, Ernest Hemingway, and Cesare Pavese, were fascinated with suicide. Long before their deaths, they indicated in their communications with others, in their poetry, writings, and artistic projections their preoccupation with death and the conceptualization of a wonderful artistic triumph that supposedly would be served by their suicide.

Exhibit one's self as an extraordinary person. Jo Roman, a conspicuous artist, had collected data and wrote about her anticipated suicide for 10 years before she actually killed herself in a highly publicized event. Her ostensible reason to die was that she had been diagnosed as suffering from cancer of the breast.

Roman assumed that she was terminally ill and allegedly wanted to save her family from the stress of standing by while they watched her go through the rigors of chemotherapy. Actually, her cancer had not spread to the axillary lymph nodes, and her cancer was considered at a stage that has a high incidence of successful response to treatment.

The cancer gave Roman the pretext to foster her projection of self and to call attention to suicide, giving the public through her death an opportunity to view the phenomenon as a valid technique which she called "a human right." Ten years before, Roman began a 250-page manuscript that asserted her intention to die by suicide. She made videotapes of her presentation, wrote her own obituary for *The New York Times*, and held a party for friends on the night of her death. The author seemed to need an excuse to display herself to the world. Her suicide provided consummation of the need to self-exhibit.

The "man on the ledge" demonstrates his pain and distress to all the world by his conspicuous display and seems to simultaneously beg for and defy rescue. He has a compulsive need to be on view, forcing attention to himself to the widest possible audience. In effect, the suicide insists, "You would not take me seriously as I lived, now you have to pay attention to me as I die."

Force others to love. By exercising the option of suicide, the rejected lover attempts to cope with his feelings of desolation. By attacking the agent who withholds love, he threatens to punish with the hammer of inflicted guilt. The display of suffering is expected to accomplish acceptance and restoration of love from whoever has withheld it.

Self-determination. If freedom to live also includes the freedom to die, the ethical question arises whether society ever has the right to prevent a person from taking his own life. Thomas S. Szasz, professor of psychiatry at the Upstate Medical Center, State University of New York, insists that no matter what the mental or psychiatric state of a person may seem to another, his wish to die must not be contradicted and his act of suicide must not be opposed against his will or wish.

Dr. Szasz insists that no one, the state, the medical profession, family, or community has the right to intervene to prevent a person from suicide. In his view, curtailing liberty to the extent necessary to save a life is in every instance a more serious abridgment and compromise of what is good and right in human affairs than the virtue of saving life. He argues that interference with the suicide is paternalistic and constitutes unwarranted interference with personal freedom.

Select suicide or murder. A 14-year-old boy recovering from severe neurological sequelae after an extended episode of glue and naphtha sniffing was asked if he ever considered any other way of dealing with his unhappiness. Slowly the boy responded, "Yes, by killing my father."

Sometimes the suicidal person sees his choice as not between living or dying but among murdering another or himself or both. The adolescent at odds with parental figures who have withheld acceptance; the supplicant agonized with the pain of rejection by a loved person; the husband or wife abused by guilt for angry and vengeful thoughts directed with destructive anticipation against the spouse defined as the source of pain—such persons convert the psychic energy of despair into aggression. First, the hatred is directed against the self and then it rebounds to the other. Then follows the emergence of murderous intent to to punish the self for vengeful thoughts and fantasies unjustly directed against the beloved person, then once again the sense of guilt and remorse fades and rage again focuses on the loved one.

Either murder of self, of the rejecting lover or of both may occur. "Father kills wife and children, calls police, then shoots himself" is not an uncommon headline or an uncommon exercise of the choice to commit suicide or murder or both.

Examination of the arguments

Those who insist on the right to suicide are constrained in our society by logical considerations. It's generally agreed that there are no absolute rights. Philosophically, the rights of the individual, however precious, may be compromised, modified, or curtailed, should they conflict substantially with the rights of others or of the community. The exercise of rights by the individual is expected to be conducted as a matter of rational deliberate choice, with reasonable knowledge and acceptance of the probable consequences.

When the suicidal person insists on imposing his own rules of logic and defines freedom as his absolute right to convert impulse and wish into action, without considering the alternatives or understanding facts and consequences, he will be opposed.

A seven-year-old child who plays with a high-voltage outlet will, if necessary, be forcefully restrained from pushing a bobby pin into the socket. A mentally retarded adolescent who does not know how to drive a car will be stopped from experimenting with the ignition key left in the lock. A delirious patient who tries to pull himself out of his hospital bed will be restrained by drugs or by Posey belts or hand-held in his bed, if necessary.

The child, the mentally retarded person, and the confused patient are forcefully restrained from exercising their assumed right to do whatever they want with their own lives.

The obvious inability of each to know the probable consequences of his action, electrocution for the boy, wrecking the car and experiencing injury to self and others for the mentally retarded person, and worsening of illness for the delirious patient, warrants the suspension of freedom and intervention of representatives of society who will protect the ward from injury and preserve life, even if he is indifferent or uncaring of the probability of serious personal penalty.

Whoever is treating the would-be suicide should confront him with the demand that he justify the premises for his intended act. The self-destructive individual may not understand that suicide is an irreversible way of dealing with problems that frequently have reversible and changeable options. He may not truly comprehend the finality of death nor appreciate that a lethal act will result in an end to life.

Assumptions that the act of self-murder will result in transcendental beatitude, life everlasting, incorporation into absolute union with the infinite love of God or that it will result in the crushing and humbling of enemies and bring the world to ashes or that it is an ultimate act of artistic creation may be contradicted as perversion of true religious faith, self-deception, philosophical misunderstanding, or flat-out delusional thinking.

The subjective impression that the patient may have of his illness and of his prognosis may be quite erroneous. A patient who has interpreted glances passed between nurses, statements between doctors in arcane doctor-language he cannot understand, or the setting-up or discontinuance of certain equipment in his cubical, may assume that he is not being told his prognosis is hopeless and may conclude, since he is doomed to die, that suicide is a logical choice.

The claimed reason for self-destructive planning may by no means actually be the true motivation. "My family will be better off without me." "After all, if my husband prefers his love affair to me, I'll just ease myself out of their way; by dying I can let him free." "I'm such a failure at everything, my death at least will stop the bad influence I have on everyone around me." The self-deception inherent in these rationalizations may be glaringly apparent to the uninvolved, but they are not always obvious to the patient.

The psychotic patient who believes he's the target of a monstrous plot to destroy him may flee torture and death at the hands of his hallucinated tormentors by dying by his own hands. He's not making a rational judgment of his true situation. His death would be unnecessary, unjustified, immoral—a calamitous waste. The fact is that people do suffer short-circuited knowledge of themselves and cannot know the true meaning of their urge to die by suicide. The decision to end life is often done at a time when a person is experiencing maximum intrapersonal chaos. It's committed with minimal preparation and forethought in the midst of turmoil and stress. People make the most momentous decision of their lives—to live or to die—with less input of reliable and accurate information than they would use in buying a kitchen gadget.

When suicide is held forth as a panacea for all ailments of spirit and body and a corrective device for all adverse circumstances and injustices, then it ought to bear the same tests as any other product marketed for consumer use: Does it fulfill its advertised promise? Is it what it is represented to be? Is it worth the cost?

The decision to commit suicide, if it is indeed rational, requires that the same criteria be met for risk/profit ratio as one would put to proffered surgery for the relief of disease or to an investment promising a good return. The consumer of suicide as an alleged beneficial investment is advised to seek at least a second opinion and to expect and demand full disclosure of all the facts, as well as positive and negative consequences, before making a commitment to buy the idea.

The artist who toys with the concept of death and dying may become fascinated and morbidly habituated to the subject. Whereas at first it was an exercise of mild intellectual curiosity, it may insinuate itself in preconscious ways into value judgments and eventually grow into a commitment. Casual interest in snakes may develop into either a scientific expertise in herpetology or the embrace of a fanatical religious cultism that exposes the devoted to rattlesnake bite as an act of devotion and faith.

Similarly, the artist, while claiming and believing himself involved in an ultimate work of creativity through destruction of self, may become entrapped in the vortices of a self-created whirlwind of confused thinking about dying, death, and rebirth, and not truly realize there is no poetry, no music, no esthetics, no love, no creation in death, just a dull thud, a blank canvas, a crumpled sheet, an undistinguished lump of clay.

A physician or other health professional who has discounted the possibility of irrationality in his patient's thinking about suicide either has been seduced into the same delusional system that abuses and enmeshes his patient or has validated what he knows to be a contrived thesis.

In the former case, the physician or other professed rescuer needs consultative help from an uninvolved colleague, and in the latter,· truly convinced, he would be on shaky ethical grounds. The physician should in good conscience at this point retire from the case.

CHAPTER 15

Suicide and the law

American criminal penalties for suicide derive from the common law of England. At one time, English common law punished the crime of suicide by requiring burial of the remains of the deceased at a crossroads with a stake impaling the body, a stone placed over the face, and amputation of the hand that committed the self-murder. The king confiscated the suicide victim's property. The justification for this ignominious burial was ostensibly to prevent the body from rising from the grave at full moon as a ghost or vampire.

Forfeiture of property reflected the king's view of suicide as contrary to his interest in preserving the lives of his subjects. It was not until 1961 that the English Parliament abolished the crime of suicide by statute, realizing that such penalties served more to punish and stigmatize the surviving families of suicides, rather than as a deterrent.

Although the statutes in a few states still describe suicide as a crime, only one, Massachusetts, ever prescribed actual punishment. This law was repealed in 1823. Although punishing sui-

This chapter was written in collaboration with Gregory T. Victoroff, J.D., who also helped prepare the state-by-state breakdown of laws regarding suicide, which appears in Appendix B.

cide is contrary to modern penal and psychological theory, the fact that it is still referred to as a crime in some statutes may indicate the reluctance of legislators to accept the view that suicide attempters should be treated in hospitals, not punished in prisons.

Attempted suicide

The legal definition of attempt is an effort or endeavor to accomplish a crime, amounting to more than mere preparation, which, if not prevented, would bring about the attempter's ultimate design. Most states that do not consider the completed act of suicide criminal do not punish attempters. This bias is generally not written into the state laws, but applied by judicial interpretation of statutes that abolish the crime of suicide.

States that once recognized the crime of suicide considered it a felony and unsuccessful attempts as misdemeanors. Many states have expressly rejected all common law crimes by statutes. Some states have enacted laws that cite punishment for the act of attempted suicide, but such statutes are seldom enforced. Punishment for an attempted crime is calculated by reference to the punishment for the completed offense.

Civilized laws are drafted to punish only those who are blameworthy, or culpable. In criminal law, this culpability is called *mens rea*, meaning evil mind or evil intent. The intent or state of mind of the person who commits an act of injustice should determine if they should be punished. This reasoning is the basis for the defense of insanity.

Society now generally regards the insane as not wholly responsible for their acts, and thus they are not culpable and not the proper subject of criminal penalties. Where it is accepted that the mentally ill lack the capacity to form culpable intent and that, generally, suicide is a manifestation of mental illness, suicide and attempted suicide are considered acts derived from mental illness that should be medically treated rather than deliberate crimes to be punished.

Accidental death of another

If one accidentally kills another during a suicide attempt, in some states he is guilty of criminal homicide. This result occurs most often, but not exclusively, in those jurisdictions where suicide and suicide attempts are felonies. When one attempts suicide in an unusually dangerous and reckless manner and unintentionally kills an innocent bystander, there is generally justification to invoke criminal penalties.

Aiding, advising, and encouraging suicide

In most states, it's a criminal act to knowingly aid, advise, or encourage suicide. Depending on the state court's interpretation of operative statutes, this prohibition may encompass acts ranging from supplying poison to firing the fatal bullet. Whether the suicide or attempt is itself criminal does not affect the criminality of the aider or adviser. As in the case of suicide attempts, several states have proposed diverse reasons for punishing an aider or adviser.

In some states where suicide is a felony, both aider and adviser may be considered accessories to murder, since the act involves the killing of another. Cases have appeared in the courts in which persons who knowingly provide the instrument of death, such as poison or a gun, were found guilty of murder, even though they did not administer the fatal dose or shoot the victim. The consent of the suicide victim is not a defense. A minority view requires the aider or adviser to actually administer the poison supplied to be guilty of murder.

In some states, aiding or advising suicide is a felony. Some expressly label the felony as manslaughter, and stipulate a prison term of seven to 15 years. Others classify aiding and abetting suicide a Class C felony, and will reduce the charge to a Class E felony if the suicide is unsuccessful. A few statutes invoke criminal sanctions specifically for furnishing the weapon or poison.

If the aider or adviser uses force, fraud, deception, or duress to effect the victim's suicide (such as in the Guyana tragedy of 1978), he may be found guilty of criminal homicide. The *mens rea* or evil intent, absent in one who is mentally ill and attempts suicide, is presupposed in one who knowingly aids or advises suicide. For this reason, the law finds adequate justification for the imposition of severe criminal penalties upon one who aids or advises suicide.

The terminally ill patient is regarded in some states as an exception. California has enacted a Natural Death Statute, which allows an adult patient to "make a written directive instructing his physician to withhold or withdraw life-sustaining procedures in the event of a terminal condition." The law provides further that this withholding of life-sustaining procedures "shall not, for any purpose, constitute a suicide."

The suicide pact

A suicide pact is an agreement between two or more persons to mutually commit suicide. Although there are no statutes specifically devoted to suicide pacts, laws against aiding and advising suicide are usually interpreted to prohibit suicide pacts as well. Survivors of suicide pacts are generally considered guilty of murder. There are three categories of suicide-pact survivors. The mental states and intentions of the survivors are considered in arriving at a decision to prosecute.

If a suicide-pact survivor has unintentionally failed to die and it's accepted that the attempt had genuine lethal intent, punishment for murder is improper since it's assumed that the attempter was a potential victim, is mentally ill, and lacks the evil intent necessary to justify punishment. If a participant in a suicide pact reconsiders his suicidal act at the last moment and survives, he may be prosecuted and, ironically, may be punished for his exercise of rational judgment.

In the third category, if a survivor is found to have purposely deceived the deceased co-conspirator, his actions indicate the requisite evil intent and should rightfully be punished. Because it's almost impossible to distinguish a genuine, failed attempt from a failed attempt that is merely pretended, the survivors of suicide pacts are not uniformly exempt from punishment.

Civil law

Suicides can be the occasion for lawsuits against doctors, hospitals, and other health-care providers. Those bringing a lawsuit may contend that the deceased was unjustifiably maligned by an incorrect judgment that he died because of a self-destructive act, and assert that the patient died accidentally, from natural causes, or perhaps that he was murdered.

Civil law settles disputes between citizens. Criminal law involves questions of conflict between government and citizens. Civil law is frequently invoked in cases of suicide, usually in the form of lawsuits for money damages. Entities sued include physicians—especially psychiatrists—either individually or as professional corporations or both, hospitals—public, private, profit-making, or charitable—and even individuals who are alleged to have provoked the suicidal act.

For example, if an automobile accident results in intolerable pain, disability, or mutilation, which then becomes the ostensible reason for suicide, the defendant accused of liability for the accident may also have to defend against the charge he caused the suicide.

Similarly, the surgeon who informed his female patient that she has to undergo breast surgery for cancer may be accused of inducing his patient to commit suicide if she dies by a self-destructive act. Lawsuits against the physician or institution may accuse them of negligence for failing to recognize and protect a potential suicidal person, of failing to alert responsible members of the family to the hazard of suicide, of aiding and abetting suicide by providing the means, and by provoking the patient to a self-destructive act.

Injuries that could be alleged to incline a patient to suicide include violations of confidentiality by the physician or institution with consequent humiliation, psychological anguish, or family or public disgrace; brutal judgmental declarations; or poor result in treatment. Lawsuits for suicide have also been launched on the proposition that the physician failed to cause an uncooperative patient with suicidal drive to enter the hospital by nonvoluntary route, such as by legal commitment. Others have attacked the physician who successfully obtained legal commitment for a mentally ill patient who later killed himself, on the premise that had the doctor not forced the patient into a psychiatric ward, he would not have died of suicide.

Lawsuits against doctors and hospitals often take the form of suits for wrongful death. Statutes promulgated in every state fix liability for "any wrongful act, neglect, or default which causes death." Damages in wrongful-death actions are based on the pain and suffering of the deceased, medical expenses incurred, the loss of prospective earnings over the victim's projected actuarial life, and the trauma and loss to survivors. The monetary amount of wrongful-death judgments tend to be quite substantial. Suits for wrongful-death suicides that arise out of or in the course of employment are pre-empted by Workers' Compensation laws and the Federal Employers Liability Act. These laws supersede wrongful death statutes and are discussed more fully at the end of this chapter.

Negligence—a variable standard

Wrongful-death suits do not usually arise from an intentional act of the person or entity being sued. In most cases, it's the alleged negligence or failure to act by the defendant that triggers wrongful death liability.

Unlike criminal cases in which definite statutes prescribe penalties for affirmative acts, penalties for wrongful deaths are generally imposed for the defendant's negligence or failure to act. In civil trials, negligence is a broad and flexible concept, whose application is determined on a case-by-case basis by judges and juries. Without the fair warning and notice of clearly drawn statutes, variable standards of negligence cause unpredictable results in negligence actions, posing a devastating threat to the practitioner.

When a patient, under the care of a physician, commits or attempts suicide, the physician may become the target of a civil suit for damages. If the patient dies, the suit may be for wrongful death. If the patient's life is saved, the suit may be for injuries and expenses resulting from the suicide attempt.

Medical malpractice

Liability for the physician is predicated on the legal principle of professional negligence, also called malpractice. In a medical setting, malpractice is defined as bad, wrong, or injudicious treatment of a patient, in the course of rendering professional services with respect to a particular disease or injury, which results in injury, unnecessary suffering, or death to the patient, caused by carelessness, lack of professional skill, disregard of established rules or principles, neglect, or a malicious or criminal intent.

In practical application, this inclusive definition mandates a degree of skill in patient care comparable to the skill possessed by others of the same profession or specialty. The standard of skill required is gauged by the current state of medical knowledge at the time the alleged wrongdoing occurred. The physician is not a guarantor of good result unless he has promised to be. He is not liable for a bad result or adverse consequence if he has rendered the requisite degree of skill and care in the treatment of the patient.

If several methods of treatment are recognized and accepted by the current state of medical knowledge in the doctor's specialty, he may choose any of the accepted modes of treatment, even if the one chosen is not generally used, customary, or popular.

Problems in outpatient practice

General practitioners as well as psychiatrists often encounter suicide situations in which the standard of medical care may be challenged. Among such situations are the following:

- a patient confides suicidal thoughts or impulses to the physician which go unheeded or ignored;
- a physician prescribes large amounts of narcotic, hypnotic, or barbiturate medication to a known drug abuser or alcoholic, especially when suicidal tendencies are present or suicidal attempts or gestures appear in the patient's history;
- a suicidal patient is prematurely discharged from the hospital;
- treating physician and ward nurse fail to communicate;
- a physician fails to communicate with the patient's family;
- there is failure to supply guidance to the family in protecting the patient;
- a physician fails to listen and record important information volunteered by the family; and
- there is insufficient consultation with medical colleagues, especially psychiatrists or psychologists.

In outpatient practice, expressions of suicidal thoughts should be evaluated and charted. The need for psychiatric consultation should be considered and discussed with the patient and the family. In hospital practice, the possibility of suicide should be entered in the patient's records as part of the therapeutic program plan. Physicians should be sensitive to local standards for prescribing sleeping pills or other dangerous drugs and keep careful records of such prescriptions.

The best defense against allegation of malpractice is the fact that the possibility of suicide was explicitly considered, a treatment decision reached, and colleagues consulted. As a final precaution, physicians should carry adequate malpractice insurance.

"Reasonable foreseeability," predicting suicide, and the duty to warn

The law imposes upon the physician a duty to treat not only those disorders of which he has present knowledge, but also those that are reasonably foreseeable. This convention of legal thought has been interpreted to establish for doctors, especially psychiatrists, the difficult duty to predict homicide or suicidal behavior.

The *Tarasoff* decision in California was the first case to impose upon doctors a duty to warn potential victims of possible future assaultive acts by a patient. Quite apart from the violence that this requirement imposes on the principle of confidentiality, predicting violent acting out behavior to the extent demanded by law and society is not yet reliably possible. The state of the art does not allow the doctor to guarantee that the patient will or will not kill himself or another in every stated circumstance.

A similar duty-to-warn requirement has been urged in cases of suicide. Courts have not yet adopted such a rule, but the ever-expanding civil responsibility of physicians, especially psychiatrists, may be extended by trials presenting strong cases for plaintiffs contending that physicians who "know" that a patient will kill himself are obligated to protect him by notifying family or authorities for timely intervention.

The "reasonably prudent person" test invoked by some courts is a correlative of the "reasonable foreseeability" standard. In some situations, it is contended, a reasonably prudent person would anticipate suicide. Other decisions have found the determination of negligence for failing to forecast suicide to be within the "ordinary, common and general experience of mankind," and "not a highly technical question of science."

Judicial bias of this sort may further handicap health-care defendants by disallowing the introduction of expert testimony in suicide/negligence trials. But not all courts reject expert testimony or agree with this simplistic view of the variable treatment of suicidal patients.

Hospital liability and suicide

Unlike the duty of the physician, the hospital is responsible for custodial care rather than treatment. If the hospital is made aware of a patient's mental incapacity, the hospital must act to safeguard him from foreseeable dangers caused by his condition. The hospital must also exercise reasonable care to control the behavior of a patient, which may endanger himself or others. Put simply, the hospital has the duties of control and observation.

Courts are not in general agreement whether reasonable, non-negligent care of a suicidal patient means constant supervision, periodic scheduled supervision, or staggered observation with the staff on notice of a patient's condition. The determination of whether a hospital or physician has failed in the duty of vigilance begins with the doctor's assessment of the patient's condition and his resulting orders to the hospital staff. In addition to the entry in the patient's hospital record, the physician should orally communicate such orders to the head nurse.

In many hospitals, potentially suicidal patients are confined to their rooms, but if a patient has not been legally committed, the hospital may not confine him against his will.

If there has been an attempted suicide, some court decisions require the physicians to order the strictest standard of precautions, which is constant supervision. Other cases have found hospitals liable for failing to observe closely when the patient was not even considered suicidal. There is a whipsaw effect: When excessive patient restraint and restriction of movement is imposed, it actually may increase the likelihood of the patient's suicide.

Reasonable care must also be taken to prepare the premises and equipment used in patient care to be sure they are in safe condition. The specific requirements of these duties may vary from patient to patient and according to the design and staffing of the facility. Therefore, standardized policies with clearly drawn definitions of what, for instance, constitutes "safe" premises for the confinement of an acutely suicidal patient are not usually codified. In Chapters 11 and 12, suggestions are offered on how the hospital administration together with the medical staff can cope with the suicidal patient.

The vague standard of "'reasonable' care under all of the surrounding circumstances" determines negligence. Neither adequate advance notice nor fair warning is expected to be given to hospital staff and administration to guard against potential liability created by a self-destructive patient.

Liability for the hospital may also be determined not only by circumstances known to the hospital or staff, but further, deemed by facts that the hospital or staff should have known had they exercised a requisite degree of care. For example, if a patient is an acute suicidal risk and a well-meaning orderly unwittingly supplies the patient with a requested straight razor for shaving and injury results, the hospital may be liable.

An unfortunate consequence of this broad standard of hospital liability is that many hospitals refuse to admit dangerous patients, fearing the difficulty of controlling such a patient, the breadth of the hospital's liability, and the likelihood of potential litigation. For this reason, mentally ill patients who are seriously ill may be refused admission if they are a substantial threat to the safety of themselves or others. Such patients are relegated by default to a state hospital and there may receive an inferior standard of care.

Hospital staff liability

Hospitals are liable for the negligent acts of their employees acting within the scope of their employment. The negligent hospital employee is rarely sued individually, unless he has acted beyond the scope of his employment. The hospital's duty is to exercise the same degree of care, skill, and diligence exercised by other hospitals in the community, including employment of reasonably competent personnel.

If a patient's suicide or injury from attempted suicide is proximately caused by the negligence of a hospital employee, the hospital may be liable, whether it is a private, public, or charitable institution. Independent contractors, such as physicians or special nurses who are not employees or under the control of the hospital, will generally not affix liability to the hospital for negligence. Rescue teams are usually protected by "Good Samaritan" statutes that protect them from liability.

Control and observation

It's the hospital's duty also to control and observe the patient. Like the variable standard of "reasonable care," the requirement of observation of a suicidal patient is an unsettled issue. Courts are not in general agreement whether reasonable care of a patient means constant supervision, periodic scheduled supervision, or staggered observation with the staff on notice of a patient's sensitive condition. Does the duty to make the premises safe include removing dangerous objects from the patient's room and locking the windows? Need all the windows on the ward be locked, screened, or barred?

When there has been an attempted suicide, the hospital is often held to constant observation. In some cases, however, hospitals have been held liable for failing to observe closely even if the patient had not been considered suicidal. The definition of legal standards of reasonable care will derive from medical standards as the science and art of medicine develop them.

Liability is not as likely to be found when a suicide was not reasonably foreseeable. The hospital is not required to exercise a maximum degree of restraint for all potential suicides. Although direct physical restraint may be warranted in immediate crisis situations, the law is not unaware of the antitherapeutic effect of excessive restriction. Thus, the hospital may not be liable when a patient commits or attempts suicide in a "mysterious or unexpected fashion," when a calculated risk is taken for therapeutic purposes with a patient who has a known suicidal history, or when it is concluded after examination by the attending physician that a patient is not suicidal and does not require antisuicidal precautions.

Like the standard of treatment for physicians, the hospital does not guarantee a good result. The hospital's degree of control and supervision need only be reasonable by the local community standards that affect all other hospitals under all of the circumstances as they were, or should have been known. There may be instances when the physician's judgment differs from the hospital administration's in the management of the patient. For example, the physician may give open ward privileges for a patient who is known to the administration or nursing staff as a potential suicide. If the patient dies, both doctor and hospital will be held responsible for wrongful death. Therefore, it's important that clear agreement be codified between the attending physician and the hospital administration both in general hospital policy and in the particular instance of a given patient.

Obviously, the closest cooperation between medical staff and administration in the evolution of antisuicide policies and their documentation is required to maximize patient protection and minimize risks to patient, staff, physician, and hospital that a suicide may create.

Confidentiality

The law classifies communications between physician and patient as privileged in most jurisdictions, protecting the patient from compulsory disclosure of his confidences to the physician in courtroom proceedings, unless the patient consents to the disclosure or waives the privilege. Conversely, the relationship of trust or fiduciary duty between physician and patient demands that the doctor reveal all pertinent information to the patient. In some situations, the doctor's duty requires disclosure to others standing in a relation to the patient, such as parent/child or husband/wife.

Evidentiary privilege

Evidentiary privilege is created by statute and may be modified only by a legislative act. Judges may not order that the privilege be violated. Exceptions to the evidentiary privilege arise when a patient "impliedly waives" the privilege by placing his mental state in issue in a trial, as in a suit for mental distress. This is called the "patient-litigant exception."

Another exception has become the focus of controversy. Even after a patient has consented to disclosure, physicians have nevertheless refused judges' orders to testify, claiming the likelihood of harm resulting to the patient, who was unaware of what would be disclosed. Reasoning that the privilege lies with the patient rather than with the doctor, the court has imposed jail sentences on well-meaning doctors who defy court orders to testify after the patient has consented to disclosure.

State statutes establish civil penalties for the disclosure of information "obtained in the course of seeking professional services in a confidential relationship." This duty of confidentiality continues after a patient's death unless it is waived by the next of kin. Both the evidentiary privilege and duty of confidentiality apply to hospital records and medical reports relating to a patient's condition or cause of death.

Invasion of privacy

Communication of private facts about a patient's mental or physical condition to persons outside the "zone of treatment" (doctors and other necessary medical personnel) violates the patient's constitutional right of privacy and results in further liability.

Libel and slander related to suicide

Relevant civil penalties for defamation of character protect against oral (slander) or written or broadcast (libel) statements to third persons that damage or injure a person's reputation in his business or occupation, suggest physical or mental disease, or generally subject them to public contempt, hatred, or ridicule. Depending on the specific language of the statement, imputations of suicidal tendencies of a living person may be defamatory.

Although actions for defamation of character do not survive a patient, they may be brought on behalf of the family of a deceased patient. The family may recover money damages for defamation if facts about a rumored suicide tend to subject the family to contempt, ridicule, or obloquy or imply that insanity or mental disease is common to other family members.

In addition to those civil penalties already mentioned, criminal libel laws in many states punish anyone who maliciously tries to vilify the name or reputation of a deceased person.

Infliction of mental distress: Negligence

Depending upon the foreseeability of the resulting mental trauma or distress to the patient or family, communication to others of a patient's suicidal behavior may trigger liability for either intentional or negligent infliction of mental distress. Some lawsuits against doctors also claim that communications that cause foreseeable shock or mental injury to a patient may be punishable by ordinary laws of negligence, but few courts have come to such a result.

Hospital disclosures

The strict standard of confidentiality is somewhat relaxed in the hospital setting. Courts have held that a "qualified privilege" goes along with the doctor/patient relationship, permitting doctors to communicate certain information about a patient to others. A physician may properly disclose relevant information about a patient's condition when consulting with other physicians or giving orders to hospital personnel, as long as the information is disclosed in good faith and in a fair manner, is specific and necessary for the purpose disclosed, and is disclosed only to personnel necessary to the purpose for which it was disclosed.

Although the dispute over the extent of hospital administration and staff access to patient records rages on, some degree of access necessary for competent hospital care is not considered violative of the patient's rights of privacy and confidentiality. For example, the director of a hospital may view a patient's hospital records if such access is specifically required by his duties as director. On challenge, the burden of proof of such necessity would be borne by the hospital administration. Access does not extend to the physician's private office records.

In contrast to laws that prohibit and punish the disclosure of facts relating to suicide, other laws mandate disclosure in certain situations. The converse of the physician/patient duty of confidentiality requires the physician to reveal pertinent medical information to the patient himself.

In the case of minors or incompetent persons, communication of confidential information to a legal guardian or conservator, spouse, parent, or child, supposedly does not violate confidentiality. The duty of disclosure requires a warning to the patient or guardian if the patient's condition or medication renders his conduct dangerous to others, such as when driving a car. If a patient dies by his own hand while under the care of a physician, the patient's next of kin, whether parent, spouse, or child, has a right to know the cause of death. Withholding of information regarding the cause of death is considered by some courts to be tantamount to misrepresentation. The problem of the certification of death is discussed below.

By the holding of the *Tarasoff* decision and the special relationship between a physician and patient, statutes in some states have established a duty to warn—and therefore disclose confidential communications to—third persons, when the risk to be prevented is the danger of violent assault. The duty to warn does not obtain when the risk of harm is self-inflicted, as in suicide, or merely threatens damage to property. It has been said that confidentiality ends where public peril begins. Physicians and psychiatrists argue that appropriate and genuine concern for the safety of the public would allow the doctrine of confidentiality to be superior to the duty to warn, since it is impossible to carry out treatment without confidentiality. Without treatment, neither the patient nor the public is protected.

A physician is not required to disclose to others vague, indefinite, or even specific manifestations of suicidal tendencies of a patient being treated on an outpatient basis. The problem of whether to communicate a patient's suicidal tendencies to significant others best able to protect against such harm can be avoided by liberal use of informed consent forms that permit disclosure.

If the patient is competent to choose, you should ask whether he objects to the disclosure of information to significant others. Whatever he chooses, you should obtain his signature on a prepared form indicating that the matter has been discussed and that the patient has either consented or refused the disclosure. Such a procedure safeguards you from possible liability for communicating or failing to communicate the danger of potential suicide to others.

Certification and registration of death by suicide

The laws of the state control the certification and registration of death and disposal of the remains. If suicide is considered a possible manner of death, the official certification and registration of the cause of death—and the consequences—are of great concern to the survivors, beneficiaries, and the community of the deceased as well as to the certifying physician. Specific formal requirements vary slightly from state to state.

Every death must be registered with the local registrar of vital statistics in the county or district where death was officially pronounced or the body was found. Such registration is essential for public reasons and helpful in the proper administration of probate and tax laws. Registration must occur within some designated time of death, usually a few days, and is required by law prior to any disposition of the remains.

A critical step in the registration process is the filing of a completed certification of death. A funeral director registers the death by filing the death certificate, since this is a prerequisite to the issuance of a permit to bury or otherwise dispose of the body. State laws require that the physician last in attendance must report certain information on the death certificate. If no physician attended the deceased at or near the time of death, the coroner or medical examiner must supply this information and sign the certificate.

When either the attending physician or the coroner or medical examiner signs the death certificate, he attests to that portion of the document relating to the cause and manner of death. It is this determination that must be considered in a discussion of suicide.

Liability for false certification

Both civil and criminal sanctions may be imposed upon a physician who falsifies any medical information regarding the certification of death. The administering state agency is empowered to interview the source "best qualified" to supply information about the cause and manner of death.

Any person who is requested to provide such information may be criminally liable if he purposely falsifies or suppresses information relevant to the interviewer's questions. Similar criminal penalties apply to alteration of the death certificate, failure to properly deliver it to the registrar, and failure of the registrar to correctly register the certificate. Depending upon state statutes, the offense is classified as either a misdemeanor or a felony.

Notification of coroner

When suicide is considered as a possible, probable, or certain manner of death, the law requires a physician, funeral director, or any person with knowledge of the death to immediately notify the coroner or medical examiner.

Traumatic consequences sometimes flow from such notification. The coroner's investigation may lead to a formal coroner's inquest, in which a six-person jury deliberates the cause and manner of death. Any delay in the disposition of the remains is the cause of considerable anguish to some families, such as Orthodox Jews who require interment of the body as soon as possible after death. Stigmatization of the survivors may be another harsh side effect of the coroner's investigation. For these reasons, the decision to conclude that a death is a possible suicide may be a difficult and sensitive one. The situation is double-edged: Potential informants must weigh the distress to the family and the likelihood of being sued civilly if suspicions prove unfounded against the threat of criminal prosecution if the suspicions go unreported.

The legal and moral dilemmas surrounding the certification of death become more understandable in light of the need for accurate data concerning causes and manners of death. Reluctance to investigate and certify suicides may cause unnecessary grief and misery to survivors of the deceased who may be confused and uncertain whether death was the result of accident, suicide, or homicide. Unaware and unwarned of underlying psychological disturbances that may have precipitated the suicidal act, the family or community at large may fail to recognize that the same forces that were instrumental in the suicide may affect other family members. If they are not informed of this real danger, they can't take necessary precautions against self-destructive acts that vulnerable family members may commit in the future.

The duty of physician/patient confidentiality allows an exception for information reported on the death certificate, including a description of the cause of death. The cause of death appearing on a duly filed certificate of death is considered inadmissible hearsay evidence as to the actual cause of death in a courtroom proceeding.

Insurance

When an individual attempts or commits suicide, payment of various kinds of insurance to beneficiaries may become a significant issue.

Underwriting

The reaction of insurance providers varies greatly to an individual with a history of attempted suicide applying for insurance.

In some situations, a policy may be written in standard form and issued without reservation. In others, the application may be rejected outright.

Typically, cases involving suicide attempts, threats, or gestures within five years are referred to the insurance company's physician for review and recommendation. Patient's records an inquiring insurer may request from a prior-treating physician or therapist are confidential privileged communications and may not be divulged without the consent of the patient. Regrettably, insurance companies have a shaky record of protecting the assumed inviolate nature of medical information sent to them. Often data referring to the patient are transmitted to the employer who pays the premiums. Information that is committed to computer may be abstracted and—without the knowledge or consent of the patient or the physician—passed on to affiliate companies, federal officials, educational institutions, and even credit companies. The physician supplying such information should consider if the patient is generally aware of the content of records before they are divulged, the likelihood they will be exposed, and the impact of such disclosure.

Insurance contracts

Life insurance benefits are payable at times and under conditions provided in the insurance contract or policy. Various and particular exclusions in the contract may be a complete defense for the insurer, denying recovery by beneficiaries in the event of a suicide. Since the policy is primarily a contract, all the usual contract defenses, including fraud, incapacity, and misrepresentation, void a policy purchased with a prior intent to commit suicide.

Rules of contract and evidence law have established legal presumptions against suicide as a cause of death, and a presumption against facts giving force to any exclusionary clause in an insurance contract. In controversies over payment of benefits, these presumptions place the preliminary burden upon the insurer to prove that the death was by suicide, that the suicidal act was intentional, or any other facts bringing the death under a policy exclusion.

Presumptions may be rebutted by the production of even minor evidence to the contrary. Recovery may be further impeded by an archaic, though recognized, public policy against payment of insurance benefits in cases of suicide.

Other insurance policy exclusions that may be argued as defenses to payment on a policy include a common clause withholding payment for "death or injury resulting from acts in violation of the criminal law." This clause is usually limited to felonies. It's intended to apply to injuries or death suffered in confrontations with law-enforcement agencies. Only a handful of statutes refer to suicide as a crime today, and authorities agree generally that the clause is inapplicable to suicide.

If a suicide occurs within a specific time, usually one or two years following issuance of the policy, some policy clauses limit the amount of recovery to a refund of the premiums paid. In some states, this rule is codified by statute.

The most common policy exclusion excludes payment for "suicide, sane or insane." This typical policy boiler-plate, together with another exclusion, for "injury from intentional acts by the insured," is intended to protect the insurer from payments of benefits. Because judges and juries often find that suicide committed by an insane person is not "intentional," and the trend is to apply a less stringent test of insanity, insurance companies specifically exclude suicide "sane or insane."

A California case caused some controversy in this regard when a state appeals court in San Diego effectively "blasted the boiler-plate" by declaring that suicide was by definition an *intentional* taking of one's own life, and therefore could only be committed by one who was sane enough to form an intent. In this way, the judge reasoned, no insane person could ever commit "suicide" in the accepted meaning of that word, and that the phrase "sane or insane" was ambiguous and illogical and, hence, should be construed against the insurer.

Although the decision satisfied families who might otherwise have been denied benefits, its logic is not consistent with what we know about suicide. In a rehearing of the case, the Los Angeles Center for the Study of Self-Destructive Behavior argued for the reversal of the precedent.

Statutes in some states accomplish a similar result by completely prohibiting suicide as a defense to payment on an insurance policy. Such statutes are not retroactive and do not necessarily prohibit the insurer from denying double-indemnity recovery.

Double-indemnity provisions commonly award double the face value of the policy if death is occasioned by accident. To avoid payment of double indemnity, the insurer may contend that the suicide victim was sane at the time of death and acted intentionally, that the death was suicide rather than accident, or that the risk of suicide is not one assumed under double-indemnity policies and provisions.

Such arguments are countered by expert testimony finding the victim insane at the time of the suicide—therefore, the death should be deemed accidental—or that the victim was sane and either killed himself by mistake or did not intend to succeed in his suicidal gesture. The coroner's inquest or the psychological autopsy are intended to establish the true circumstances surrounding death.

Workers' Compensation and Disability

State laws control the issuance of Workers' Compensation and Disability payments for suicides or suicide attempts that result from injuries arising out of employment. The amount of Workers' Compensation death benefits is seldom substantial.

In almost every state and in the United States Employees Compensation Act and Federal Longshoremen's and Harbor Workers' Compensation Act—two federal statutes that specifically mention suicide—recovery of benefits is expressly denied for injuries caused by the willful intent of the employee. To avoid this defense in a contest over benefits, employees and their families have been required to show affirmatively that the victim did not intentionally injure himself.

Formerly, only testimony of wildly delusional behavior immediately preceding a bizarre method of attempting suicide would suffice to show unintentional self-injury. The majority rule today has been liberalized and requires only that the employment-related injury caused "mental derangement" leading to suicide, rather than requiring positive proof of the difficult legal concept of "proximate causation." Moreover, the degree of derangement may now be shown by direct evidence of psychiatric hospitalization or institutionalization or expert psychiatric testimony evincing compelling evidence for severe mental illness as consistent with depression, drug addiction, alcoholism, organic brain dysfunction, or psychosis.

Payment of disability benefits, whether from government-subsidized insurance or private insurance, arising out of a suicide attempt depends on the type of coverage in force and specific exclusions enumerated in the policy. Disability caused by self-inflicted injury is not usually excluded from standard disability-income policies. A specific policy exclusion that withholds death benefits for suicide does not automatically exclude disability insurance benefits for an attempted suicide.

Although the disability caused by a suicide attempt may be temporary, the underlying psychiatric disturbance is of greater concern. To promote needed treatment of the mentally ill, claimants and beneficiaries should understand that in disability cases a finding of insanity or mental incapacity in no way divests the beneficiaries of their entitlement to insurance benefits.

CHAPTER 16

Obligations and liabilities of the physician

The obligations of the physician regarding the suicidal patient derive from his status as a doctor. They originate in a host of rules, traditions, philosophic doctrine, and moral scruples he picks up while learning what it means to be a physician. They are present throughout the professional life of every doctor as inspiration to and context of his every decision.

His liabilities are mainly defined by law and by specific regulations imposed by all the agents to whom he is answerable. This includes the state board, which licenses him and defines his limits and privileges; the government, which establishes regulations with stated penalties if they are violated; and medical societies, which offer a forum in which changes can be debated and advances in medical art and science are shared and creates the opportunity to learn the ethics of the profession.

The societies offer guidelines to the physician regarding personal risks and potential rewards and they sometimes act as allies who defend, ameliorate, intervene, and arbitrate instances when the doctor is under critical review for allegedly failing to live up to his obligations.

Beyond these external constraints, the physician is under the dominion of his own moral system and personal conscience, which largely determines how he accepts his obligations and recognizes his responsibilities. As common denominator to all the entities that shape the physician's motivation is the prevailing morality of the society in which the doctor lives, learns, and functions.

Obligation to recognize and intervene

In light of the rising morbidity from and mortality from suicide attempts, it seems inescapable that the physician's first obligation is to do more than he now does to recognize the premorbid suicide, successfully intervene at the time of the morbid act, and cope better with the postmorbid effects of suicide. Considering the substantial number of patients who first go to their doctors, then to their clergymen, and last to psychiatrists and psychologists before they kill themselves, it's evident that opportunities for positive intervention are missed.

Pediatricians, for example, frequently discover the effects of chaotic interaction in the families of their young patients. They need to learn how to recognize decompensation in the child and take the initiative for earlier intervention to prevent the cycle of destructive behavior that can end in death.

Probably every physician can do more to detect suicide, take antisuicide action, and sensitize himself to the seriousness of the entire problem of suicide.

Obligation to know the law

The obligation to detect suicide risk and take appropriate action to intervene further requires knowledge of the laws that impose demands on the physician when he confronts a suicide. For example, notification of suspicion of suicide is required in every state. The liability of the physician who fails to notify the coroner or medical examiner may result in professional censure and legal sanctions.

Obligation to be accessible

The urge to die by suicide and the panicky cry for help does not affect patients at times necessarily convenient to the doctor. The plea on the telephone "Talk to me, Doctor, I'm frightened" may come as the physician is about to go out the door, tennis racquet under his arm, to meet his partners for doubles.

Whether to listen with empathy or disengage when immediate service is demanded is a judgment. If you're always ready to give attention to any patient in an emergency, you run the risk of being exploited by a narcissistic, dependent, controlling, or malicious patient. If you answer every demand on your time and energy with the maximum response, out of a misplaced sense of virtue and commitment, you'll be quickly exhausted, frittering away your professional gifts on false alarms. This is obviously not in the best interest of anyone—you, your family, the patient, or society itself.

Knowledge of the patient's potential for low or high lethal suicide attempt will help in deciding if you can ease away from the patient or must give up the tennis date and sit down for a serious engagement on the telephone or meet with him face-to-face. An open-ended "Tell me what is troubling you?" is preferable to setting a time limit. "I just have a minute, what's bothering you?" can only and correctly be interpreted as brusque rejection by the patient.

The immediate stimulus for the call should be determined. "My wife and I had a fight this morning, and I can't live through another day of this" or "While I was peeling apples, the urge to stab myself came over me, and I am afraid that I'll do it" or "I just swallowed the whole bottle of my heart pills."

Each of these scenarios requires a discriminating level of engagement. You're obligated to be accessible to the patient. If you're unable or judiciously believe it best to minimize your personal engagement, a continuum of attention should be assured or other options cited to the patient.

The suicidal patient thinks in terms of absolutes as his focus constricts. If you're accessory to this process, producing absolutes and reducing options, he'll accelerate the probability of acute crisis. Remarks like, "Don't call me with such complaints after regular office hours" or "I don't know what to say to you" or "There's really nothing that I can do for you" or "I'm sorry, but I can't talk to you now" have a door-slamming effect.

If you give assurance of your involvement, you'll introduce a note of hopefulness. "I know you're hurting and feel you need to talk. Let me call you later today" or "What you're going through is obviously painful. I'll arrange to see you right away."

If the situation is deteriorating, you may be quite directive and request the patient to go at once to the emergency room, or summon a member of the family to speak to him, or tell the patient he must be hospitalized and that a bed will be reserved for him at once.

In general, unless you're unwilling to continue to offer services to this particular patient, you ought to reiterate assurances of your availability. "Please call me any time. I may not get back to you right away but be patient; I will answer your call."

Even if you're annoyed by repeated demands on your time and attention, you're still ethically and legally responsible for the patient until another physician or appropriate resource is made available. The doctor who wishes to do so should announce his intention to withdraw from medical responsibility but at the same time, must offer an alternative to the patient. He should later confirm in a written memorandum what he had said on the telephone. In the event the patient is not a competent person or is a minor, the formal notification should be sent to the guardian or the parent. Here's an example:

Dear Mrs. Enderby:

This is formal notice of my withdrawal from medical responsibility in your case. Please arrange for another physician to attend to you. In view of your medical condition, I advise that you do need a physician. Your failure to follow this recommendation could have serious effects on your health and may even put your life in danger.

If you don't know whom to choose, I suggest you call the local medical association who will be glad to suggest the names of physicians in your neighborhood.

Pending arranging for an alternative physician, I shall be available for emergency service.

Your records in my possession will be made available to your new physician upon your written request.

Sincerely,

John Dolittle, M.D.

The minimum ethical obligation on a physician who is unilaterally voiding his unwritten contract to the patient is:

● Written notice of intent to resign.

- Recommendation of alternative services.
- Warning of consequences if advice is not followed.
- Assurance that the doctor will give emergency service until alternative agents are found.
- Reminder that medical records are available to the new physician consistent with the dictates of medical ethics in protecting confidentiality.

If suicide has been an accomplished fact, the physician has an obligation to be available to the survivors. They will need his explanation, consultation, assurances, sympathy, and expression of human concern. The family of a suicide needs more than conventional platitudes; they need professional intervention. Prompt and appropriate psychiatric and psychological consultation may avert symptoms of pathological grief and even sympathetic suicide among the survivors.

Obligation to notify the coroner or medical examiner

The physician who mishandles a suicidal patient faces many hazards. If he fails to identify the patient at risk and gives him drugs that are later used in committing suicide, or if the doctor fails to arrange protection for a self-destructive patient in the hospital, he may have to defend himself as having failed to use state-of-the-art skill and judgment in the treatment of his patient.

If he fails to notify the coroner or medical examiner in the event he suspects or knows suicide has occurred and files a medical certificate that contains false information, or if the doctor fails to cite the cause of death, he is guilty of a misdemeanor.

The death certificate is a formal legal document. When a physician completes the data, it's as if he had prepared it under oath. Intentionally distorting anything or creating false data is at least conduct unbecoming a physician, immoral, and may be a significant, punishable violation of the law.

If there is a delay in getting a burial permit because the doctor has filed an improperly completed medical certificate, the family of the deceased may be subject to an unexpected, unconscionable delay in the funeral ceremony, adding another injury to the trauma that suicide already has imposed upon survivors.

If the physician is at fault, he's a visible target on whom the gathering wrath of family and friends may focus, resulting in high probability that the doctor will be subject to a lawsuit.

Obligation to educate

As physicians and other health professionals become more sophisticated and confident in coping with suicidal patients and their families, an obligation arises to educate others. The technical skills of recognition and management should be shared in teaching seminars with colleagues. Beyond that, the enhancement of knowledge by research and careful documentation is certainly encouraged. An important area of education that physicians, psychologists, social workers, nurses, and others can invest their energy, skill, and time in is legislation. Legislators ought to decriminalize suicidal behavior wherever archaic laws still impose legal sanctions on mentally disturbed persons.

There may be a long interval between the time a suicidal person is first aware of his melancholy inclination to die and when, if at all, he seeks rescue. In a frightening plurality of instances, the professional comes to help *after* the suicidal act is already in progress. The rescuer has only a miniscule opportunity to intervene in the earliest stages of preoccupation and psychological turmoil out of which the impulsion to self-destruct is formed.

Physicians and other health professionals have the obligation to improve their personal skills, but they also might provide their patients, families, young people in schools, teachers, and the police with information so that prevention of suicide in our society can become a goal to which everyone can contribute.

Volunteering to lecture and demonstrate to PTA's, groups of students, and church groups, preparing material for the media, and helping a community set up suicide hotlines are a few of the ways in which physicians may help to reduce the incidence of suicide.

PART V

After the fact

CHAPTER **17**

The survivors

A newspaper series of interviews with intimates and kin of persons who had committed suicide was entitled "Hell is on earth for survivors after a suicide occurs." Whether maliciously intended by the victim of suicide or an inevitable byproduct of the act, the immediate effect of suicide is shock. Like a great stone thrown into a shallow pond, it creates turmoil long after the mopping-up and the platitudes are over. The lives of survivors will forever be changed by the action of the deceased, as intense grief and guilt rouse and battle with its neutralizer, denial.

Psychological effects

A young man had made four suicide attempts between his 14th and 21st years. His father found him dead from an overdose of barbiturates and diazepam. The boy's mother had committed suicide on his 12th birthday. He had been on multiple street drugs. Although he was bright, he had dropped out of school and had spent several years in jail for felonious assault. After each of several highly lethal suicide attempts from which he was rescued, he spent time in a hospital but remained inaccessible to therapy, grimly determined that he would "have fun and then die, like my mother did."

203

The medical examiner ruled the death to be a suicide. The grief-stricken father demanded that the medical examiner change the diagnosis, insisting that his son had died of acute drug intoxication, not by suicide, and that the death was accidental. He bitterly insisted, "They [the office of the coroner] ignored the facts; they didn't care that he has a twin sister who will be affected by this decision. I will be able to get over it. His sister will not."

An intelligent socialite publicly mourned the suicide of her 20-year-old daughter, projecting blame for the death of the girl on the alleged failure of her psychiatrist to have advised the family of suicidal risks and, even more pointedly, of having provoked the suicide. A year after her daughter's death, after eight unsuccessful attempts, the mother succeeded in killing herself.

The exasperated wife reacted to her husband who had once too often threatened to kill himself and demonstrated a loaded gun. She screamed at him, "Don't threaten me anymore. Go ahead and do it. Get it over with or stop threatening." At once, her husband shot himself in the head. She wheeled around, transfixed in horror, and developed torticollis within the hour, which became a permanent, visible stigma of her guilt.

A prominent obstetrician killed himself at the height of his career. His son since has dropped out of college, abandoning plans to pursue a medical career. His daughter has developed terminal ileitis. A younger daughter has disappeared; presumably she has joined a counter-culture group. The doctor's wife had to sell the house, has gone to work as a medical secretary, and bitterly calls her dead husband "the most malicious man who ever lived."

In a letter to a newspaper syndicated columnist, a woman described herself as touched deeply by evidence of insensitivity to suicide threats. She stated that her mother had committed suicide without warning. "It was a shock from which my father, sister, and I will never recover."

A survivor of her brother's suicide became severely mentally ill, refused to eat or drink, and was hospitalized as her brother had been before. She identified so closely with him that she needed to imitate his suicide. She said, "How could I ever prove how much he mattered unless I did the same thing. Here . . . I show you how much I care. I kill myself."

There are profound tragic consequences of suicide in the family of the deceased. There is intense guilt and shame as members of the family, particularly the surviving spouse, have stressful confrontations with the physician, the hospital authorities, neighbors, friends, employers, insurance agents, the police, and the coroner's or the medical examiner's office.

In contrast to the loving support that the community ordinarily gives the bereaved when there is death, neighbors and friends are ambiguous and try to avoid contact.

Because of the time it may take the medical examiner to come to a decision and release the body, funeral arrangements may be postponed. If the deceased was prominent or if the suicide was bizarre or unusual, newspaper reporters and TV cameramen and commentators will haunt the home, pry, and in their quest for news become offensive in their violation of the family's privacy.

The survivors are turned against themselves and sometimes against each other, pointing the finger of blame. There is no truce for the guilty. Anger in the presuicidal family may have generated hostile wishes against the deceased. Now they seem to have come true, and there are both guilt feelings and a heady, almost intoxicating conviction of omnipotence, which in turn engenders further guilt. Sometimes family members are drawn closer together, even relieved, by the death of the suicide victim, but in the main, the event of suicide is destructive to ties that hold a family together.

The anger that the survivor experiences has no place for expression. There is no counter-aggressive effective action to take. There is no way to cancel the dreadful doubts, no object for the expression of love.

One survivor put it, "The conventional funeral was hypocritical from start to finish. The eulogies were ridiculous." Survivors are isolated from society, unable to do what needs to be done to work out their grief. They find their own ego strength eroded. Defenses against these painful affects are hard to come by. The first, of course, is denial. A strenuous effort is made to reject the hypothesis of suicide and to suggest that either the death was an accident or perhaps the deceased was murdered.

Even before the event, family and friends of a prior attempter, manipulator, or threatener already have begun to set up unconscious or even conscious defenses against the increasing probability of suicide. A nurse who made abortive suicide attempts with overdoses of various drugs teased her friends, telling each that she had made a suicide attempt but asked secrecy and that the matter be kept confidential.

By accident, each of several nurse-associates discovered that the mutual friends did know. The friends confronted the nurse. They said, "You've put us on a guilt trip. You've not been honest about yourself. You must see a consultant regarding what you are doing. We'll not be guilty for your death if you kill yourself."

Psychological adaptive mechanisms include *incorporation* in which the dead person is imitated. His habits become adopted, his standards and esthetic taste replicated. Sometimes there is *substitution*. Members of the family will keep the artifacts of the dead person as symbols of his previous life. Closets full of clothes of the deceased may be saved indefinitely after a death if pathological grief has not been adequately resolved. In Alfred Hitchcock's *Psycho*, the demented son made the ultimate substitution for his dead mother by keeping her body in his possession. This symbolized his refusal to admit that she had in fact died.

Sometimes a loved object, a strain of music, a place to go, a passage in a book, a photograph may become a *symbolization*. Investing in objects is a way of postponing grief and refusing to admit the permanency and irrevocability of death. *Mystification* occurs when a strange horror is attributed to the dead and the act of suicide is assumed to have an occult purpose beyond the ken of the survivors. The implication is that the death was for some magnificent or noble purpose not yet understood and judgment should be reserved until all the facts have been clarified. Such mysteries are usually entirely fantasized and represent psychological techniques of postponing the task of grief. In more severe cases of depression and illness among survivors, *depersonalization* may occur. They feel numb and withdraw to a point where they brood about the deceased in an obsessional exaggeration of normal mourning.

Practical effects

There are profound practical consequences that affect the survivors of a suicide. The suicidal person contemplating and justifying death may say, "They'll all be better off without me."

The greater probability is that the death will turn the family into a chaotic state with loss of security for nearly all members.

To begin with, there is some mopping up to do. Some suicides are extremely punctilious and neat, as was the young woman who lay in a bathtub, let the water run, then cut her wrists and bled to death while the water carried away the blood. Other suicides are not so tidy. Most leave the gross evidences of their mutilated bodies on display staining the carpets, floors, walls, or bedding with blood. Aside from the grossness of it, there may be the implication that the survivors are being punished by having to clean up the mess. Also, it's not easy to find car keys and insurance policies, cancel subscriptions to publications, and meet the curiosity of the community.

Studies on the social effects of suicide show that a high percentage of families in which an adult died by self-destruction suffered serious reduction in their standard of living, in many cases having to move away from the parental home. In other instances, families have had to separate, further aggravating the consequences of the one-parent household.

There are negative consequences of the psychological autopsy or inquest. However worthy its objective and necessary for satisfying legal requirements, the examination is most stressful for the next of kin. To begin with, it's sometimes necessary for some member of the family to view the body for identification. This is sometimes a shocking and punishing experience. A man whose drowning was not discovered for weeks after his disappearance was a hideous sight after the crayfish had eaten away the soft parts of his body. His identification in the morgue by his wife constituted brutal punishment. Nonetheless, the verdict of the medical examiner is generally conclusive. As painful as it may be, at least it helps to reduce rumor mongering.

Some families take offense at the fact that suicide notes left by the deceased are retained by the coroner. Sometimes they are returned when the case has been terminated. In some jurisdictions, they are not.

Effects on children

A remarkable feature in many families is the attempt of the surviving parent to conceal from children the fact of the suicide, though this is virtually impossible to do. It's generally done to reinforce the denial mechanism, the defense of a parent against accepting the self-destructive act for what it was. The consequence to the children is a state of doubt, confusion, and mistrust. Disturbed communication of this nature deprives the children of an outlet for their intense feelings and their real or fantasized guilts or a way to validate reality.

In a presuicidal family with pathology, children are sometimes made responsible for preserving the life of the depressed parent, with the result that when there is a suicide the children are held accountable by implied or outright accusations. The reason for suicide is sometimes attributable to the children. Some badness, naughtiness, or delinquency that they may have displayed shortly before the death is assumed to have been the primary reason for the suicide and becomes a heavy burden for a child. Such guilts are inconsolable. Effects may be serious in both mental and physical consequences. In very young children, head-banging, excessive weeping, sleep disturbances, regressive toilet control, school failure, despondency, and psychosomatic illness are but one set of reactions. Another is a counter-aggressive defiance manifested by angry acting out, delinquency, even violence.

Children need psychiatric and psychological counseling as the degree of pathology increases for the first several years, peaking approximately five years after the event. But the morbid effect of the death lingers on throughout life, carrying with it the shadow of a much higher vulnerability to self-destruction.

What can a child think of a parent who in the act of killing himself attempts to destroy the child? "I love my daughter," said the middle-aged woman whose husband had deserted her. "Therefore, I am going to take her with me." When she turned on the gas and died, the daughter almost died too. Was her attempt to kill the child an act of love or a manifestation of hatred?

A mother flung her 10-year-old boy into a river running with spring flood waters, then she jumped in after him. By remarkable good fortune, the boy was rescued, but the mother drowned. In the mind of such a suicide, there is an assumption of proprietorship, of identification with the child, and an assumed right to use the child as a weapon of punishment against survivors. When children are rescued, knowing that they were intended as sacrificial victims, the psychological trauma is severe and the task of rehabilitation is arduous.

Therapy with survivors

The urgent message to give to survivors is that life is for the living. It's only in the living memory, thoughts, and deeds of survivors that any significance, any good or promise, or compensation for the loss of the deceased can ever be constructed. The major immediate task of the therapist is to give hearing to the guilt, the grief, and the anger of the survivors.

The moment-by-moment, obsessively detailed recollection of the death may have to be recounted many times until it has been worked through. Truths need to be exchanged and justice administered. Speaking ill or speaking well of the dead ought not to follow some conventional expectation, but should be expressed as it's truly felt.

Friends and family as well as the physician ought to give what they can of their time, empathy, and compassion to the survivors. They should encourage reminiscence and offer whatever practical aid they can, even if it's relatively modest, in bringing the family to relative stability after adjustment to the death.

The offices of the coroner, the medical examiner, or the forensic pathologist should employ tact, reassurance, kindness, and consideration for the family of the deceased in performing their duty. In all transactions and any way possible, the clarification of the status of the deceased, completion of the medical certificate, and the release of the body for burial should be expedited. Physicians who treat cardiac arrhythmias, gastrointestinal distress, persistent and nagging skin reactions, loss of appetite, nagging joint and muscle pains are aware that survivors undergo great psychological stress and may be expected to suffer somatic disorders.

Gently and with assurance that the ventilations of feelings will be welcomed, even months after a suicide, the survivor should be encouraged to talk. Various communities have set up group therapy for survivors. These may be sponsored by professional agencies and suicide-prevention centers. Such support groups offer time and assistance for people who have lost a relative or friend by suicide. Their purpose is to promote a positive resolution of the grief experience and to foster emotional health. The feelings that survivors experience are openly shared in a nonjudgmental atmosphere. The goal is to help members live with the loss and grief. Such ventures are most valuable but not well-publicized within the community.

Religious counselors frequently carry the burden of grief-resolution. Many priests, ministers, and rabbis are experienced and comfortable in the role of bereavement counselor. When acceptable and solicited, the implication of the existence of an all-forgiving, all-knowing, loving God who is the ultimate spiritual resource may offer security and hope as well as strength to tolerate the painful affects that afflict the survivors of suicide for some time after the incident.

The psychological autopsy

After any suicide, whether it occurs in the doctor's private practice, in the hospital, in the county jail, or in the street, an investigation is required. The contributing causes must be researched to clarify the cause and manner of death and reported in such a manner to make the review as valuable as possible for prevention of suicide in the future. Investigators are generally based in the coroner's or the medical examiner's office. They may be forensic pathologists or social scientists. The decedent's personality, habits, associations, and relevant history are sought out by these expert investigators. Not only does the psychological autopsy assist the medical examiner in determining whether the deceased killed himself, it also allows the methodical sorting of important demographic data that help to define behavior related to injury and death, relevant statistics, as well as important behavioral details that mental health scientists can utilize in suicidology research.

The next of kin are interviewed usually as soon as possible after a death. Frequently, calls of this nature may be disturbing and require considerable skill on the part of the interviewer to evoke a cooperative attitude from the survivors. Further contacts with friends and acquaintances of the deceased are obtained following the initial visits. The medical examiner's office may also solicit medical history in depth from physicians and hospitals where the patient has been treated in the past.

An 18-year-old boy is found dead on a highway, killed when he "appeared out of nowhere" and was struck by a truck whose driver had no chance of avoiding him. Was it accident or suicide? A 22-year-old girl was cleaning a brand-new revolver intended as a birthday gift to her brother. The gun went off, and the girl suffered a fatal wound. Accident or suicide?

The aching doubt in the minds of survivors regarding whether the deceased died of self-murder or accident may require that they receive counseling for their grief. The empathy, warmth, and concern shown by the investigative members will allow the relevant data to be abstracted and obtained more easily, and may reduce the suffering, guilt, and anger that must be managed by the bereaved.

Families may participate actively and cooperatively in the psychological autopsy or may manifest a hostile and repudiating attitude, refusing even to consider the possibility that the death occurred by suicide.

In hospitals, self-criticism and self-scrutiny inevitably follow a suicide of a patient or of a staff member. Whether the responsibility is assigned to an ad hoc committee or to an already created standing committee, responsible persons should be assigned to conduct a psychological investigation whenever there is a serious suicide attempt and a psychological autopsy whenever there is a death by suicide.

The knowledge that the committee is not on a witch hunt to assign blame, but rather is attempting to learn from the experience will engender confidence and cooperation among members of the staff. It's important to allow staff members, particularly those who are close to the person who died, to express and work through their feelings.

Each person involved should be interviewed singly and in private and persuaded to give any information he can, explaining, for example, lapses or seeming contradictions in the patient's chart, particularly in the sections of physicians' and nurses' notes. A clear understanding of the patient's personality, life-style, prehospital course, and other data relevant to his suicide ought to be documented.

Interviews with the family and friends may be solicited, but this must be done delicately and with tact. If a member of the hospital staff who has been exposed to the suicide or intimates of the deceased show evidence of painful psychological reactions, such as depression and pathological mourning, psychological and psychiatric consultation may be appropriate.

After the information-gathering team has accumulated data, a meeting of all persons, particularly staff immediately involved in the deceased patient's care, should be held. Two goals are to be frankly stated. First, to determine as reasonably and accurately as possible the cause of the patient's suicide. Next, to establish if possible how the death might have been averted.

The staff assembly is likely to be mutually supportive and may reduce the threat to morale, improve the capacity of staff members to take care of their patients in the future, and restore their sense of competence.

In any psychological autopsy report the ad hoc committee may submit to the governing board of the hospital, the same question that pertains to a pathological autopsy ought to inspire it: "What can we learn by examining the deceased that will further our skills in caring for the living?"

CHAPTER 18

Afterword

People write books for a variety of reasons. They may need to demonstrate their verbal skills, tell a good story, communicate ideas, provoke dobate, commit an aggression, make an apology, exhibit themselves symbolically, or make money. I've written this book to keep a promise.

When we were barely in our teens a friend of mine and I were inseparable buddies. His father was a severe asthmatic who was a furrier. My friend and his mother came home one day and found him dead of illuminating gas poisoning. Although I never told my friend how helpless I felt in attempting to console him, I resolved then that I would someday do something to prevent suicide.

As a physician I have seen suicide in many guises. It's variously an act of consummate self-indulgence, of oppression, a violent transgression of the rights of others, the last shout of a hypocrite, the statement of a liar belligerently demanding credibility. It may also be a gift of benevolence, an act of benign loving, a refuge against unendurable pain. As Buddha presumed to attain Nirvana through cremation, some believe that through what may be a pathological, masochistic, or exhibitionistic act they, too, will find eternal bliss.

There's a conviction in our culture that no one, under any pretext, should provoke another to take his life. I take a giant step from that position and contend that most suicides can and should be prevented. However, I have no assurance that any tactic or technique, even those I describe and advocate in this text, is always a successful intervention against suicide.

A woman came to me after her daughter had died by suicide. She suffers from bipolar affect disorder. The daughter had ignored suggestions that she should see a psychiatrist when, at the age of 18, she began to show signs of cyclic depression. In her grief, the mother sat across the desk from me. She pleaded that she felt totally alone and could obtain no solace from her husband, a rather crude fellow without much empathy. She put her head down on my desk and wept. Then she reached across the desk, her hand moving toward me in a desperate gesture, like a drowning swimmer grasping a board. There was no hesitation. It was a fair, just, therapeutically sound intervention I then performed. At that instant I don't believe I was primarily thinking of psychoanalytic mechanisms and strategies. They would come later. I took her hand and held it for a long moment. She seemed to take strength from my offering and I said simply, "I don't want you to die as your daughter died." She thoroughly understood the meaning of my moment of sharing with her. In the end, the patient made a reasonably good resolution of her daughter's death.

An 82-year-old man made a serious attempt at killing himself five years after his wife had died. Eventually he recovered from the physical effects of severe drug intoxication and became my patient on the psychiatric ward.

After many weeks of psychotherapy, he was discharged and was taken in by one, then another of his sons. He saw me in the office several weeks after his release from the hospital. He had a sparkle in his eye and remarked that he had a surprise for me. He said, "I know now why I didn't die when I tried to kill myself." Several days before he had been in the kitchen of his son's home. His five-year-old grandson ran into the kitchen on some impulse and accidentally struck at the handle of a pot on the stove which contained boiling water. The old man said, "The instant I pulled the boy away from the stove, and saved him from severe scalding, I knew that what I had done—my suicide—was wrong. There is a reason I need to be alive."

A random thought worries me. The cause of many suicidal acts is an aggressive intent that is turned from the object, another person, to the self. Examples are the new mother who commits suicide rather than kill her infant, the adolescent boy who runs the car into an abutment rather than turn his wrath against his perpetually dissatisfied father, the girl who cuts her throat instead of killing her unfaithful boyfriend. In each instance, murderous impulsions are converted by the alchemy of hate, love, or fear into suicidal acts.

When we rescue a self-destructive person who is in a reflexive, suicidal mode, is there significant danger we may reconstitute the original, other-directed hostile intent? Is there a possibility we may make murderers out of potential suicides? I do not know, but the responsibility to learn the answer is grave.

Carl Sagan and other students of the universe may find conclusive evidence that life exists elsewhere than on earth. Pending such momentous news, for all we know all the life there is exists right here among us. All we personally have is the spark within ourselves. It seems reasonable that if life is so rare, its destruction for any reason is an act of reckless, wanton, awful vandalism. For each of us, if there is only "one to a customer, no exchanges, no returns," we should make the most of the life we have for as long as it is our fortune to possess it.

But why not suicide? Why does anyone bother to stay alive? The imperative seems to be baked into our genetic material. Any living form that does not have, or loses, this unarguable mandate, cannot, does not, survive. Evidently, the programming of everything living requires that it persist until its vital processes are somehow frustrated by running out of raw materials, such as protein and oxygen; or the breaking down of parts by injury, age, or disease; or changes in environment that become inimical to the individual.

Whether produced by the fortuitous concatenation of incredible coincidences or by the will of God, life—that is, being alive—is the main, perhaps the only real reason for living.

Man may be the *only* species that questions the value of life, and with varying degrees of volitional and knowing intent assumes the right to terminate it prematurely.

Though I have stressed the somber nature and maleficent effects of suicide, the optimistic view is that those who commit suicide are a small minority. Sinister as it is, suicide ranks fairly far down the list of causes of death, perhaps 10th. When asked, a majority will admit having fleeting thoughts of self-destruction

215

or of being dead. However, a surprising number of people deny they have ever had suicidal ideation, even under the most grievous circumstances. This sentiment has been voiced by those who have been badly injured, suffered painful and disfiguring mutilations or terrible personal losses, are in the last stages of terminal diseases, or who have been abused victims of war, pestilence, or political oppression.

What special psychological binding forces hold their egos together? How did these forces develop, from what root did they grow? How can they be taught or implanted in others? We don't know, but the study of suicidology will address itself to such immunity in expanding research.

In addition to the inertial pace that keeps living beings alive from the moment the little chemical explosion kicks the spark from the germ plasm of sperm and egg to a new living entity, the experience of sensory, spiritual, and intellectual pleasures makes existence worthwhile. Beyond these pleasures, granted or promised, in the near and distant future, there is also the satisfaction of curiosity. The optimism that makes old men plant new trees is commingled with the exclusively human rousing interest in exploration, in wanting to know everything humanly knowable, which can only be implemented in a state of life.

There are many authorities who offer reasons to choose to live. Sir William Schwenck Gilbert, who believed suicide is a bit of folly, ironically and highly ridiculed it in *The Mikado:*

"He sobbed and he sighed, and a gurgle he gave,
   Then he plunged himself into the billowy wave,
   And an echo arose from the suicide's grave—
   'Oh willow, titwillow, titwillow!' . . .
   There's a fascination frantic
   In a ruin that's romantic;
Do you think you are sufficiently decayed?"

The Bible has some strong and appropriate observations which validate how good it is to live, how abysmally final it is to die. In Ecclesiastes, Chapter 7: "Be not overmuch wicked, neither be thou foolish; why should thou die before thy time?" And in Chapter 9: "For to him that is joined to all the living there is hope: for a living dog is better than a dead lion." And: "For the living know that they shall die; but the dead know not anything, neither have they any more a reward; for the memory of them is forgotten." And further: "Also their love, and their hatred, and their envy, is now perished; neither have they any more a portion for ever in any thing that is done under the sun."

Living isn't always easy, but dying, especially by suicide, is even more difficult. As the singer reflects in George Gershwin's "Ole Man River," "I'm tired of livin' and scared of dyin' . . ." A reason that blocks some suicides is the high probability of botching the job, either because of ignorance of the effectiveness of the suicidal means or because of gross inefficiency. Undoubtedly, the ambivalence that haunts many depressed patients provides a strong if unconscious guard against self-destructive acts. Further, remarkable medical advances make it possible to rescue many self-injured patients who, 20 years ago, would have died but are now saved by effective medical and surgical emergency interventions. In one year I attended four suicide victims who shot themselves in the head with handguns. All four have survived with varying permanent mental, physical, and cosmetic deficiencies.

Then, of course, there is the matter of chance. O. Henry wrote a story about a would-be suicide who was down on his luck and turned on the gas. The meter turned off because he didn't have a quarter, and he survived. Clive of India in his early career suffered setbacks. He resolved to kill himself and put a revolver to his head. Five times he pulled the trigger, five times the gun misfired. He assumed he was not meant to die. What can be said of the caprice of fate that saved a woman who jumped from the Empire State Building in New York? A strong gust of wind blew her falling body back against the facing, and she landed on a parapet, suffering only a fractured leg.

The final word was written by a contemporary humorist, Dorothy Parker, who admonishes:
"Razors pain you;
Rivers are damp;
Acids stain you;
And drugs cause cramp.

Guns aren't lawful;
Nooses give;
Gas smells awful;
You might as well live."

Appendices

APPENDIX A Administrative policy regarding suicide and homicide

I. **PURPOSE:** To keep a suspected or confirmed suicidal and/or homicidal patient from harming himself and others.

II. **SCOPE:** This policy affects the physicians and all staff personnel involved in providing patient services.

III. **RESPONSIBILITY:** The attending physician or his designee and the nursing staff are responsible for carrying out this policy and procedure.

IV. **PROCEDURE**

A. **Admitting**
1. Patients who are suicidal/homicidal may be admitted to any nursing division and remain if:
   a) no bed is available on the psychiatric unit;
   b) the patient is cleared medically by a physician for transfer to the psychiatric unit; or
   c) the responsibility for the care of the patient has not been accepted by a designated psychiatrist.
2. Admit the patient to a room as close as possible to the nurses' station and block the other bed. Assign to a private room if available.
3. Contact psychiatric division personnel for consultation.

4. The physician's admission note and nursing staff observations must state presence and indicate the relative severity of suicide/homicide risk.

5. The physician must state on the order sheet that suicidal and/or homicidal precautions shall be taken in relation to the estimated degree of risk.

B. **Care of the patient: Once the patient is admitted and while waiting for a psychiatric consult and disposition, the following steps should be taken:**

1. Request a family member or friend to stay with the patient or make arrangements for a sitter, unless otherwise ordered by the psychiatrist.

2. If family member/friend is not available, arrangements shall be made to obtain a sitter unless otherwise ordered by the psychiatrist. Note: A sitter shall be responsible for observing the patient at all times, under the supervision of the nursing staff, but the presence of a sitter *does not* release nurses from full responsibility.

3. If none of the above arrangements can be made, obtain an order from the attending physician and/or designee or the psychiatrist for restraints.

C **Nursing responsibilities**

1. Restrict patient to his room.

2. A member of the nursing staff must observe patient at least every 30 minutes—more often if alone and in restraints. Documentation shall be noted on the chart on a separate sheet and also on the inside of the patient's closet door.

3. Free room of objects potentially dangerous to the patient:
   a) Two (2) staff members check room for restricted items. See Restricted Items list.
   b) Remove overbed stand.
   c) Remove light cords and eliminate hazards from electrical sources.
   d) Remove signal cord and replace with tap bell.
   e) Have housekeeping remove blinds and drapes with cords.
   f) Remove radio pillow speaker.
   g) Remove telephone and table or support bracket.

RESTRICTED ITEMS

Glass vases	Glass items
Nail files	All spray containers
Nail clippers	Mirrors
Nail polish	Crochet hooks
Nail polish remover	Knitting hooks

Perfume	Electric equipment (except
Picture frames	battery-powered radio)
Matches	Alcoholic beverages
Scissors	Pins
Needles	Pop cans
Knives	Hangers
Guns	Plastic bags
Tweezers	Lighters
Electric razor	Razor blades

4. Place patient's belongings in personal belongings bag, label, and keep at the nursing station.
5. Take only rectal or axillary temperatures. Keep thermometers locked in bathroom out of patient's reach.
6. Meal trays
   a) Mark or stamp diet sheet *Special Precautions.*
   b) When serving meal to patient, assure that paper or styrofoam service and plastic utensils are on the tray *before* and *after* the meal. Document on the chart. *Report any missing items to the charge nurse STAT.*
7. When administering oral medications, observe that patient swallows the drugs. Do mouth check if necessary. Do not leave ointments and lotions in the patient's room.
8. Maintain side rails and restraints as needed.
9. Remain with patient until completion of any routine procedure.
10. Document relevant conversations and observations accurately in nurses' notes. Any statement about intention to do violence must be accurately stated.

V. IDENTIFIED SUICIDAL/HOMICIDAL PATIENTS: Potentially violent patients should be reported immediately to the attending physician or designee. Implementation of suicidal/homicidal precautions is to be initiated with the least possible delay.

If the physician is not available and/or refuses to acknowledge the risk, the charge nurse shall notify the nursing supervisor. The chief of staff shall then be notified of the special hazard.

If the threat is recognized:

A. **8:00 a.m.–4:30 p.m.: Nursing supervisor also shall notify department head, the chief executive officer, and the president of the executive committee.**
B. **4:00 p.m.–12:30 a.m.; 12:00 p.m.–8:30 a.m.; weekends and holidays: Nursing supervisor shall notify the administrator on call.**

VI. ELOPEMENT OF SUSPECTED SUICIDAL/HOMICIDAL PATIENT

A. Staff member shall immediately notify the nurse in charge.
B. Nurse in charge:
  1. Requires the ward clerk to notify security and the information desk with a description of the patient.
  2. Notifies the nursing supervisor.
  3. Notifies the attending physician and/or designee.
  4. Assigns staff members to search within the hospital grounds.
     a) If unable to locate the patient within thirty (30) minutes, staff members return to the nursing division and inform the charge nurse.
     b) If the patient is found, the staff member should attempt to persuade him to return to the ward voluntarily. Physical effort to detain, restrain, or return the patient to the hospital against his will is not permitted unless legal sanction for involuntary status has been previously established.
  5. Notifies the family of the facts regarding the situation.
C. If the patient has committed an act of violence against himself or others, resulting in injury or damage to property in the act of elopement, or if the patient has been admitted by a legal restraining order, the police are to be called by the nursing supervisor and/or security and asked to assist in the search for and apprehension of the patient.
  1. The attending physician will be notified of this action.
  2. The nursing supervisor will decide if and when the hospital administrator will be called.
  3. The immediate family is to be notified of developments as they occur.
  4. Disposition of the patient to be determined, depending on condition and prevailing circumstances, by attending physician in consultation with the administrator.
D. The nurse in charge is to complete incident reports and submit them to the nursing service office and ensure that accurate documentation has been completed on the patient's chart.

VII. SUICIDE/HOMICIDE RISK LABEL

A. The chart of any patient deemed to be suicidal, homicidal, or potentially violent is to be identified with a special chart label.
B. The label is an informal signal that alerts all personnel that the patient may be violent or dangerous to self and others.
C. Label may be applied by a nurse with approval of a supervisor or by a physician.

1. No physician's written order is required.
2. Physician should be notified within 24 hours of application of label.
3. Label is automatically instituted when suicidal precautions are ordered by a physician.
4. The reason for instituting the label will be documented in either the nurses' notes or the physician's progress note.
5. Label will be removed by physician's order only.
6. Label will be affixed to the front of the chart for as long as it is in effect and will read in capital letters ADMINISTRATIVE POLICY IN EFFECT. No other wording is to be used.

VIII. SUICIDE/HOMICIDE PRECAUTIONS

A. **Suicide/homicide precautions are protective procedures to be instituted for any patient who may be considered a potential threat to himself or others. This will include suicidal, assaultive, or homicidal patients.**
B. **The procedure is divided into three categories:**
   1. Grade I—suspected suicide/homicide risk,
   2. Grade II—serious suicide/homicide risk, and
   3. Grade III—extreme suicide/homicide risk.
C. **A nurse may institute this procedure at any time, if deemed necessary.**
   1. The physician must be notified, and a written order is to be obtained.
   2. Procedures remain in effect until discontinued by a written order of the physician.
D. **The names of all patients on suicide/homicide precautions are written in red ink on the observation list.**
E. **The Kardex care plan of these patients carries a green tag with written specification of Grade I, Grade II, or Grade III.**
F. **The status of these patients shall be discussed daily by the treatment team.**
G. **The patient should receive an explanation of the procedures and should be advised what to expect in regard to day-to-day care.**

IX. GRADE I—SUSPECTED SUICIDE/HOMICIDE RISK: The patient whose ideational trend and verbal content suggests rumination and consideration of death by suicide or of other violent acts.

A. **The patient is ambivalent about wanting to live or die, but has no definite plan to commit suicide or other act of violence, and there** has been no suicide attempt or overt act of violence. The patient acknowledges he is fearful of his thought content and impulse control.

B. The following policies relate to this level of suicide precaution:

1. The patient must be seen by a nurse (RN), licensed practical nurse (LPN), or nurse attendant (NA) no less often than every half-hour.

2. Nurses' notes on the patient's chart will include a résumé of the patient's behavior and activities and a statement that the patient was seen every half-hour. This shall be instituted on each shift.

3. Some items on the Restricted List may be used. However, the RN, LPN, or NA must make checks while the patient is using any restricted item and must assure that the item is returned to the nurses' station immediately after use. The patient's assigned RN, LPN, or NA will be responsible to issue the restricted item and assure control and supervision.

4. The patient may go off the ward, accompanied by an RN, LPN, or NA, if:
   a) the RN, LPN, or NA judges the patient is under control and compliant, and
   b) the patient indicates to the RN, LPN, or NA that he feels in control of his thought processes and will be compliant.

5. The patient may go on therapeutic home visits, accompanied by a person specifically requested by the physician, if the person responsible for the patient understands and accepts the need for protecting the patient away from the hospital and agrees not to leave the patient alone at any time while away from the hospital.

6. The patient may have visitors.

7. The patient may participate in general ward activities.

8. The patient may have regular dishes and utensils.

9. The patient may wear his/her own clothing.

10. A room search is to be done by two (2) staff members whenever it is suspected that the patient may have a dangerous item in his possession.

X. **GRADE II—SERIOUS SUICIDE/HOMICIDE RISK:** The patient whose thought content is primarily and admittedly suicidal.

A. **The patient is no longer ambivalent about wanting to live or die, but has arranged a plan of action. The patient's actions are directed toward self-destruction (e.g., saving medications, attempt-**

ing to hide silverware, failure or refusal to return razor to RN,
LPN, or NA after use and then denying it).
B. The following policies relate to this level of suicide precaution:
1. The patient must be seen by the RN, LPN, or NA every quarter-hour or less.
2. Nurses' notes on the patient's chart will include a résumé of the patient's behavior and activities, with a statement that the patient has been seen every quarter-hour. This shall be in-stituted on each shift.
3. Restricted items may be used but only in the presence of the patient's RN, LPN, or NA. For example, the RN, LPN, or NA must remain with the patient who is shaving with a razor.
4. The patient may go off the ward for procedures and treatments ordered by the physician, such as X-rays, scans, EEGs, con-sultations, only if accompanied by one or more staff members.
5. The patient may not go home on therapeutic home visits.
6. The patient may have visitors. However, the assigned care-giver should check with the visitors to make certain they understand that they are not to give the patient any items on the Restricted List. It should be determined that the visitor is welcome by the patient and is not upsetting to him/her.
7. The patient may participate in general ward activities unless ordered otherwise by the physician.
8. The patient may wear his/her own clothing.
9. Regular dishes and utensils may be used. However, they may not be left unattended with the patient. A utensil count should be done before and after the meal.
10. The patient should be assigned to a room close to the nurses' station and the intercom turned on at all times while the patient is in the room.
11. A room search is to be done by two (2) staff members at least once a day and whenever it is suspected that the patient may have a dangerous item in his/her possession.

XI. **GRADE III—EXTREME SUICIDE/HOMICIDE RISK:** The patient whose behavior, both verbally and nonverbally, is almost totally in the direction of self-destruction.

A. **The patient must have constant nursing attendance or constant attendance by a family member or close friend under close super-vision of the nurse. There shall be documentation to this effect in the nurses' notes on the patient's chart for each shift.**
B. **No restricted items may be used unless specifically ordered in writing by the physician.**

C. The patient may not go off the ward except when specially ordered by the physician. When he leaves the ward at least two competent attendants shall accompany the patient.

D. No visitors shall be permitted except as sitters, as noted in A. above.

E. Paper dishes and plastic utensils shall be used. If necessary, plastic utensils may be restricted and finger foods ordered for the patient.

F. The patient is to wear a hospital gown at all times.

G. The patient is to be placed in a seclusion room with reduced environmental stimuli.

   1. All extra furniture and other articles should be removed from the room.

   2. If necessary, the mattress may be removed from the bedframe and placed on the floor.

   3. Restraints should be used for further protection, if necessary, by order of the physician.

   4. The intercom is to be turned on and monitored at all times.

APPENDIX B Index of state laws regarding suicide

CRIMINAL STATUTES	KEY TO INDEX
Suicide:	Criminal penalties for completed suicide.
Attempted suicide:	Criminal penalties for attempted suicide.
Aiding or advising suicide; suicide pacts:	Criminal penalties for aiding another in committing suicide or for forming suicide pacts.
May use force to prevent suicide:	Statutes expressly permitting the use of reasonable force to prevent another from taking his/her own life.
Coroner or medical examiner must be notified immediately:	Statutes providing criminal penalties for anyone with knowledge of a suicide who fails to immediately notify the coroner or medical examiner.

CIVIL STATUTES

Natural death: Statutes allowing individuals to refuse extraordinary life-support measures in certain cases. "Not a suicide" by legislative fiat.

Life insurance: Statutes that limit an insurance company's denial of payment on life insurance or double-indemnity policy claims in cases of suicide.

Workers' Compensation: Statutes affecting recovery of Workers' Compensation payments in cases of suicide.

Nonforfeiture of estates of suicide victims: Statutes expressly abolishing common laws of escheat or forfeiture of the land and property of suicide victims to the state.

New York and Oklahoma lead the nation in statutes dealing with legal aspects of suicide. In Texas, it is a misdemeanor to threaten to commit suicide within earshot of a law-enforcement official. Alabama, California, and Minnesota have criminal penalties for the accidental death of another in connection with a suicide attempt. For current information in your state, consult an attorney.

	Criminal statutes					Civil statutes			
	Suicide	Attempted suicide	Aiding or advising suicide; suicide pacts	May use force to prevent suicide	Coroner or medical examiner must be notified immediately	Natural death	Life insurance	Workers' Compensation	Nonforfeiture of estates of suicide victims
Alabama			■					■	
Alaska			■				■		
Arizona			■			■			
Arkansas			■						
California			■	■	■				■
Colorado			■				■		■
Connecticut			■	■					
Delaware			■						
District of Columbia									
Florida			■				■		
Georgia				■	■		■		
Hawaii			■	■	■				
Idaho									
Illinois									
Indiana			■						
Iowa							■		
Kansas			■		■		■		
Kentucky									
Louisiana									
Maine			■						
Maryland				■					■
Massachusetts							■	■	
Michigan									
Minnesota			■				■		
Mississippi			■				■		
Missouri				■			■		
Montana			■						

231

| | Criminal statutes | | | | | Civil statutes | | | |
State	Suicide	Attempted suicide	Aiding or advising suicide: suicide pacts	May use force to prevent suicide	Coroner or medical examiner must be notified immediately	Natural death	Life insurance	Workers' Compensation	Nonforfeiture of estates of suicide victims
Nebraska									
Nevada			■						
New Hampshire			■	■					
New Jersey				■					
New Mexico			■				■		
New York			■				■		
N. Carolina						■			
N. Dakota							■		
Ohio					■				
Oklahoma	■	■			■		■		
Oregon									
Pennsylvania									
Rhode Island				■	■				
S. Carolina									
S. Dakota			■				■		
Tennessee									
Texas	■				■		■		
Utah									
Vermont									
Virginia							■		
Washington			■				■	■	
W. Virginia			■					■	■
Wisconsin			■	■	■				
Wyoming									
Puerto Rico			■						
Virgin Islands			■						

APPENDIX C Bibliography

A manual on how to commit suicide. *Newsweek*, April 7, 1980, p 77.

Adelson L: The forensic pathologist: Family physician to the bereaved. *JAMA* 237:1585–1588, 1977.

Akiskal HS, Bitar AH, Puzantlan VR, et al: The nosological status of neurotic depression. *Arch Gen Psychiatry* 35:756–766, 1978.

Albert N, Beck AT: Incidence of depression in early adolescence: A preliminary study. *J Youth Adolesc* 4:301–307, 1975.

Aleksandrowicz MK: The biological strangers: An attempted suicide of a seven-and-a-half-year-old girl. *Bull Menninger Clin* 39:163–176, 1975.

Allen MD, Greenblatt PJ, Noel BJ: Overdosage with antipsychotic agents. *Am J Psychiatry* 137:2, 1980.

Alvarez A: *The Savage God. A Study of Suicide.* New York: Random House, 1970.

Ansel EL: *Correlates of Volunteer Performance in a Suicide Prevention/Crisis Intervention Service.* Unpublished thesis, University of Florida, 1972.

Babescu S: The threat of suicide in psychotherapy. *Am J Psychother* 19:99–105, 1965.

Bagley C, Greer S: Black suicide: A report of 25 English cases and controls. *J Soc Psychol* 86:175–179, 1972.

Baker R: Adolescent depression: An illness or developmental task? *J Adolesc* 1:297–307, 1978.

Bancroft J, Hawton K, Simkin S, et al: The reasons people give for taking overdoses: A further inquiry. Br J Psychiatry 52:353–365, 1979.

Barraclough BM, Shepard DM: The immediate and enduring effects of the inquest on relatives of suicides. Br J Psychiatry 131:400–404, 1977.

Bauer AC: Emotional disorders among doctors. New York Times, May 19, 1981, pp 13–14.

Beck AT, Beck M, Kovacs M: Classification of suicidal behaviors, I: Quantifying intent and medical lethality. Am J Psychiatry 132:285–287, 1975.

Beck AT, Kovacs M, Weissman A: Assessment of suicidal intention: The scale for suicidal ideation. J Consult Clin Psychol 47:343–352, 1979.

Beck AT, Kovacs M, Weissman A: Hopelessness and suicidal behavior: An overview. JAMA 234:1146–1149, 1975.

Beck AT, Schuyler D, Herman I: Development of suicidal intent scales. In The Prediction of Suicide, Beck AT, Reswick HLP, Lettieri DJ (eds). Bowie, Md: Charles Press, 1974, pp 45–56.

Beck AT, Weissman A, Lester D, et al: Classifications of suicidal behaviors, II: Dimensions of suicidal intent. Arch Gen Psychiatry 33:835–837, 1976.

Beck AT, Weissman A, Lester D, et al: The measurement of pessimism: The hopelessness scale. J Consult Clin Psychol 42:861–865, 1974.

Beck R, Morris J, Beck AT: Cross-validation of the suicidal intent scale. Psychol Rep 34:445–446, 1974.

Bergman J: The suicide rate among psychiatrists revisited. Suicide Life Threat Behav 9:219–226, 1979.

Berman AL: Dyadic death: Murder-suicide. Suicide Life Threat Behav 9:15–23, 1979.

Berman AL: Let me die not alone. Unpublished, 1981.

Bittker JE: Reaching out to the depressed physician. JAMA 236:1713–1716.

Blachly PH: Suicide as seduction: A concept for evaluation of suicidal risk. Hosp Med 5:117, 1969.

Bremer WS: Help for the impaired physician. Postgrad Med 67: 39, 1980.

Brook M: Dilemma: Suicide threat during psychoanalysis. Bull Phil Assoc Psychoanal 23:189–207, 1973.

Bruyn HB, Seiden RH: Student suicide: Fact or fancy? J Amer Coll Health Assoc 14:69–77, 1965.

Burke AW: Clinical aspects of attempted suicide among women in Trinidad and Tobago. Br J Psychiatry 125:175–176, 1974.

Bush JA: Similarities and differences in precipitating events between black and Anglo suicide attempts. Suicide Life Threat Behav 8:243–249, 1978.

Cain AC, Fast J: Children's disturbed reactions to parent suicide. *Am J Orthopsychiatry* 36:873–880, 1966.

Canton PC: Personality characteristics found among youthful female suicide attempters. *J Abnorm Psychol* 85:324–329, 1976.

Cantor P: The effects of youthful suicide on family. *Psychiatr Opin* 12:6–11, 1975.

Carpenter RG: Statistical analysis of suicide and other mortality rates of students. *Br J Prevent Soc Med* 13:163, 1959.

Cohen W: *The Substance Abuse Problems.* New York: Haworth, 1981.

Combrinch-Graham L: Suicidal children. *Clin Pediatr* 19:447, 1980.

Comstock BS: Suicide in the 1970s: A closer look. *Suicide Life Threat Behav* 9:3–13, 1979.

Corder BF, Shorr W, Corder F: A study of social and psychological characteristics of adolescent suicide attempters in an urban, disadvantaged area. *Adolescence* 9:1–6, 1974.

Cranshaw R, Bruce JA, Eraker PL, et al: An epidemic of suicide among physicians on probation. *JAMA* 243:1915–1917, 1980.

Current opinions of the judicial council of the American Medical Association, 1981.

Daniel WA: Suicide in adolescence. *Acta Paediatr Scand* 256:36–38, 1975.

Deaths according to cause. *World Health Statistics Annual,* 1980.

Delano JG: Psychiatric implications of the teen-agers' problems. *JAMA* 184:539–539–543, 1963.

Dictor RM: Suicidal patients among admissions to Louisville General Hospital (1961–1970): Incidences and diagnostic conclusions. *J Ky Med Assoc* 70:773–776, 1972.

Diller J: The psychological autopsy in equivocal deaths. *Perspect Psychiatr Care* 17:1–6, 1979.

Dorpat TL, Ripley HS: The relationship between attempted suicide and committed suicide. *Compr Psychiatry* 8:74–79, 1967.

Drye RC, Goulding RL, Goulding MR: No-suicide decisions: Patient monitoring of suicidal risk. *Am J Psychiatry* 130:171–174, 1973.

Duboin LI: *Suicide: A Sociological and Statistical Study.* New York: Ronald Press, 1963.

Durkheim E: *Suicide.* New York: Free Press, 1951.

Eisenberg L: Adolescent suicide: On taking arms against a sea of troubles. *Pediatrics* 66:315–320, 1980.

235

Appendices

Epstein LC, Thomas CB, Shaffer JW, et al: Clinical prediction of physician suicide passed on medical student data. *J Nerv Ment Dis* 156:19–29, 1973.

Farberow NL: Suicide prevention in the hospital. *Hosp Community Psychiatry* 32:99–104, 1981.

Fawcet J, Leff M, Bunney WE: Suicide: Clues from interpersonal communication. *Arch Gen Psychiatry* 21:129–137, 1969.

Feggetter G: Suicide in opera. *Br J Psychiatry* 136:522–557, 1980.

Flanagan MD, Greenblatt PJ, Noel BJ: Overdosage with antipsychotic agents. *Am J Psychiatry* 137:2, 1980.

Flanagan P: Hopelessness, a key to potential suicide. *Prac Psychol Physician* 3:60–61, 65–67, 1976.

Fleming JC: It can happen here. *Postgrad Med* 67:27–31, 1980.

Frederick CJ: Current trends in suicidal behavior in the United States. *Am J Psychother* 32:172–200, 1978.

Frederick CJ: The suicide-prone depressive: The widening circle. In *Depression in the '80s, a Symposium.* New York, 1980, pp 33–46.

French AF, Steward SM: Family dynamics, children, depression, and attempted suicide in a 7-year-old boy. *Suicide* 5:29–37, 1975.

Gibbs WF: Therapy for suicidal patients. *Va Med Month* 85: 139–141, 1958.

Goldberg EL: Depression and suicide ideation in the young adult. *Am J Psychiatry* 138:35–40, 1981.

Harris R, Linn MW, Hunter KI: Suicide attempts among drug abusers. *Suicide Life Threat Behav* 9:25–32, 1979.

Heinz L: Annotated bibliography of suicide: AJPH, 1911–1978, and PHR, 1930–1978. *Suicide Life Threat Behav* 8:257–262, 1978.

Hellon CP, Solomon MI: Suicide and age in Alberta, Canada, 1951 to 1977. *Arch Gen Psychiatry* 37:505–510, 1980.

Henderson S, Lance GN: Types of attempted suicide (parasuicide). *Acta Psychiatr Scand* 59:31, 1979.

Hendin H: Student suicide: Death as a life style. *J Nerv Ment Dis* 160:204–219, 1975.

Hendin H: Suicide: The psychosocial dimension. *Suicide Life Threat Behav* 8:99–117, 1978.

Hirsch CS, Rushforth NB, Ford AB, et al: Homicide and suicide in a metropolitan county, I: Long-term trends. *JAMA* 223:900–905, 1973.

Hitchcock J, Wolford JA: Alternatives to the suicide prevention approach to mental health. *Arch Gen Psychiatry* 22:547–549, 1970.

Hoffman A: Adolescents in distress: Suicide and out-of-control behaviors. *Med Clin North Am* 59: 1429–1437, 1975.

Holinger PC: Adolescent suicide: An epidemiologic study of recent trends. *Am J Psychiatry* 135:754, 1978.

Holinger PC: Suicide and adolescence. *Am J Psychiatry* 134:1433–1434, 1977.

Holinger PC: Violent deaths among the young: Recent trends in suicide, homicide, and accidents. *Am J Psychiatry* 136:114–117, 1979.

Hospitals' duty to the suicidal. *Br Med J* 4:754, 1970.

International rise in suicide. *Statistical Bulletin*, March 1967.

Jacobziner H: Attempted suicides in adolescence, *JAMA* 191:101–105, 1965.

Jenkins J, Sainsbury P: Single-car road deaths: Disguised suicides? *Br J Psychiatry* 201:1041, 1980.

Kelly WA: Suicide and psychiatric education. *Am J Psychiatry* 130:463–468, 1973.

Kendra JM: Predicting suicide using the Rorschach ink blot test. *J Pers Assess* 43:452–456, 1979.

Kerfoot M: Parent-child role reversal and adolescent suicidal behavior. *J Adolesc* 2:337–343, 1979.

Kiev A: Psychotherapeutic strategies in the management of suicidal patients. *Am J Psychiatry* 29:345, 1975.

Kitchen LW: Suicide among medical students. *West J Med* 129:441–442, 1978.

Kovacs M, Beck AT, Weissman A: Hopelessness: An indicator of suicidal risk. *Suicide* 5:98–103, 1975.

Kovacs M, Beck AT, Weissman A: The communication of suicidal intent. *Arch Gen Psychiatry* 33:198–201, 1976.

Kraft DP, Babigian AM: Suicide by persons with and without psychiatric contacts. *Arch Gen Psychiatry* 33:209–215, 1976.

Krueger DW, Hutcherson R: Suicide attempts by rock-climbing falls. *Suicide Life Threat Behav* 8:41–45, 1978.

Lester D, Beck AT: Attempted suicide in alcoholics and drug addicts. *J Stud Alcohol* 36:162–164, 1975.

Lester D, Beck AT: Early loss as a possible "sensitizer" to later loss in attempted suicides. *Psychol Rep* 39:121–122, 1976.

Lester D, Beck AT: Suicide and national holidays. *Psychol Rep* 36:52, 1975.

Lester D, Beck AT, Mitchell B: Extrapolation from attempted suicides to completed suicides: A test. *J Abnorm Psychol* 88:78–80, 1979.

Lifschutz, 85 Cal Rptr 829,476P 2nd 557 (Cal Sup Ct, 1970), discussed in 22 The Citation 49 (1970).

Lifton RJ: The appeal of the death trip. *New York Times Magazine*, January 7, 1979.

Litman RE: Psycholegal aspects of suicide. In *Modern Legal Medicine*, Curran CE et al (eds). Philadelphia: Davis, 1980, pp 841–853.

Litman RE, Curphey T, Shneidman ES, et al: Investigations of equivocal suicides. *JAMA* 184:924–929, 1963.

Loughlin H: Suicide: A case for investigation. *J Psychiatr Nurs* 18:8–12, 1980.

Lukianowicz N: Attempted suicide in children. *Acta Psychiatr Scand* 44:415–435, 1968.

Lyons HA: Civil violence: The psychological aspects. *J Psychosom Res* 23:373–393, 1979.

Mackay A: Self-poisoning: A complication of epilepsy. *Br J Psychiatry* 134:277–282, 1979.

McIntire MS, Angle CR: Evaluation of suicidal risk in adolescents. *J Fam Pract* 2:5, 1975.

Management in hospital after attempted suicide. *Drug Ther Bull* 17:78–80, 1979.

Mannes M: *Last Rights*. New York: Morrow, 1974.

Maltsberger JT, Buie DH: Counter-transference hate in the treatment of suicidal patients. *Arch Gen Psychiatry* 30:625, 1974.

McCandless FD: Suicide and the communication of rage: A cross-cultural study. *Am J Psychiatry* 125:197–205, 1968.

McIntyre MS, Angle CR, Schlicht ML: Suicide and self-poisoning in pediatrics. *Res Staff Physician* 26:72–80, 85, 1980.

Metropolitan Life Insurance Company: Recent trends in suicide. *Statistical Bulletin* 57, 1976.

Miles CP: Conditions predisposing to suicide: A review. *J Nerv Ment Dis* 164:231–246, 1977.

Miller JP: Suicide and adolescence, *Adolescence* 10:11, 1975.

Minnaar GK, Schlebusch L, Levin A: A current study of parasuicide in Durban. *South Afr Med J* 57:204–207, 1980.

Mishara BL: The extent of adolescent suicidality. *Psychiatr Opin* 12:32–37, 1975.

Moore JT, Judd LL, Zung WW, et al: Opiate addiction and suicidal behaviors. *Am J Psychiatry* 136:1187–1189, 1979.

Motto JA: Newspaper influence on suicide. *Arch Gen Psychiatry* 23:143-148, 1970.

Motto JA: The psychopathology of suicide: A clinical model approach. *Am J Psychiatry* 136:516–520, 1979.

Motto JA: Treatment and management of suicidal adolescents. *Psychiatr Opin* 12:14–20, 1975.

Murphy GE: Clinical identification of suicidal risk. *Arch Gen Psychiatry* 27:356–359, 1972.

Murphy GE: The physician's responsibility for suicide, II: An error of commission. *Ann Intern Med* 82:301–304, 1975.

Murphy GE, Armstrong JW, Hermole SL, et al: Suicide and alcoholism. Interpersonal loss confirmed as a predictor. *Arch Gen Psychiatry* 36: 65–69, 1979.

Murphy GE, Robins E: Social factors in suicide. *JAMA* 199:303–308, 1967.

Murphy GE, Wetzel RD: Suicide risk by birth cohort in the United States, 1949 to 1974. *Arch Gen Psychiatry* 37:519–523, 1980.

Murphy GE, Wetzel RD, Swallow CS, et al: Who calls the suicide prevention center: A study of 55 persons calling on their own behalf. *Am J Psychiatry* 126:314–324, 1969.

Neill K, Benensohn HS, Resnik HL: The psychological autopsy: Technique for investigating a hospital suicide. *Hosp Community Psychiatry* 25:33–35, 1974.

Neuringer C: Problems in predicting adolescent suicidal behavior. *Psychiatr Opin* 12:27–31, 1975.

O'Brien PJ: A study of low-dose amitriptyline overdoses. *Am J Psychiatry* 134:66–68, 1977.

O'Brien PJ: Increase in suicide attempts by drug ingestion: The Boston experience, 1964–1974. *Arch Gen Psychiatry* 34:1165–1169, 1977.

Osgood NJ: Suicide in the elderly. *Postgrad Med* 72:123–130, 1982.

Pao PN: The syndrome of delicate self-cutting. *Br J Psychiatry* 42:195–206, 1969.

Papa LL: Responses to life events as predictors of suicidal behavior. *Nurs Res* 29:362–369, 1980.

Pasnau RO, Russell AT: Psychiatric resident suicide: An analysis of five cases. *Am J Psychiatry* 132:402–406, 1975.

Peck J: Youth suicide. Unpublished, 1980.

Pepitone-Rockwell F: Medical student suicides. *Mind Med* 8:7, 1981.

Perlin S (ed): *A Handbook for the Study of Suicide.* New York: Oxford University Press, 1975.

Perlstein A, Brozovsky M: Hospitalized suicidal adolescents—two generations. *J Am Acad Child Psychiatry* 14:268–280, 1975.

Perr IN: Suicide and civil litigation. *J Forensic Sci* 19:261–266, 1974.

Pfeffer CR: Suicidal behavior of children: A review with implications for research and practice. *Am J Psychiatry* 138:2, 1981.

Pfeffer CR, Conte HR, Plutchik R, et al: Suicidal behavior in latency-age children: An empirical study. *J Am Acad Child Psychiatry* 18:679–692, 1979.

Pfeffer CR, Conte HR, Plutchik R, et al: Suicidal behavior in latency-age children: An outpatient population. *J Am Acad Child Psychiatry* 19:703–710, 1980.

Plea from an impaired physician's wife. *Postgrad Med* 67:39, 1980.

Pokorny AD: Suicide rates in various psychiatric disorders. *J Nerv Ment Dis* 139:499–506, 1964.

Pritchard PB, Lombroso CT, McIntyre M: Psychological complications of temporal lobe epilepsy. *Neurology* 30:227–232, 1980.

Rado TA: Stress common to medical school students. *Psychiatry Dig* 38:16, 1977.

Reich P, Kelly MJ: Suicide attempts by hospitalized medical and surgical patients. *N Engl J Med* 294:298–301, 1976.

Resnik H: Suicide: A national epidemic. *Prac Psychiatry* 2:1–4, 1974.

Rich CL, Pitts FN Jr: Suicide by psychiatrists: A study of medical specialists among 18,730 consecutive physician deaths during a five-year period, 1967–1972. *J Clin Psychiatry* 41:261, 1980.

Richman J: Suicide and infantile fixations. *Suicide Life Threat Behav* 10:3–9, 1980.

Roberts JC, Hawton K: Child abuse and attempted suicide. *Lancet* 19:882, 1980.

Robins E, Murphy GE, Wilkinson RH, et al: Some clinical considerations in the prevention of suicide based on the study of 134 successful suicides. *Am J Public Health* 49:888–899, 1959.

Robins E, Schmidt EH, O'Neal P: Some inter-relations of social factors and clinical diagnosis and attempted suicide: A study of 109 patients. *Am J Psychiatry* 114:221–231, 1957.

Rosen DH: The serious suicide attempt: Epidemiological and follow-up study of 886 patients. *Am J Psychiatry* 127:764–770, 1970.

Rosen DH: The serious suicide attempt. *JAMA* 235:2105, 1976.

Rosenberg PH, Latimer R: Suicide attempts by children. *Ment Hygiene* 50:354–359, 1966.

Ross JR, Hewitt WL, Wahl CW, et al: The management of the presuicidal, suicidal, and postsuicidal patient. *Ann Intern Med* 75:441–458, 1971.

Ross M: Suicide among college students. *Am J Psychiatry* 127:220–225, 1969.

Rotov M: Death by suicide in the hospital: An analysis of 20 therapeutic failures. *Am J Psychother* 24:216–227, 1970.

Rounsaville BJ, Weissman MM: A note of suicidal behaviors among intimates. *Suicide Life Threat Behav* 10:24–28, 1980.

Rucker CM: How to prevent suicide. *Reflections* 12:55–60, 1977.

Ryndarson EK: Suicide internalized: An existential sequestrum. *Am J Psychiatry* 130:04–87, 1981.

Schizophrenics who try suicide at high risk for second try. *Clin Psychiatr News*, November 1979.

Schrut A: Suicidal adolescents and children. *JAMA* 188:1103–1107, 1964.

Seiden RH: Campus tragedy: A study of student suicide. *J Abnorm Psychol* 71:389–399, 1966.

Seiden RH: The problem of suicide on college campuses. *J Sch Health* 51:243–248, 1971.

Seiden RH: Where are they now? A follow-up study of suicide attempters from the Golden Gate Bridge. *Suicide Life Threat Behav* 8:203–216, 1978.

Seiden RH, Freitas RP: Shifting patterns of deadly violence. Proceedings of the Conference of the American Public Health Association, New York, November 6, 1979.

Shapiro S, Waltzer H: Successful suicides and serious attempts in a general hospital over a 15-year period. *Gen Hosp Psychiatry* 2:118–126, 1980.

Shepard DM, Barraclough BM: The aftermath of parental suicide for children. *Br J Psychiatry* 129:267–276, 1976.

Shneidman ES (ed): *Suicidology: Contemporary Developments*. New York: Grune & Stratton, 1976.

Shneidman ES, Dizmang LH: How the family physician can prevent suicide. *The Physician's Panorama*, June 1967, pp 5–10.

Shneidman ES, Farberow NL (eds): *Clues to suicide*. New York: McGraw-Hill, 1957.

Shupin S: Cults: Why so appealing? *Today in Psychiatry* 7:1–7, 1980.

Silver MA, Boynert M, Beck AT, et al: Relation of depression on attempted suicide and seriousness of intent. *Arch Gen Psychiatry* 25:573–576, 1971.

Stetten IW, Barton JL: Suicidal patients in the emergency room: A guide for evaluation and disposition. *Hosp Community Psychiatry* 6:407–411, 1979.

Stetten IW, Brown ML, Evenson RC, et al: Suicide in mental hospital patients. *Dis Nerv System* 30:324–334, 1972.

Steen LH: Physician suicide. Report of the Board of Trustees of the American Medical Association, Resolutions 49 and 50 (I–79), 1980.

Stein M, Levy MT, Glasberg ML: Separations in black and white suicide attempters. *Arch Gen Psychiatry* 31:815–821, 1974.

Steppachner RC, Mausner JS: Suicide in male and female physicians. *JAMA* 228:323–328, 1974.

Stone ML: The suicidal patient: Points concerning diagnosis and intensive treatment. *Psychiatr Q* 52:52–70, 1980.

Strong RW: Gunshot wounds of adolescents. *Med J Aust* 1:113–115, 1980.

Suicide and the Samaritans. *Lancet* 2:772, 1978.

Suicide in prisons. *Psychiatr News*, October 5, 1979.

Suicide: International comparisons. *J Health and Soc Behav* 13:99–104, 1972.

Suicide rates. U.S. Department of Health and Human Services, Vital Statistics, 1978.

Szasz TS: The ethics of suicide. *Antioch Rev* 21:7–17, 1971.

Tabachnick N: Subintentioned self-destruction in teenagers. *Psychiatr Opin* 12:21–26, 1975.

Tabachnick N: The crisis treatment of suicide. *Calif Med* 112:1–8, 1970.

Tarasoff v Regents of the University of California, 118 Cal Rptr 1'29, 529 P2d 553 (Cal Sup Ct, 1974).

Teenage suicide. *Pediatrics* 66:144–146, 1980.

Teenage suicide: A tragic impulse. *MD* 25:49–52, 1981.

Teicher JD, Jacobs J: Adolescents who attempt suicide: Preliminary findings. *Am J Psychiatry* 122:1248–1257, 1966.

Toolan JM: Suicide and suicidal attempts in children and adolescents. *Am J Psychiatry* 188:19, 1962.

Troutman EC: Suicide attempts of Puerto Rican immigrants. *Psychiatr Q* 35:544–554, 1961.

Valko RJ, Clayton PJ: Depression in internship. *Dis Nerv System* 36:26–29, 1975.

Vandivort DS, Locke PZ: Suicide ideation: Its relation to depression, suicide, and suicide attempt. *Suicide Life Threat Behav* 9:205–218, 1979.

Victoroff J, Victoroff VM: A report on the recognition and management of suicidal patients at a metropolitan hospital, July 1974–December 1975. Unpublished.

Vital statistics. *Statistical Abstract of the U.S.*, 12th ed, 1979.

Wall JH: The psychiatric problem of suicide. *Am J Psychiatry* 101:404–406, 1944.

Weiner A, Marten S, Wochnick, et al: Psychiatric disorders among professional women. *Arch Gen Psychiatry* 36:169–173, 1979.

Weissman A, Beck AT, Kovacs M: Drug abuse, hopelessness, and suicidal behavior. *Int J Addict* 14:451–464, 1979.

Welti CV, Bednarcyzk: Deaths related to propoxyphene overdose: A 10-year assessment. *South Med J* 73:1205–1209, 1980.

Wenz FV: Multiple suicide attempts and informal labeling: An exploratory study. *Suicide Life Threat Behav* 8:3–13, 1978.

Wexler L, Weissman MM, Karl SV: Suicide attempts 1970–1975: Updating a United States study and comparison with international trends. *Br J Psychiatry* 132:180, 1978.

Zung WK: A self-rating depression scale. *Arch Gen Psychiatry* 12:63–70, 1965.

Zung WK, Richards CB, Short MJ: Self-rating depression scale in an outpatient clinic: Further validation of the SOS. *Arch Gen Psychiatry* 13:508–515, 1965.

Zung WW: A cross-cultural survey of symptoms in depression. *Am J Psychiatry* 126:116–121, 1969.

Zung WW, Moore J: Suicide potential in a normal adult population. *Psychosomatics* 17:37–41, 1976.

INDEX

Index

246

Index

Emergency telephone numbers

Suicide hot line or crisis intervention center _____

Police _____

Fire department _____

Sheriff's department _____

State highway patrol _____

Federal Bureau of Investigation _____

Emergency ambulance service _____

Out-patient psychiatric clinic _____

Admitting office, psychiatric hospital _____

Psychiatrist _____

Psychologist _____

Social worker _____

Psychiatric nurse _____

Clergy _____

Poison control center _____

Drug abuse information hot line _____

Alcoholics Anonymous _____

Rape crisis center (counseling for victims)_____

Women Together (for battered wives) _____

Safe Space Station (for runaways) _____

Senior information center _____

Parents Anonymous (for child abusers) _____

Child abuse hot line _____

Community information service _____